MAKING CONNECTIONS

TEACHING AND THE HUMAN BRAIN

RENATE NUMMELA CAINE
GEOFFREY CAINE

ASCD

ASSOCIATION FOR SUPERVISION
AND CURRICULUM DEVELOPMENT
Alexandria, Virginia

The Authors

Renate Nummela Caine is Associate Professor of Education at California State University, San Bernardino (CSUSB). She is also the Executive Director of the CSUSB Center for Research in Integrative Learning/Teaching.

Geoffrey Caine is a consultant specializing in adult learning. He is also an Adjunct Member of Faculty at the University of Redlands, California, Whitehead Center for Lifelong Learning, where he teaches management and law.

Printed in the United States of America. Text and cover design by Weber Design. Printed by Banta Company.

Ronald S. Brandt, *Executive Editor*
Nancy Modrak, *Managing Editor, Books*
Carolyn R. Pool, *Associate Editor*
Stephanie Kenworthy, *Assistant Manager, Production Services*
Valerie Sprague, *Desktop Specialist*

Price $15.95
ASCD Stock No. 611-91025

Library of Congress Cataloging-in-Publication Data

Caine, Renate Nummela.
  ` Making connections: teaching and the human brain / Renate Nummela Caine, Geoffrey Caine.
      p.   cm.
  Includes bibliographical references.
    ISBN 0-87120-179-8 (pbk.)
    1. Learning, Psychology of. 2. Learning—Physiological aspects. 3. Brain.
  4. Teaching.   I. Caine, Geoffrey.   II. Title.
  LB1057.C33   1991
  370.15'23—dc20   91-7631
                                                                        CIP

MAKING CONNECTIONS
TEACHING AND THE HUMAN BRAIN

FOREWORD

In these times, when reform and restructuring are on everybody's lips, a treatise that provides insight into the rationale for educational change from the perspective of the recipient and appropriate teacher responses is most relevant. Here, the wife-and-husband team of Renate Nummela Caine and Geoffrey Caine discuss the fascinating functioning of the brain in optimal and depressed conditions and how the brain and therefore learning is affected by health, stress, and teaching approaches.

Intuitively, I have known for some time now that many capable youngsters are either so bored with their education or so stressed out by their experiences, that optimum learning cannot take place. I have also seen many students "flower" in a learning environment that builds on their current knowledge base and personal experiences. The authors not only explain why this is so but also show how a reconceptualization of teaching, based on a knowledge of brain functioning, can enhance students' learning. At the same time, we can more successfully produce the worker requested by business and industry—with open-endedness, flexibility, and resourcefulness. Teachers must become facilitators of learning, and they must expect students to go beyond the surface knowledge frequently achieved through rote memorization of unconnected content. By integrating the curriculum, we can assist students in their search for deeper meaning and thus enhance the brain's quest for patterning. Other helpful practices include incorporating stress management, nutrition, exercise, and relaxation into the learning process.

The implications of this seminal work for teaching, testing, and remediation are far reaching. Repeated practice on isolated skills becomes inappropriate as an option for acquiring knowledge. It becomes obvious that skills and content must be presented in a context that is familiar to the learner. This contextual approach also supports authentic modes of assessment.

As a side benefit of this work, the authors have legitimized the right of a learner not to fit the mold of the "average American student" and have challenged teachers and students to find those familiar contexts, "schema," within which to embed new learning.

Also of note, the authors openly discuss the benefits to learning provided by the regular practice of meditation and other methods of achieving a state of relaxed alertness, from the perspective of the positive physiological impact on the brain of such efforts—a bold step.

Finally, the clarity and easy style with which this book is written cannot mask the substantive content. This work may be the most powerful work written this year in terms of its potential to produce a long-range impact on education. It certainly invites a dramatic shift in the conceptualization of the teaching and learning paradigm— one that undoubtedly will have a positive impact on our educational system and the lives of the students who experience it.

DONNA JEAN CARTER
ASCD President, 1990–91

INTRODUCTION: TIME FOR A CHANGE

This book is for educators and others who know that schools must change. It adds to the growing body of knowledge and research suggesting that we need to move beyond simplistic, narrow approaches to teaching and learning. The book contributes to this knowledge base by focusing on information from the neurosciences that can help educators understand their role more fully.

From the very outset, it became clear that direct translation from the neurosciences into educational practices would be impossible. We have therefore taken the liberty of extrapolating the educational significance of the research we have explored. We have done this in three ways. In the first part of the book, we examine education today in light of critical findings of brain research. In Part II, we select specific topics, theories, and models of brain functioning that appear to address current issues in education and provide implications for curriculum restructuring and design. We then reorganize major aspects of such research for the purpose of eliciting a useful and practical set of general principles. In Part III, we describe elements of instruction that we believe more fully use the brain's capacity to learn. These later chapters serve as guides for translating what we know about how the brain learns to actual orchestration of the learning environment.

We challenge some strongly held beliefs. For example, the brain does not separate emotions from cognition, either anatomically or perceptually. Hence, brain research challenges the belief that teaching can be separated into the cognitive, affective, and psychomotor domains. Such artificial categorization may be helpful in designing research projects, but it can actually distort our understanding of learning. A physiological model of memory also calls into question the notion that learning must take place through rote memorization. In addition, by understanding properties of our spatial memory system, educators can understand that teaching to behavioral objectives ignores other functions of the brain and other aspects of memory and learning. Indeed, we have come to the conclusion that educators, by being too specific about facts to be remembered and outcomes to be produced, may prohibit students' genuine understanding and transfer of learning.

We need to expand our notion of learning and teaching. The brain is far from simple, and implications are always more complex than we initially perceive. It is not so much that what we are doing in education is right or wrong, it is more a matter of seeing beyond our heavily entrenched mode of doing business. We therefore invite educators to move beyond what Ivan Barzakov of Optimalearning™ calls "the fallacy of the familiar." This requires that in order to genuinely expand our knowledge and understanding of an issue, we avoid the tendency to reduce the new to something we already know and to practices that are familiar. Given that learning and teaching involve multifaceted human beings in complex interactions, we have no choice but to acknowledge and comprehend this complexity and move beyond narrow definitions and practices to genuinely improve education on a large scale. This is why coming to terms with complexity, tolerating ambiguity, and accepting active uncertainty are so critical and why these, rather than the actual information, may be the principal opportunities provided by this book.

Educators do not need another method or approach or model guaranteed to "save" education. From the point of view of educational theory and methods, much of what we say has been said or done before. What is needed is a framework for a more complex form of learning that makes it possible for us to organize and make sense of what we already know. In addition, such a framework has to have "bottom line" integrity; for us, that means it must integrate human behavior and perception, emotions and physiology. To make our point, we borrow heavily from cognitive psychology, education, philosophy, sociology, science and technology, the new physics, and physiological responses to stress, as well as the neurosciences. We believe this book contributes to the creation of such a framework.

Both in the neurosciences and in education, we will no doubt learn more in the years to come. Though we make strong recommendations and suggestions, the book has an open-ended quality. For example, we do not directly deal with the question of consciousness or the brain/mind issue. We use the two interchangeably and in a metaphoric sense. This suits our purpose but leaves the issue for others to unravel. Our translation of the research also raised many questions, which we hope will serve as the link between the neurosciences and education as we begin a critical, but tentative, bridge of communication between these disciplines.

Strangely enough, understanding the enormous complexity of issues in the neurosciences left us with an even deeper respect for the job teachers must do in the classroom. Properly understood, the issues plaguing the neurosciences become the inside mirror image of what educators deal with on the outside with ongoing behavior. Teaching in the traditional way, dependent on content and the textbook, is demanding but not very sophisticated. Teaching to the human brain, however, based on a real understanding of how the brain works, elevates teaching into a challenging field requiring the finest minds and intellects.

A word of thanks is due to many people. California State University, San Bernardino, supported Renate with a creative leave grant. Our friend and colleague, Sam Crowell, devoted a great deal of time to the exploration of these ideas with us; and we would like to thank Les Hart for his work and his encouragement. Many others have reviewed this book in some valuable capacity. Diana Caine gave us excellent advice and some appropriate words of caution about extrapolation from the neurosciences. Peggy Atwell has been a continuous source of encouragement and support. Other welcome assistance came from Tennes Rosengren, Betty Snow, Lynn Dhority, and Donald and Peggy Caine. Lynn Nadel gave generously of his time for several years; without his help, this book would not have been possible. Renate wishes to acknowledge the outstanding group of humanists who contributed to her education at the University of Florida in the 1970s, among whom were Art Combs and William Purkey. Renate dedicates this book to the memory of Donald L. Avila.

I

ACCESSING THE BRAIN'S POTENTIAL

1

MAKING CONNECTIONS

There are perhaps about one hundred billion neurons,
or nerve cells, in the brain, and in a single human
brain the number of possible interconnections
between these cells is greater than the number
of atoms in the universe.

Robert Ornstein and Richard Thompson,
The Amazing Brain, 1984, p. 21

We are given as our birthright a Stradivarius and
we come to play it like a plastic fiddle.

Jean Houston, "Education," in *Millenium,*
1981, p. 151

WHAT IS BRAIN-BASED LEARNING?

In many ways, the brain is like the heart or lungs. Each organ has a
natural function. The brain learns because that is its job. Moreover,
the brain has a virtually inexhaustible capacity to learn. Each healthy
human brain, irrespective of a person's age, sex, nationality, or cultural
background, comes equipped with a set of exceptional features:

- the ability to detect patterns and to make approximations,
- phenomenal capacity for various types of memory,
- the ability to self-correct and learn from experience by
  way of analysis of external data and self-reflection, and
- an inexhaustible capacity to create.

If, then, everyone has these capacities, *why are we struggling in our ability*
to educate?

One essential reason is that we have not yet grasped the
complexity and elegance of the way the brain learns, especially when

3

it is functioning optimally. When we understand both the possibilities and the available processes, then we can access the vast potential of the human brain and, in a very real sense, improve education. In the words of Leslie Hart (1983), there can be "brain-compatible" or "brain-antagonistic" education. Understanding the difference is critical.

Many educators, for example, have assumed that learning takes place primarily through memorization of facts and specific skills. This is like looking at the moon and believing that we have understood the solar system. There is more. Almost ignored is the immense capacity of the brain to deal with and instantly remember the moment-to-moment events that constitute life experience. Even more neglected and underused is the innate predisposition of the brain to search for how things make sense, to search for some meaning in experience. This translates into the search for common patterns and relationships. It is a matter of finding out how what is being learned relates to what the learner already knows and values and how information and experiences connect. In essence we have to come to terms with meaningful learning and the art of capitalizing on experience. Although all learning is brain based in some sense, to us *brain-based learning involves acknowledging the brain's rules for meaningful learning and organizing teaching with those rules in mind*. That is when we are teaching to the human brain.

Here is a simple example of the distinction between ignoring and capitalizing on experience. Children live with parallel lines long before they ever encounter school. By the time parallel lines are discussed in geometry, the average student has seen thousands of examples in fences, windows, mechanical toys, pictures, and so on. Instead of referring to the parallel lines students and teachers have already experienced, most teachers will draw parallel lines on the blackboard and supply a definition. Students will dutifully copy this "new" information into a notebook to be studied and remembered for the test. Parallel lines suddenly become a new abstract piece of information stored in the brain as a separate fact. No effort has been made to access the rich connections already in the brain that can provide the learner with an instant "Aha!" sense of what the parallel lines they have already encountered mean in real life, what can be done with them, and how they exist other than as a mathematical abstraction.

Currently literature, mathematics, history, and science are often seen as separate disciplines unrelated to the life of the learner. And much of what we presently accept as teaching is based on the mistaken belief that students can be taught reading and writing as separate from meaning and purpose, and that somehow what happens in the classroom is unaffected by the real world children and adults inhabit. Brain-based learning, on the other hand, rests on the fact that the various disciplines relate to each other and share common information that the brain can recognize and organize. This, for instance, is at the heart of thematic teaching.

Because the learner is constantly searching for connections on many levels, educators need to *orchestrate the experiences* from which learners extract understanding. They must do more than simply provide information or force the memorization of isolated facts and skills. The changes to be made in education will usually be substantial, and teaching to the brain will therefore require most of us to make a major perceptual shift.

TAKING ADVANTAGE OF BRAIN RESEARCH

Much of what we say about learning has been said before and is supported by a significant amount of research in education, as well as by the anecdotal experience of many educators. Brain research is invaluable, therefore, in part because it confirms that many of the criticisms of education are correct. It endorses what we already know and can be used to support the many innovative educators and members of the community who have been and are striving for change.

Equally important, the brain itself can be a guide and a metaphor. The findings can help us be more precise about what is not working in education and what we need to do. As we become more familiar with the brain's capacity to seek and perceive patterns, create meanings, integrate sensory experience, and make connections, we can also become more adept at solving practical problems, such as selecting appropriate methodologies, effectively assessing learning, designing schools, and administering education.

IS THERE ANY GENERAL GUIDING PRINCIPLE?

Brain research establishes and confirms that multiple complex and concrete experiences are essential for meaningful learning and teaching. Optimizing the use of the human brain means using the brain's infinite capacity to make connections—and understanding what conditions maximize this process. In essence, students learn from their entire ongoing experience. In many ways, content is inseparable from context.

Every complex event embeds information in the brain and links what is being learned to the rest of the learner's current experiences, past knowledge, and future behavior. The primary focus for educators, therefore, should be on expanding the quantity and quality of ways in which a learner is exposed to content and context. The best word we have found for this process is "immersion." We know from other sources, for instance, that the more children can talk about what they are doing (Cohen 1984) and the more their teachers use the appropriate vocabulary in teaching, the greater the learning (Harste 1989, Moraes 1986). The learner needs to be engaged in talking, listening, reading, viewing, acting, and valuing. Brain research supports this.

Let us look at one basic example to explore the nature and power of the interconnectedness of experience. Millions of times every school day, students are asked to deal with specific issues. We'll examine an aspect of English literature, although any subject will do. Students are asked to read Shakespeare's *Hamlet* and come prepared to discuss the play and answer critical questions. A test will follow to check on their ability to understand and recall parts of the play. What can a teacher do? And what else is influencing the student's learning?

Excellent teachers do more than teach to the test. The best teachers use the background and information students bring to class, including their experiences with parents, power, and love. Such teachers attempt to help students recognize the deeper meanings and issues in *Hamlet* and make genuine personal connections with the play. These connections include increasing familiarity with a somewhat different vocabulary, society, and period in time. Students also learn about themselves and life in the process. Thus, immersion in the subject, linking the information to other subjects and personal meaning, and expansion of vocabulary, history, and psychology has begun.

What we tend to ignore is that this immersion process can itself be hindered or helped. Do the students ever discuss Shakespeare with friends or peers? Is that a "weird" thing to do? How often or frequently do they discuss *Hamlet* outside of class? Is the school an exciting intellectual environment where topics of this nature are mirrored in the interests of teachers and administrators and discussions among them? Does the physical environment reflect deep appreciation and valuing of the arts, science, and the social sciences? Can students discuss *Hamlet* (or any other subject) at home? How does the family allow for the student to make additional connections and to be further immersed in using and exploring the information and understanding gleaned in class? Does the community support the arts, provide good plays for students to attend, or fund community science projects in which children of all ages can participate? And what of our society? Does television encourage abstract and creative intellectual thought? Do our politicians merely call for educational reform, or do they engage learners in critical thinking and reflection on the issues affecting our society? Do adults within our society give students other opportunities to engage their brains more fully and immerse them in broader learning? Is the content of schooling compartmentalized and separated from life? All these questions illustrate other aspects of the experience in which a student is immersed. All have a bearing on how *Hamlet* will be perceived and understood and on the number of rich connections made in the learning brain.

People can and need to grasp the larger patterns. The part is always embedded in a whole, the fact is always embedded in multiple contexts, and a subject is always related to many other issues and subjects. The capacity of schools and society to optimize learning and realize the potential of the human brain depends on their capacity to deal with this interconnectedness. Such an approach, however, calls into question many of the foundations on which the educational system has been built.

What Is the Objective?

Our general objective is to improve learning and teaching. More specifically, we want to see the emergence of learners who can demonstrate a high level of basic competence, as well as deal with complexity and change. People in business, such as John Sculley, the CEO of Apple Computers, have been saying for some time that students need to acquire judgment skills. For this to happen, education needs to accommodate both the needs and design of the human brain. The overwhelming need of learners is for meaningfulness.

To accomplish that objective, we have to more clearly distinguish between the types of knowledge that students can acquire. The main distinction, which we examine in more depth in Chapter 8, is between *surface knowledge* and *meaningful knowledge*. The former, involving memorization of facts and procedures, is what education traditionally produces. Of course, some memorization is very important. Meaningful knowledge, however, is critical for success in the 21st century.

Surface knowledge is anything that a robot can "know." It refers to programming and to the memorization of the "mechanics" of any subject. It results in specifiable performance. Meaningful knowledge, on the other hand, is anything that makes sense to the learner. A child who appreciates a plant as a miracle approaches the study of plants differently from a child who "engages in a task." It is impossible to deal with complexity and change and to make sound judgments if the tools and knowledge at our disposal do not make sense. We do not come to understand a subject or master a skill by sticking bits of information to each other. Understanding a subject results from perceiving relationships. The brain is designed as a pattern detector. Our function as educators is to provide our students with the sorts of experiences that enable them to perceive "the patterns that connect" (Bateson 1980).

An essential problem is that almost all our testing and evaluation is geared toward recognizing surface knowledge. We tend to disregard or misunderstand the indicators of meaning. Thus a person who plays around with a formula may have a better appreciation for what is actually happening than the person who can memorize it but cannot manipulate it creatively. Present testing procedures tend not to accommodate both types of knowledge.

Even more tragic is the fact that, by teaching to the test, we actually deprive students of the opportunity for meaningful learning. Testing and performance objectives have their place. Generally, however, they fail to capitalize on the brain's capacity to make connections. By intelligently using what we call *active processing*, we give students many more opportunities to show what they know without circumscribing what they are capable of learning. Testing and evaluation will have to accommodate creativity and open-endedness, as well as measure requisite and specifiable performance.

WHAT ARE THE COMPONENTS OF BRAIN-BASED LEARNING?

The brain processes information all the time. It digests experience to some extent in the same way that we digest food. It is always responding to the complex global context in which it is immersed. Educators must come to grips with that fact. Brain-based education, therefore, involves:

1. Designing and orchestrating lifelike, enriching, and appropriate experiences for learners.
2. Ensuring that students process experience in such a way as to increase the extraction of meaning.

The specific elements are spelled out more fully in Chapters 9–11.

Among the features of brain-based learning are active uncertainty or the tolerance for ambiguity; problem solving; questioning; and patterning by drawing relationships through the use of metaphor, similes, and demonstrations. Students are given many choices for activities and projects. Teaching methods are complex, lifelike, and integrated, using music and natural environments. Brain-based learning is usually experienced as joyful, although the content is rigorous and intellectually challenging; and students experience a high degree of self-motivation. It acknowledges and encourages the brain's ability to integrate vast amounts of information. It involves the entire learner in a challenging learning process that simultaneously engages the intellect, creativity, emotions, and physiology. It allows for the unique abilities and contributions from the learner in the teaching-learning situation. It acknowledges that learning takes place within a multiplicity of contexts—classroom, school, community, country, and planet. It appreciates the interpenetration of parts and wholes by connecting what is learned to the greater picture and allowing learners to investigate the parts within the whole. Brain-based learning is meaningful to the learner. What is learned makes sense.

It follows, then, that a particular procedure or methodology may or may not be brain based. For example, cooperative learning is brain based if it incorporates the intellect and the emotions and calls for spontaneous adaptations to meaningful, intellectually challenging issues. It is not necessarily brain based if parameters are strictly defined, the learning process is constricted and controlled, and students engage in specified activities for the purpose of identifying predetermined outcomes. Obviously, the brain is also involved in such learning, but it may not engage in enough "mapping" processes to create the type of connections that we seek.

Who Does Brain-Based Teaching, and How Successful Is It?

Many schools and individuals are engaged in brain-based teaching to some extent, often not consciously. One example is New Jersey's Hightstown High School, which has a humanities program with an integrated curriculum (Shalley 1987). In 1988, the program won the Christa McAuliffe Grant for Excellence in Education. Les Hart's Brain Compatible Learning, based on proster theory (1975, 1983), has been successfully implemented at Drew Elementary School in New Jersey. Susan Kovalik and her group boast of over 45 schools that have implemented the integrated thematic approach to learning based on Hart's proster theory (S. Kovalik, personal communication 1990). Stanford's Complex Learning is also brain based, and results are impressive (Cohen and Lotan 1990).

The Colorado School of Mines has integrated the humanities into a beginning engineering course (Olds and Miller 1989, 1990). It is team taught by engineering and humanities instructors. Results to date show that students can deal with more complex issues in their decision making and like the course and their new profession more. Another successful example is the Horton School in San Diego, which has adopted a model of accelerated learning based on Lozanov's work, as translated by Stephanie Merritt (Merritt 1989). Integrative learning, a model developed by Laurence Martel and Peter Kline at Syracuse

University, produced remarkable results at Guggenheim Elementary School in Chicago. This inner-city school qualifies for Chapter 1 funding for disadvantaged and low-income students. Between 1986 and 1987, student achievement rose significantly when compared with other schools in the district. In 1988 students gained the equivalent of one year's development in eight months (Martel 1989).

Literally hundreds of schools around the country are using some form of brain-based learning. Some are low-income schools, like the New Orleans Free School; Public School District 4 in New York; the City Magnet School in Lowell, Massachusetts; and Clara Barton School in Minneapolis. Others are suburban, middle-income schools, like Tanglewood School in Golden, Colorado; Peninsula School in Palo Alto, California; Nueva School in Palo Alto; the Open Magnet School in Los Angeles; and Graham and Parks School in Cambridge, Massachusetts. These schools demonstrate that success is not restricted to race, cultural background, or income.

Many successful individual teachers also stand out. Jaime Escalante, the mathematics teacher made famous in the film *Stand and Deliver*, is an example. Although we question his textbook approach to the content of the subject, he understands his students and the world students live in. In his classes, calculus becomes a way of life, is a source of pride, and is linked to deeper understanding of how mathematics opens doors to further study and the individual student's future. Another example is Lynn Dhority, who has developed a superb program for teaching German at the University of Massachusetts in Boston. A third is Leo Wood, who teaches chemistry in Tempe, Arizona, using the theme "Life Is a Miracle." We describe his delightful class, and others, in more detail in Chapter 12.

THE FUTURE

Unfortunately, many teachers who are aware of the complexities of learning and teaching have been intimidated into ignoring what they know. They have had to fight both a factory model that places a premium on low-quality output and a research model that implies that their observations of what actually happens are invalid. It takes a strong personality and enormous conviction to ignore such pressures.

Yet, there are signs of an emerging awareness that creating educated human beings is a complex and skillful process, warranting a grasp of how the brain learns. Examples include the *California Frameworks in History/Social Science* (1988), *English/Language Arts* (1988), and *Science* (1990), which spell out the need to acknowledge information on brain functioning in designing the curriculum. The *History/Social Science Framework* calls for incorporation of the arts into the social

10

studies classroom and encourages holistic approaches. These are brain-based approaches because they acknowledge the brain's ability to relate vast amounts of information to what is already "in" the learner, through the identification of underlying patterns and relationships among the sciences, humanities, and arts.

The problem is that the education edifice has been constructed on a set of assumptions that prevent us from perceiving what people can do and therefore interfere with our capacity to adequately teach to the human brain. We must, therefore, add our voices to those calling such assumptions into question.

2

QUESTIONING FUNDAMENTAL ASSUMPTIONS ABOUT EDUCATION

Nature is like a radio band with infinite stations; the reality you are now experiencing is only one station on the band, completely convincing as long as you stay tuned to it, but masking the other choices that lie on either side.

Deepak Chopra, *Perfect Health,* 1990, p. 14

Do not confine your children to your own learning For they were born in another time.

Hebrew Proverb

The pivotal issue is why we tend to overlook interconnectedness and "whole" experiences in teaching. One reason is that education has been designed and operates with a cluster of interactive, but restrictive, assumptions in mind. Most of us take these assumptions for granted. In operation, however, they actually interfere with the learner's ability and opportunity to see relationships and make connections.

ASSUMPTIONS

ASSUMPTION 1. THE FACTORY MODEL IS AN APPROPRIATE MODEL FOR THE ORGANIZATION AND OPERATION OF SCHOOLS.

Public education has always been tied to economic and social trends. With the advent of industrialization, public schools were largely concerned with producing a work force to staff and operate the factories. It was only natural, perhaps, that schools would also adopt the basic tenets of the industrial model as guides for effective education.

In traditional factories, products are manufactured on an assembly line, and the final product is the combination of readily identifiable parts that are made using precisely measurable materials. Work is done according to specific schedules, with precise times for beginning, taking breaks, and ending. Speed, accuracy, and the amount of output are rewarded.

Similarly, in most schools, we still find that subjects are dealt with separately; and each subject is "taught" at a separate time. The students move through subjects in the schedule in an assembly-line routine. Times and places for learning and taking breaks are specifically allocated according to the need to cover subject matter—not according to a student's thirst for knowledge. And just as content is predetermined, so are outcomes specified in terms of general standards, skills, and facts, which make it relatively easy to test for success. In both the factory and the school, decisions are made by individuals who have acquired specific authority to evaluate the work done. Some interconnectedness, as between math and physics, does become apparent over time. In most other respects, however, interconnectedness is not emphasized.

In factories, the rewards for work tend to be perks and financial incentives. In schools, rewards are free time, extra credit, and grades. Moreover, students identify what they do in school as "work" and escape from it as soon as the bell rings. This is the same response seen in people who are freed from custodial institutions. In effect, schools operate as though the most crucial aspect of education is the informational content that they purport to teach students. Schools concentrate on memorization. The products are the facts that students memorize.

Today, as 50 years ago, any student, from elementary school through college, can complete this series of questions in exactly the same way without prompting:

Q. How do you study?
A. I read, I take notes, I make outlines, and I memorize.
Q. Why do you do this?
A. For the test.

Why the Factory Model Is Inappropriate. The school based on the factory approach fails to prepare students for two reasons. First, the relevant skills and attributes students need for this century and the next tend not to be addressed. Second, the organization and methods of teaching content and skills are inadequate because they fail to take advantage of the brain's capacity to learn.

Indeed, business and industry are themselves having to respond to technological innovations and change. They are now demanding a very different worker. Life in the workplace has changed enormously. The words that come to mind are not "stable and predictable," as indicative of a segmented, controlled factory workplace, but rather "fluid and dynamic."

Tomorrow's employees will be doing what robots *can't* do, which means that their work will call for the exercise of sophisticated intelligence. What we now appear to need is not individuals trained for the hierarchical and mechanical workplace but individuals who can govern themselves. Tomorrow's successful employees will have to be problem solvers, decision makers, adept negotiators, and thinkers who are at home with open-endedness, flexibility, and resourcefulness. They must be able to deal with uncertainty, complexity, the global village, the information explosion, other technologies, and many different cultures—and still maintain a set of values that foster an adequate degree of individual stability, integrity, and social harmony. It will not be enough for people to have acquired a store of nontransferable facts. They must have understood and internalized content, such as math, economics, and history, sufficiently to make it available spontaneously, appropriately, and in many different contexts.

We do not wish to give the impression that the business world, at this point, is prepared to accommodate the type of complex learner we have been describing. Business itself is still inappropriately dominated by the factory model. Schools need to prepare students who have these skills and who take the "basics" for granted. Preparing students for this changing world requires much more than memorization for tests. Because many skills and attributes interpenetrate every subject in the curriculum, their implementation in one subject requires an understanding of many others. A fragmented and assembly-line education actually inhibits the grasp of the link between subjects and life that is essential for complex learning.

The need to change from the factory model has been raised repeatedly by educators and others concerned with the future of American education. More than ten years ago, the *1979 Yearbook* of the Association for Supervision and Curriculum Development spelled out the frustration with the present, single-minded approach to teaching. Overly (1979) put it this way:

> As practiced, schooling is a poor facilitator of learning. Its persistent view of learning as product interferes with significant learning connected to such complex processes as inquiry and appreciation. What often passes for education is noise that interrupts the natural flow of learning. Schooling too often fragments learning into subject areas, substitutes control for the natural desire to learn, co-opts naturally active children for hours in assembly line classroom structures, and ignores both individual and cultural differences. . . . The formal education system often destroys

opportunities for learning from elders, from each other, and from the new generation. . . . Much is known about the learning process but little has been applied to education. . . . The American education system is not making use of brain research findings (p. 107).

The Emergence of New Technologies. Despite laser discs, bioengineering, computer technology, magnetic resonance imaging (MRI) scans, a new world economy, emerging ecological approaches in science and technology, and literally hundreds of new fields of study, this narrow and bureaucratic approach to teaching persists. It is powerfully ingrained in our society and serves as the foundation for countless textbooks, teaching models, teacher inservicing, lectures, and testing procedures.

The lack of student preparation is but one reason that industry is now so concerned about upgrading the basic skills of employees, as evidenced by the "Train America's Workforce" program recently launched by the American Society for Training and Development. The ironic point is that memorization, particularly as practiced in our schools, does not work to provide a foundation in basic skills and knowledge. The previous dialogue inevitably concludes as follows:

Q. What do you do after the test?
A. I forget it!

Schools organized on the factory model do not open doors to the future; they imprison students in their own minds.

ASSUMPTION 2. BEHAVIORISM IS AN APPROPRIATE MODEL OF HOW PEOPLE LEARN.

The factory model provided fertile soil for the behavioral approach to learning, which has dominated educational practices for the past 50 years. It is an approach predicated on the beliefs that what we learn can be reduced to specific, readily identifiable parts and that equally identifiable rewards and punishments can be used to "produce" the desired learning.

Behavioral approaches, by ignoring the power and vitality of the inner life of students and their capacity to create personally and intellectually relevant meanings, have interfered with the development of more challenging and fulfilling approaches to learning and teaching. New definitions of behavior have blurred the lines between behaviorism and cognitive psychology. According to Morton Hunt, author of *The Universe Within* (1982): "The wonder of wonders is that so many intelligent and thoughtful people could have believed that behaviorism was an adequate explanation for human behavior" (p. 53). And in their book, *The Hippocampus as a Cognitive Map*, O'Keefe and Nadel (1978) simply say, "Skinner was wrong."

We elaborate on these issues throughout the book. It suffices, for *now*, to make three central points:

• Behaviorism, particularly as incorporated into schools, is largely based on rewards and punishment; but these are extremely complex, not simple. A smiley sticker is not just a single reward for a single act. The use of a sticker may well influence the formation of expectations, preferences, and habits having impact far beyond any single event. Thus, a single teacher behavior may have vast, but initially invisible, consequences. One of many problems with the behaviorist approach is that it does not provide for a way to acknowledge those consequences.

• When rewards and punishments are controlled by others, most children are influenced to look to others for direction and answers. In fact, we now seem to have an entire generation working for the grade or rewards of an immediate and tangible nature. One consequence is that they are literally *demotivated* in many respects, as we show in Chapter 6. In particular, their innate search for meaning is short-circuited. Another consequence is that they are actually deprived of some major rewards, namely the joy and excitement that are the consequences of real learning (Deci and Ryan 1987).

• We query the design of questions and lectures where all answers and outcomes are predetermined. For any skill to be deeply mastered, students must have substantial opportunity to create their own meanings and organize skills in their brains in their own ways. That is only possible when they have a significant amount of creative opportunity. When all options are determined in advance, students are actually deprived of the opportunity to do some of the innovative and creative things that are essential for adequate learning. That forces them back into memorization for tests.

ASSUMPTION 3. SCHOOLS RESPOND ADEQUATELY TO, AND ARE SUFFICIENTLY IN TOUCH WITH, THE NEEDS OF THIS GENERATION.

> We have used our wealth, our literacy, our technology, and our progress to create the thickets of unreality which stand between us and the facts of life. . . . Experiences of our own contriving begin to hide reality from us, to confuse our sense of reality, taking us headlong from the world of heroes to a world of celebrities, transforming us from travellers into tourists (Daniel Boorstin, *The Image: A Guide to Pseudo-Events in America,* 1988).

One function of schooling should be to prepare students for the real world. They need to have a sense of what will be expected of them, how they will be challenged, and what they are capable of doing. The assumption is that, by and large, schooling as we know it meets those goals. The reality is that it does not. On the contrary, it fosters illusions and obscures the real challenges. In particular, it fails to deal with the impact of electronic media.

Take a close look at American teenagers. For a moment, let time run backwards to deprive teenagers of gadgets that are in some way dependent on electricity. One by one, we remove the television, the CD player, the computer, the videodisc, the radio, tape player, record player, electronic games, airplanes, air conditioning and automatic heating, shopping in large malls, and the opportunity to acquire large numbers of possessions. How well do you think our teenagers could cope? How would their lives be different? And what about our own? One of the only places that would reflect scarcely any difference in the scenario we've painted—and that would be operating largely as it did more than 50 years ago—would be the local school!

Children growing up with "electronic miracles" are different. They live in a world of vast media and technological input that entertains and influences them in both conscious and unconscious ways. The information they listen to contributes to the ideas they formulate, influences the makeup of their personalities and values, and ultimately influences how they see and interact with the world. It is important to note that all the electronic items mentioned previously, with the possible exception of very sophisticated computers, are limited to one-way communication. Unfortunately, television, audiotapes, and CD players do not allow students to raise searching questions, enter into debate, formulate their own opinions, develop a moral philosophy, engage in problem solving or critical thinking, or test their view of reality.

> When you plug something into the wall, someone is getting plugged into you. Which means you need new patterns of defense, perception, understanding, evaluation. You need a new kind of education (Postman and Weingartner 1969, p. 7).

We allow our children to experiment in the social arena with new morals and a remarkable number of possessions. But how much do we manage to motivate students to participate enthusiastically in the intellectual/thinking arena on issues that affect their own moral and ethical development? Where, in life, do they learn about nurturing, the positive aspects of responsibility, and the realization that hopes and dreams take time to come to fruition?

Such issues may once have been dealt with in the family, but this is not a matter of returning to the "good old days." For one thing, U.S. family statistics are discouraging, and a turnaround is unlikely. Fifty percent of children age five or younger have two parents who work. For 58 percent of children in the 6–13 age group, both parents work. Three out of five children born today will live with a single parent by age 18, and 58 percent of children age five or younger have a single parent who works. That number increases to 68 percent for the 6–13 age group (*U.S. News and World Report,* October 27, 1986). Further, current estimates suggest that by the time American children reach the age of 16 years, they will have spent six hours in front of the television for every one hour spent with parents.

Although television could be used constructively to educate our young, most educators and parents do not look to that medium for mentally challenging input. On the contrary, the television industry produces great profits through programming and commercials that influence people, while denying that program content has any influence.

Regrettably, most schools do not engage students in the reflection, inquiry, and critical thinking needed to help them cope with and take charge of the influences of technology and the media. In an interview in the *Los Angeles Times*, Merlin Wittrock, the educational psychologist at UCLA, simply expresses the obvious when he says, "Teaching is more than knowing a subject matter and presenting it in clear language; . . . teaching involves knowing how students think, their preconceptions and misconceptions. . . . It involves learning what motivates students and what genuinely gets their attention" (*Los Angeles Times*, March 16, 1988). The result of continuous input without realistic engagement in interactive experiences may well be a generation that has access to a great deal of superficial information but has no deeper sense of how that information connects to ecological issues, a global economy, the quality of life, or even the joy of learning.

Some of this lack of deeper understanding may be reflected in the fact that most 11th graders have extremely unrealistic career goals when measured against standards established in the profession of their choice. Although U.S. children ranked last in mathematics among 14 nations tested in 1988, they ranked highest in their own assessment of how good they were in mathematics. Sixty-eight percent thought their knowledge was "excellent," compared with 22 percent of the Korean students who had, in fact, performed best (International Association for the Evaluation of Educational Achievement 1988, cited by Finn 1989). Although such facts are subject to multiple interpretations, we contend that it is symptomatic of a generation that has not had the opportunity to test itself against realistic challenges.

ASSUMPTION 4. CURRENT APPROACHES TO RESEARCH IN EDUCATION ARE SUFFICIENT AND APPROPRIATE.

Much research in education has been productive, but it has been dominated by a mechanistic approach that is no longer adequate. Educational research, like teaching, has focused heavily on the pieces without giving us a greater sense of how those pieces interact in more complex "wholes." Our most recent past has been dominated by what

Donald Schön (Doll 1989) calls the "rational/experimental" model. Translated into a model for social science research, the "true" experiment is one in which a sufficient number of independent variables can be held constant in both an experimental and control group while at least one independent variable can be manipulated (Van Mondrans et al., cited in Biehler and Snowman 1986).

Research guided by this approach has focused largely on identifying individual characteristics or factors relating to learning and teaching by way of quantitative measures. Education researchers have tried to use the same objective modes of inquiry devised for the natural sciences. Research tends to be based on the Newtonian notion that the world is like a great machine. The implication is that we can deal with one variable, such as class size, while we hold all the other variables stable. This approach, by definition, is limited.

The traditional approach to research is being challenged on several fronts, in part because the view of reality as a machine is being called into question in almost every field of scientific endeavor. Researchers in quantum mechanics have had to face the fact that the observer influences and is a part of the experiment. Prigogine (Prigogine and Stengers 1984) has demonstrated that systems in equilibrium and disequilibrium behave differently, and that order can emerge out of chaos. And indeed there is an emerging science of complexity that is built in part on the fact that hidden in apparent chaos are complex types of order (Gleick 1987). Whenever we seek to control for one variable, we end up influencing the entire system, often in unpredictable ways. Thus, one of the major recent developments in the world of science has been an appreciation of how complex, interactive, and open ended social systems are. Although the Newtonian or mechanical paradigm has proven fruitful, it is much too limited as a vehicle for understanding these more complex situations.

As William Doll writes in "Curriculum Beyond Stability: Schön, Prigogine, Piaget" (1986):

> But to give meaning and substance to the language of disequilibrium, reflective intuition, surprise, puzzlement, confusion, zones of uncertainty, non-rationality, and metaphoric analysis is hardly possible within a model structured around behavioral objectives, competency based performance, accountability, mastery learning and effective teaching (p. 16).

As a practical matter, we all know this. It can be classically illustrated by the fact that technique is not sufficient for the creation of great art, although it is indispensable. Similarly, defining aspects of attraction does not give us love.

Emerging trends in educational practice both acknowledge and work with the complexity that actually exists in the classroom. These are more "process" oriented approaches to education, such as thematic teaching, whole-language approaches to literacy, and the integration of the curriculum. Yet we are not adequately benefiting from them because process can be neither easily understood nor measured with the rational/experimental research model. Hence a limited approach to research frustrates us in our search for ways to improve education.

Why have these global, contextual models been so poorly supported? As early as 1969, Pribram wrote in *On the Biology of Learning*:

> Every psychologist who has explored the problem has found that the context, the set of events in which information occurs, is as important a determinant of the outcome of his experiment as the information- carrying signal itself. And yet it is usually this context that remains unspecified, unstudied, and often hopelessly shrugged off as being impossible to study.
>
> Why? . . . Behavioral scientists of the hard-headed variety rarely want to take such a large system into account. For this would only point up the limitations of their data (p. 194).

Research restricted to controlled environments could not adequately explain what happens in a natural setting that fully uses the experimental animal's spatial and contextual memory systems. And Hart (1983) states:

> Usually the first step was to put the animal in some form of captivity, in the best "scientific" tradition of simplifying and controlling the conditions and variables. This of course ignored the plain fact that all higher animals have brains developed to deal with complex conditions in a state of freedom, not with strange, unnatural boxes in a state of confinement (p. 21).

We urgently need more qualitative measures in education. Ethnographic research is one promising solution. We must record not only the products and identifiable parts, but give genuine credence to the larger human experience.

Although cognitive psychology is having a substantial impact on educational theory and practice at the moment and is largely replacing the behavioristic research as the potential determiner of future approaches to learning and teaching, its basically mechanistic approach is of some concern. As Nadel (1989) points out:

> Thoughts, however, have more than formal structure. They are *always* about things, referring to specific objects, their features, their changes of state and/or location, their interaction with other objects. Additionally, our thoughts often reflect feelings of pain, of hunger, of ecstasy, of despair, of hope. The ability, or unwillingness, of behaviorism to account for the influence or conscious experience of these, or indeed any, thoughts was one of the driving forces behind the cognitive renaissance. Cognitive science has, however, had relatively little to say about the fact that activities of the mind/brain reflect beliefs and desires about the world we live in. The relative lack of attention given to these subjective

aspects of cognitive function reflects the fact that modern cognitive science is ruthlessly mechanistic; the computing machine is after all its guiding metaphor.

Roger Sperry (1986), the Nobel Prize laureate responsible for the initial "split brain" research, echoes Nadel's comments when he insists that brain cells are not simply excited by biophysical forces. They also "obey a higher command involving feelings, wants, choice, reasoning, moral values and other 'things of the mind.' "

The question is whether research helps us to create healthy, humane, and supportive environments that foster more integrated human beings with a greater wish to remember, or focus on developing memory pills that are given to children each morning to help them memorize information more efficiently. At the very least, the brain engages in both global and discrete processes. We need research that focuses on both.

WHAT PRICE DO WE PAY FOR ADHERING TO THESE ASSUMPTIONS?

Some of the greatest minds of our time, ranging from Eccles (1989) to Bohm (1987), are telling us that we are more than machines. "The question of capacity looks very different if we consider it from the perspective of biology rather than of engineering; if we regard the mind as something living and growing (which it is) rather than a machine (which it is not)" (psychologist Ulrich Nuisser, quoted in Campbell 1989, p. 17). The problem is that the assumptions discussed here conspire to have learners treated as machines and, therefore, to severely inhibit effective education and the functioning of students' brains.

A corollary is that educators cannot afford to stay in the memorization business. One consequence, we believe, is that it would ultimately lead to the replacement of many of them, often by the computer. We do not say that lightly. Our travels around the country and contacts with software developers have left us deeply aware of the fact that software designers rarely include the teacher in any role other than that of caretaker. This is not necessarily done out of conscious intent to eliminate teachers, but because people do not really see what teachers do other than "put information into children." Many software developers also understand very well how to create challenging, low-stress software that motivates students, makes learning fun, and teaches in ways the children remember. And in a clash between two modes of information "inputters," teachers can often be replaced because computers are cheaper and, in many respects, easier to control.

This is harsh truth telling. Educators must redefine their role and become seen as generators of meaningful, connecting, and linking knowledge, who can not only use the appropriate software but far surpass its performance in interactive questioning and exploration of information. Otherwise, the future looks bleak. We believe in the power of teachers, and brain-based learning focuses heavily on the teacher as the major facilitator of learning. But real facilitating, which engages more of the abilities and capabilities of the human brain, will require much more than the level of teaching that has become standard in most of our schools.

For teachers to become facilitators, as Doll (1989) suggests, "a new model for educational theory and practice is desperately needed." Because it is the brain that learns, it is the brain that we use as the basis for our model. The question, then, is what do educators need to know about the brain? They do not need to be familiar with all the anatomical features of the brain. What is vital, we believe, is an appreciation of essential functional theories and basic operations and processes that help us to better understand learning and teaching. We look next at some underlying theories and brain facts that allow us to develop a solid and basic set of assumptions about how to teach to the way we all learn best.

II

FACTS AND THEORIES ABOUT
THE HUMAN BRAIN

3

BRAIN BASICS

*Our schools . . . are not ineffective because they do not
know what happens at synapses or the chemistry of
neurotransmitters, but rather because they have yet to
address the brain as the organ for learning, and to fit
instruction and environment to the "shape" of the brain
as it is now increasingly well understood. We know that
as the consequence of long evolution, the brain has
modes of operation that are natural, effortless, effective
in utilizing the tremendous power of this amazing
instrument. Coerced to operate in other ways, it
functions as a rule reluctantly, slowly, and with
abundant error.*

Leslie Hart, *Human Brain, Human Learning,*
1983, p. xiv

There is an old German saying: "Jede tag beginnt ein neues Leben."
It means that each day marks a new beginning. Back in the early
'70s, a Harvard professor who was conducting a workshop on the
physiology of dreaming suggested that every morning upon waking
our brains were physiologically different because they had assimilated
our experiences from the day before. He implied that our memories
actually altered our brains. At the time, such ideas were very radical;
but as it turns out, brain research is beginning to prove that the professor was right and the point is critical. Learning is, in fact, a physiological process, and every day *can* make a difference.

SHOULD ALL EDUCATORS UNDERSTAND
BRAIN ANATOMY?

Learning about the brain should improve teaching. If it does not, it
becomes pointless information. Educators do not need to be experts
on brain anatomy, especially since even those who study the anatomical intricacies of brain functioning update their own knowledge

almost daily. However, what educators must have is some appreciation of how multifaceted the brain is in order to more fully appreciate the complexities involved in education. That is the thrust of this chapter. We begin with an analogy that can guide us in placing brain "facts" in perspective. By comparing the brain to a city, we can gain a better sense of how truly complex the brain is.

CITY IN THE MIND

Imagine a distant planet where scientists are using a powerful telescope to examine a large city on Earth. The first things they notice are the physical structures of the city. Further analysis of the function of these structures reveals them to be institutions like factories, banks, schools, utilities companies, and shopping centers. They are connected by streets, rails, and wires. The scientists notice that people are also vital elements—they are the agents that make the city and organizations "work." They direct the transmission of information and materials from one area to the next, and they execute essential functions.

The observers also notice that cities are divided into neighborhoods and that most people work in clusters or groups. Specific organizations such as the telephone company employ people with special skills to perform functions related to communication. Of course, not all people are parts of groups. And the functions of some are hard to pin down. Such clustering is also typical of the brain.

Now, notice all the simultaneous functions within the city. On any given day, large numbers of groups and individuals are working at the same time. The utilities companies are active at the same time that schools are open, and the working of the bank does not interfere with the library. Similarly, in the brain many things are happening at one time or "in parallel." Different parts are monitoring hormone levels, temperature, and digestion at the same time that we may be watching the screen and typing an emotionally arousing dialogue on the computer. Thus, the brain is regarded as a *parallel processor*.

INTERCONNECTIONS

Again, as in the brain, the centers in the city are interconnected and dependent on each other. The bank depends on the electric company, the telephone company, the gas company, and the water company. Schools require electricity, water, a sewage system, books that are printed elsewhere, products for chemical experiments, and food for the cafeteria. In fact, it is difficult to mention any specialized group that is not also highly dependent on many others. There is a greater degree of organization still. Some centers handle the most critical or important functions, while other branches in the same building or in outlying areas provide support. And in every process there are decision-making bodies, such as committees and subcommittees, with varying degrees of power and influence. The brain also has an infinite number of possible interconnections. It is because this parallel and interrelated processing is typical of the brain, as of the city, that the brain is described as "holographic" or "global" or "interconnected." It is very busy. And because every element influences every other element, an understanding of this complexity is paramount for education.

THE CHANGING BRAIN

By the time of birth, there is a definite organization to the human brain. We arrive with some of the basic equipment that allows us to interact with the world around us. In fact, research on infants is showing that they are much more alert and interactive than had previously been thought (Papalia and Wendkos Olds 1981). The developed areas of the brain are largely survival oriented. They control basic functions, such as eating, elimination, breathing, the maintenance of body temperature, and sleep. In addition, we appear to have some basic capacities that already allow us to look for patterns. Thus very young infants have the ability to identify faces (Stucki, Kauffman, and Kauffman 1987).

These basic, natural ways of responding to the external world begin to expand as the brain continues its development. Vast numbers of nerve cell connections are made in the developmental years, and there is some evidence that we have periods of "brain spurts," followed by periods of consolidation and rest (Epstein 1978; Klausmeier and Allen 1978; Levey, B. 1972), similar to the stages of cognitive development that Piaget suggested. The dates for these spurts vary enormously—as do the arguments over exactly what this means. Brain spurts occur in animals as well as people.

BRAIN PLASTICITY

At least as important as genetically programmed brain development is what has been called "brain plasticity." It means that the *physical structure of the brain changes as the result of experience.*

We now have evidence to illustrate the details of the anatomical changes that do occur with modification in the environment. This evidence addresses many of the questions that concerned the early sociologists and educators, including the effects of the environment on the young as well as the elderly, sex differences, and the effects of nutritional deprivation, isolation, or crowding. It is now clear that the brain is far from immutable (Diamond 1988, p. 2).

One of the most exciting findings in brain research was originally reported by a group of researchers at the University of California–Berkeley (Bennett, Diamond, Krech, and Rosenzweig 1964). Over a period of roughly 40 years, they examined the brains of rats to study anatomical features. Quite by accident, the researchers discovered that rats who lived in "enriched" environments had brains that weighed more than those of rats from "impoverished" environments.

Researchers have since accumulated a substantial amount of data indicating that the brain will grow physiologically if stimulated through interaction with the environment. In the rat experiments, the impoverished conditions consisted of individual cages for each rat, with solid walls so that the animals could not see or touch each other. Cages were in separate, quiet, dimly lit rooms. In the enriched environments, rats were housed in groups of 10–12 in large cages and given toys consisting of ladders, wheels, boxes, platforms, and so on. Cages were in large, brightly lit rooms; and toys (selected from a large inventory) were changed each day. In super-enriched environments, rats had 30-minute exploratory sessions each day in large fields, in groups of 5 or 6, with sets of barriers in patterns that were changed daily. The most enriching environment for any rat appeared to be its natural habitat, presumably because natural environments present maximum complexity.

Here are some of the reported differences. The brains of rat pups growing up in enriched conditions had changed from those in impoverished conditions after only two weeks. They had 10 percent more thickness in the general sensory area and 14 percent more thickness in the sensory integration area. Adult rats placed in enriched conditions had a 4 percent change in net weight of the outer layers of the brain, a 6 percent increase in thickness, and increases in enzymes dealing with transmission of impulses. Enzymes found in glial cells changed by 10 percent, and the total number of glia by 14 percent. Glial cells are critical to brain function in that they provide nourishment to the neurons or brain cells that transmit the signals required for all brain functioning. Diamond, Scheibel, Murphy, and Harvey (1985) hypothesize that one of the significant differences between Einstein's brain and that of the average human is that Einstein had far more glial cells.

Brains of enriched rats also showed an increase in the diameter of blood vessels in the brain, another important factor in brain cell nourishment. Animals who had lived three-fourths of their lifetime before being placed in enriched environments showed positive changes in somatosensory, frontal cortex, and visual spatial areas. These changes differed from rat to rat, but changes showed consistent overall growth—leading to the conclusion that *the brain maintains its plasticity for life*. Another remarkable fact from the research on rats that has interesting possibilities for people is that it is apparently also possible to selectively modify one or another region of the cortex, depending on the particular program of enrichment used.

This helps us to understand why neither inherited characteristics nor the environment can ever be the sole determinant of development and behavior. Children are not blank slates. They change, both psychologically and physiologically, as they "absorb" life. Winston Churchill is reputed to have said to Parliament, "We shape our houses and then they shape us." We could as easily say that our experiences shape our brains, and then our brains shape our experiences.

WHAT ARE THE IMPLICATIONS FOR EDUCATION?

1. THE BEGINNING IS CRITICAL.

Freud insisted that the first five years of life were the most critical to the development of a psychologically healthy adult. Piaget and cognitive psychologists tell us that there are critical periods of cognitive development in the early years. Generally speaking, brain research supports and augments that point.

2. LEARNING AND MATURATION CANNOT REALLY BE SEPARATED.

The moment we interact with our environment, including mommy, daddy, toys, and the baby-sitter, our biologically growing brain also builds new connections based on what we experience. These new connections constitute a part of what we bring to other experiences. Thus, our genetically programmed development is inextricably connected with what and how we learn.

The entire process is immensely complex but can be demonstrated conceptually with the following formula:

A—a unique brain + B—a unique environment =
C—a unique brain organized on the basis of $A + B$.
Then we have
C—a unique brain organized on the basis of $A + B$, interacting with B_1—the unique (ever changing) environment, and we get D—a unique brain now organized on the basis of $C + B_1$, and so on.

Leslie Hart (1983) developed a theory of brain functioning called "proster theory" ("proster" stands for "programmed structures") that gives expression to this process.

3. THE ENVIRONMENT AFFECTS THE BRAIN PHYSIOLOGICALLY.

For the purposes of education, we can no longer afford to separate brain development from life experience. Although many implications still need to be worked out, the bottom line is that experience changes the physiological structure and operation of our brains. As we suggest in Chapter 1, children from enriched environments will have more highly developed brains, and that in itself increases the ability to learn. However, this point is to be treated with extreme caution. First, stimulation here refers to complex events, not isolated pieces of information fed to the brain. Second, it is not necessarily true that a person from a middle-class home with lots of toys will have a more highly developed brain than a person who plays in the streets. Because there are many interacting factors, most children are likely to be impoverished in some ways and enriched in others.

In general, we suggest that early development requires safe, "consistent" environments that provide opportunities for a variety of rich emotional, social, and cognitive interactions. **If, beginning tomorrow, we did nothing more than protect children from destructive experiences closely linked to some form of abandonment, we would have an emotionally healthier, brighter generation 20 years from now.** When we finally understand and accept this notion, we begin to see high-quality preschools and early intervention as an absolute priority for our society.

4. THE TIME SCALE OF CHANGE VARIES ENORMOUSLY.

There is an enormous difference in rates of development in "normal" children. There can be as much as a five-year difference in the early years. One consequence is that assessing children by reference to chronological age is often worse than useless. Each brain appears to have its own pace, which renders the "failing" of a child in the first year of school entirely inappropriate. At the other end of the spectrum, connections in the healthy brain continue to be made throughout life; we can learn as long as we are alive. There are many myths about aging. The central truth is still "use it or lose it."

REST AND ACTIVITY

Rest and activity are different sides of the same coin. Effective, ongoing, long-term activity requires an adequately rested brain. By "rest" we mean *deep physiological rest*. With the great emphasis on outcomes and high test results in education, many schools eliminated nap time for small children, presumably to take advantage of every minute for instruction. From the point of view of good sense and a growing brain, this is poor teaching because it fatigues the entire physiology, including the brain—which therefore becomes less responsive. The brain is a physiological organ, and its rules for functioning include an emphasis on health and respect for its rhythms. Thus, it has also been shown that adolescents who get minimal sleep have a more difficult time absorbing new information and demonstrate less creativity (Horne 1989).

STATES OF MIND

The distinction between rest and activity is actually very complex as we use it here. In the waking state, deep metabolic rest helps the brain experience a variety of different states of activity and excitement indicative of a general state of alertness. We can be excited in different ways and to different degrees. Technically these are called *states of arousal*. Again, the city analogy will help. Cities never stop everything completely, but most reduce their activity at night. During the day, there are also different intensities and types of activity. Some are local, some are citywide. Thus there is a period of waking up, of rush-hour traffic, of deadlines such as those for the news and stock markets, of common events such as the times of schools opening and closing. Other activities occur around the clock, such as police patrols and service station operations.

In the same way, the brain has many states of arousal, which affect the ways the brain deals with signals and information. These states of arousal are closely linked to what are called *states of consciousness*. Moss and Keen (1981) define consciousness as meaning "openness to the world."

States of consciousness are not Eastern phenomena, nor are they experienced by a few enlightenment-seeking souls—although mystic states also qualify. Most of them are experienced frequently by everyone. Charles Tart (cited in von Eckartsberg 1981) identifies several. They include creative states, meditative states, dreaming, and rationality (which here means being functional and effective in the world).

States of arousal are influenced, among other things, by our degree of physical well-being and by our emotions. We are aroused in one way when we have a sense of urgency caused by deadlines. We are aroused in another way when we have that sense of the "timeless now" that people have when they are deeply engrossed in a project and feel that they are "in the flow." Different parts of the brain may be dominant when we are in different states, but it is the brain as a whole that is functioning.

Effective learning always involves the alternation of several states of arousal. One of the fundamental reasons schools fail is that they impose on learners a single state of unrelieved boredom. The comparative importance of states of arousal can be seen in the power of entertainment and the arts. A good movie triggers a range of states with a series of buildups and releases. The power of great theater lies to a large extent in the way in which it uses this tension. Intelligent orchestration in teaching includes an understanding of these states of arousal and borrows from the theater such elements as timing and the ability to create anticipation, drama, and excitement.

ARE MALE AND FEMALE BRAINS DIFFERENT?

Research reveals that there are anatomical differences between male and female rat brains. For instance, females have millions more cells in a broader corpus callosum. The corpus callosum is the largest of several "bridges" joining the left and right hemispheres of the brain. Female brains tend to develop fairly uniformly; male brains do not. In sexually mature male rats, the right hemisphere is thicker than the left. This is also true of the human male and includes particularly the visual spatial cortex. Interestingly enough, as the male gets older, he loses much of his asymmetry; as the female ages, there is some indication of a tendency toward right-hemisphere dominance like the male. If we take the ovaries out of the female rat, her brain will develop more like the male. Without testes, the male rat brain will reflect similar development to the female. The outer portions of the brain are extremely plastic and can therefore be changed by external experiences, interactions with the environment, and changes in internal hormone levels (Diamond 1987). Administration of steroids will change brain development.

There are probably some corresponding differences in the brains of men and women. As yet the differences are too tenuous and too subject to different interpretations (Diamond 1988, Wittrock 1980). However, it is conceivable that some approaches to education may favor one sex over the other. Educators need to continue to track such research for possible implications for teaching.

HOW THE BRAIN IS ORGANIZED, OR WHATEVER HAPPENED TO LEFT BRAIN/RIGHT BRAIN?

I do not impugn the motives—though I do question the judgment of the brain's great dichotomizers. Many, for example, sincerely detect faults in our society, especially in its educational system, and are eager to use any method at their disposal to bring about desired changes. But the scientific enterprise is too precious to be sacrificed to any cause, however worthy it may appear. It is high time for investigators conversant with brain lateralization to announce that the unknowns in the field dwarf the little that is known, and the little more that is suspected. Once we concede the improbability of a brass ring's existing, we can, perhaps, get down to brass tacks (Gardner 1982, p. 285).

A Brief Recap

Most educators and teachers will have experienced some encounter with left brain/right brain enthusiasts. To be absolutely fair, the original research appeared to justify the conclusion that the brain, even in the normal person, tended to be highly left-hemisphere or right-hemisphere dominant. But the original research was based on the severing of the corpus callosum to provide relief from epileptic seizures. Scientists had performed commissurotomy or split-brain surgery in animals with apparently no observable change in behavior. According to Springer and Deutsch (1985), most researchers basically believed "that the corpus callosum's only function was to hold the halves of the brain together to keep them from sagging" (sort of like a brain brassiere). Roger Sperry and his colleagues at California Technological Institute went beyond the operation itself to see if there were any changes in perception in their patients (Sperry 1968). The rest, of course, is history.

The severing of the corpus callosum prevented the normal interchange of information between the two sides in the way it occurs in an intact brain. Once the two sides were isolated, scientists were able to study the two hemispheres separately. Each hemisphere seemed to have highly specialized functions. For example, since the left hemisphere is specialized for verbal expression, patients could verbally describe anything presented to that hemisphere. If a picture was presented to the right hemisphere, on the other hand, then the patient would have a nonverbal reaction, with no words to describe what was seen. In one example, a patient fixated on a dot while a picture of a nude woman was flashed to her right hemisphere. Her reaction was one of embarrassment, accompanied by giggles; but when asked what she saw, she could only reply, "Oh, doctor, you have some machine!"

Neurophysiologists, psychologists, educators, and business trainers generalized from Sperry's original research and similar experiments. They divided mental and personality characteristics according to which hemisphere appeared to be dominant within any individual, similar to whether someone was right or left handed:

• *Left-hemisphere Dominant*—Someone who is highly verbal, is primarily a sequential learner who is time conscious, all-or-none (outcome) oriented, prefers logical and analytical thinking, and is basically rational.

• *Right-hemisphere Dominant*—Someone who is not easily able to express experiences in verbal form, has excellent spatial memory and highly developed sensory (particularly spatial) recall. This person tends to experience the "whole" before noticing the parts. Hence this person is adept at synthesis and intuitive processing.

LEFT AND RIGHT TOGETHER

The most accurate statement we can make is that research on hemisphericity, at this point, is inconclusive. There is probably something to the distinctions made, but they are extraordinarily simplistic because both hemispheres are involved in all activities (Levy, J. 1985). For example, consider a poem, a play, a great novel, or a great work of philosophy. They all involve a sense of the "wholeness" of things and a capacity to work with patterns, often in a timeless way. In other words, the "left brain" processes are enriched and supported by "right brain" processes. Similarly, great artists do not just set up an easel and paint; they may do a significant amount of preliminary design and analytical thinking. That is why we have so many sketches from, say, Picasso and da Vinci, before the final product was painted. The artistic process involves a substantial amount of analytical and segmented thinking. The "right side" relies on the left for success.

We must recognize that intuition, holistic images, and synthesis over time, which are supposedly right-hemisphere functions, are within everyone's grasp. At the same time, analytic detail, verbal expression, and the ability to articulate, as well as engagement in critical and logical thinking, can all add a wealth of richness to our lives. Schools—or any place where learning is being encouraged—should therefore provide the opportunity to develop all abilities even as we continue to prefer some things over others.

WHAT DID OUR LOVE AFFAIR WITH HEMISPHERICITY LEAVE US?

What the split-brain research and the resultant hemispheric speculations did for education was quite earthshaking. For the first time, educators used brain research as a source for curriculum assessment and design. Admittedly, they also learned that the brain does not lend itself to simplistic explanations. But the door to the brain was opened, and many educators were determined to learn more about what represents the focus of their work.

LEARNING STYLES

This research also lent support to the belief that traditional education favors an all-too-narrow approach to teaching. When observing any group of human beings, we see an incredible variability in preferences, inclinations, opinions, and talents. The controversy over hemisphericity fostered acknowledgement of the fact that there are differences in styles of learning. Reading styles (Carbo, Dunn, and Dunn 1986), learning and creative/perceptual styles (McCarthy 1981), and management styles inventories (Hermann and Hanwood 1980) were originally developed with a left/right brain theoretical foundation. Such approaches have done a great deal to show that narrow or rigid teaching methods do not help all children.

Once again, however, educators may be jumping the gun by developing elaborate "how to's" before these findings have been thought out more carefully. Styles and preferences are immensely complex to understand. Preferences are expressed on the basis of moods, sleeping needs, time of peak activity during the day, sensory diversity, developmental factors, physical health, and on and on. No teacher can adequately deal with all of these variations or attempt to reach one child at a time with customized teaching methods. Variation and creativity in school, as well as a teacher's thorough knowledge of content, are all critical ingredients in helping the learner pattern correctly, regardless of personal style or preference. We agree with Hart (1983) that the more we approach meaningful, challenging, and relevant learning in the classroom, the more likely that children of all types will learn well.

DEFINITIONS OF INTELLIGENCE

Closely related to our acknowledgement of learning styles is a willingness to look at intelligence differently and admit that our definition of intelligence may be far too limited. Howard Gardner's (1985) "seven intelligences" is perhaps one of the most useful models to have emerged out of the controversy over learning styles. Gardner is the head of Project Zero at Harvard University. The project was so named because researchers wanted to begin studying intelligence without any preconceptions. Gardner's model of seven intelligences takes us away from our outmoded focus on only logical-mathematical and verbal intelligence. He suggests that the different intelligences are linguistic, musical, spatial, body-kinesthetic, mathematical, interpersonal, and intrapersonal.

We are not in a position to comment on precisely how many intelligences there might be. Moreover, it is clear that they, too, interpenetrate each other. The point is that the brain is capable of much more than has been realized. The broader definition responds to the fact that different brains are organized differently. In addition, without such broadening of the meaning of intelligence, we continue to send deeply conflicting messages to students and parents. How can we encourage students to believe that we really want them to develop their unique talents when we use such a limited measure of success?

PARTS AND WHOLES

As a result of split-brain research, we began to understand that parts and wholes always interact. Arthur Koestler (1972) coined the word "holon," which means that everything is a part of something bigger and is itself made up of parts. The arm is a part of a human being, which is part of a family, a community, a city, state, and country. Embedded in the arm are skin, cells, blood, oxygen, molecules, and so forth. The part contains the whole, and the whole, the parts. All knowledge is "embedded" in other knowledge. When we translate this to school subjects, we see that there is an enormous degree of overlap in that literature is deeply embedded in history, as are mathematics, science, and art. And art uses the knowledge of chemistry and science to create its paintings, sculptures, or pottery. The ability to perceive this interpenetration and both understand it and teach it constitutes one of the cornerstones of brain-based learning.

The split-brain research helped us to appreciate that the brain has an enormous innate capacity to deal with parts and wholes simultaneously. The brain can deal with the interconnected, interpenetrating, "holographic" world, provided it is encouraged to do so. One common thrust of many new methods of teaching is that they have this sense of "embeddedness"—a sense of wholeness that emerges out of seeing how academic subjects relate to each other and how human beings relate to the subjects (Crowell 1989). Thematic teaching and the integration of the curriculum are only two approaches to learning that epitomize this kind of teaching. That is why they are so powerful and effective when they are done well. In effect, such approaches orchestrate complex experience in a way that takes advantage of what the brain does well. They do not limit the brain by teaching the memorization of isolated facts and skills.

* * *

By grasping the interconnectedness of so many facets of our being, we appreciate how much learning is a product of everything that we are. Physical health is important. So is emotional health. Experiences actually shape our brains and therefore shape future learning. Relaxation and stress play a part, as do the ways we communicate and our sensory preferences. The body is, in fact, "in the mind." The brain's capacity to learn is vast. The brain is constructed for much more demanding intellectual activity than it usually experiences. We use the brain better when we enrich our experiences so that our brains can extract new and more complex ways of communicating and interacting with the world.

4

THE FORGOTTEN MEMORY SYSTEM

Space plays a role in all our behaviour. We live in it,
move through it, explore it, defend it. We find it easy
enough to point to bits of it: the room, the mantle of the
heavens, the gap between two fingers, the place left
behind when the piano finally gets moved. . . . Is space
a feature of the physical universe, or is it a convenient
figment of our minds? If the latter, how did it get there?
Do we construct it from spaceless sensations or are we
born with it? Of what use is it?

John O'Keefe and Lynn Nadel,
The Hippocampus as a Cognitive Map, 1978, p. 1

Many of us associate the word *memory* with the recall of specific dates or facts or lists of information and sets of instructions, requiring memorization and effort. What most of us tend to ignore and take for granted, however, is the ability to recall the thousands of bits of information we constantly accumulate in daily experience. Grasping that difference, however, is critical to understanding how to improve the ways that we teach the human brain.

Natural Memory Versus Memorization

When we compare memorizing a list of words with recalling facts about our meal last night, we notice a fundamental difference between the two tasks. Recalling the list will usually require repetition and some concerted effort at memorizing. The second task, recalling dinner, on the other hand, is almost ridiculously easy. Details such as the type and quality of food, who served, the furniture, floor, room layout, and so on are embedded in our memory. Yet never once did we repeat to ourselves during the meal: "Peas, peas, peas" or "blue carpet, blue carpet" to ensure memory of the meal.

For all of us, even when specific recollections fade away, we quite naturally and easily retain vast amounts of this sort of "ordinary" information that we can call on at any time.

The point is that there are different ways of dealing with new information. Education that focuses on memorization disregards the immense "natural memory" that everyone has for the events of life. The key to enhancing education is to find out how, most effectively, to have the two processes working together. A very useful investigation of the differences between memorization and effortless, natural memory was conducted by O'Keefe and Nadel (1978). Their initial work was done with rats, but they have also extended many of their findings to humans. Although their view of memory does not exhaust the field, we begin with their research because it is both biologically based and highly illuminating. And it allows us to draw some additional inferences that are extremely useful to educators. Their essential message is that we have at least two different types of memory systems, with different properties. Although they interact, the differences need to be appreciated.

Taxon Memory

We begin by focusing on the type of memory that involves storage in what O'Keefe and Nadel call *taxon memory systems*. Taxon derives from "taxonomies" or lists. These memories consist of items that do not depend on a specific physical context. They include prototypes or categories that represent a generic item, such as bird or house or dog; the contents of categories, such as types of trees and cars; and routines and procedures, such as driving.

Information-Processing Model

There are numerous taxon systems. For example, there appears to be one system that is specialized for the memory of faces. However, all the systems have many characteristics in common. The most pervasive characteristic is that taxon memories must be rehearsed. The system is accurately represented by the traditional information-processing model of memory (Figure 4.1).

The information-processing model is based on the notion that, of all the signals that reach our sensory register, we focus on a few that seem important (normal capacity is about seven "chunks" of information). Those signals or items move into short-term memory (Miller, G.A. 1956). If we rehearse them long and well enough, they are then stored in long-term memory. The memorizing of telephone

Figure 4.1 Information-Processing Model

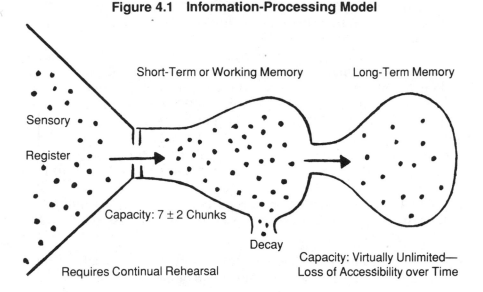

numbers is usually invoked to demonstrate how repeated rehearsal results in memory, while lack of rehearsal results in forgetting.

SOME FEATURES OF TAXON MEMORY

1. Information in taxon memories is placed there through practice and rehearsal. One example is the way some people recall the steps in starting a computer without actually understanding what is happening inside the box.

2. Taxon learning is linked to extrinsic motivation and is powerfully motivated by external reward and punishment. The behavioral approach to learning and, in fact, all rewards such as grades or privileges, tend to invoke and support learning via these memory systems. This is evident when students memorize for tests instead of seeking to understand ideas.

3. Our taxon memories are set in a way that makes them quite resistant to change, as anyone who has tried to change a habit knows. It is also why applying what we have learned in new and complex contexts is not automatic. Transfer of knowledge stored in the taxon systems does not occur easily. The ice skater practices for hours to get a movement correct so that it can be replicated as often and as perfectly as possible. Animal trainers ensure that animals can perform even with boisterous audiences present. The military services teach specific skills and responses that ensure uniform performance

under threat. All of these skills are extremely specific and habitlike, and it is assumed that they can be recalled and invoked with minimal variation.

4. Items in our taxon systems are relatively isolated. That is, they exist as stable entities, such as driving a car and memorizing phone numbers, that can be called on and used in a fairly predictable manner. The items are only relatively isolated because they can be highly organized and do interact with other items stored in memory so that they can be called on as needed during ongoing events. Thus we recall a specific phone number in a life context that calls for it.

5. Much of what we store in taxon systems is not initially meaningful. What matters to us is that the information can be recalled or skills used, on demand, irrespective of meaning. Such learning forms the basis of operant and classical conditioning and has greatly influenced our schools.

Information housed in taxon systems differs substantially from our memory for locations and interconnected events.

LOCALE MEMORY

O'Keefe and Nadel (1978) point out that everything that happens to us happens in space. This is so fundamental that we overlook it, and it needs to be made apparent. It means, in part, that we are always operating in a very rich physical context. We do not simply select furniture in a store. We select specific furniture in specific stores in specific malls and so on, all of which surround us and are in a precise, yet ever-changing relationship to us. We can substitute any action for selecting furniture in a store, such as attending a concert or reading a book, and the same principle holds true. Regardless of what we are doing, we are always in a physical context—and this affects our comprehension. "The scope of 'context' ranges from local linguistic constraints . . . to the physical and social milieu of an utterance" (Anderson, R.C., Reynolds, Schallert, and Goetz 1976, p. 3).

CREATING SPATIAL MAPS

We are all genetically endowed with the capacity to "navigate" through space. According to O'Keefe and Nadel, we do this by constantly creating and testing spatial maps that give us information about our surroundings. Maps are constructed within what they call the *locale memory system*. This system relies heavily on the hippocampus, which is part of the limbic system, almost in the center of the brain.

We rely on spatial maps to guide our movements and inter-actions within our surroundings. We use "maps" here to describe an interconnecting representation of places in the external world. The presence of these maps is absolutely crucial to the operation of our lives. After all, we *must* remember where we are in order to interact with the world safely and effectively. Thus we may become frustrated with the particulars of a strange airport, but from prior experience we remember about ticket counters, standing in line, security checks, smells, and the feel of the escalator under our feet. We know that airports have newsstands, some places to buy food, lounges, and sched-ules. We continuously call on our past experiences with airports to construct and update our ongoing interactions and to help us find our way through a new one. Perhaps the closest term in cognitive science is "schema" (Spiro 1980, p. 33).

The locale memory system is not adequately represented by the information-processing model of memory. In particular, it is clear that we continuously monitor a great deal of sensory information, much more than can be specifically attended to. We automatically form long-term memories of events and places without deliberately attempting to memorize them. This is shown by the example, referred to previously, of our recollections of our meal last night (even if we had a unique meal in a totally new or strange setting). It is in the recognition and use of the power of our locale memory that we begin to give credibility to the complex forms of instruction that are needed to upgrade education.

SOME BASIC FEATURES OF LOCALE MEMORY

1. Every human being has a spatial memory system. It is survival oriented, and its capacity is virtually unlimited.

2. Locale memories are never limited to static, context-free facts. They are memories that exist in relationship to where we are in space, as well as what we are doing. Thus they are records of ongoing life events, whether a trip through the Alps or the two hours we spent last night reading a good mystery. There is always a complex set of relationships among all these items.

3. Initial maps tend to form very quickly. This is an example of one-trial, or "instant," learning. Thus, when we first visit a friend's house and look around, we can gain an almost instant sense of the layout of the room we are in, and it will "stay" with us.

4. We update our maps on a continuous basis. Our spatial memory system is instantaneously and constantly monitoring and comparing our present surroundings with past, similar surroundings. It is always moderately open ended and flexible. For example, we create

a preliminary map of a restaurant when we first step into it. The comings and goings of people will be loosely monitored, but sometimes their behavior (such as taking the table next to us and speaking loudly) will generate a significant change in our map—whether or not we like the people.

5. Map formation is motivated by novelty, curiosity, and expectation. We expect the world to be a particular way because of the preliminary map that we form and the memories we recall of similar environments or events. For example, we might expect a person who is not from our native country to speak some other language, and we expect the traffic that we see to stay on the appropriate side of the road. We guide our behavior by those expectations and keep checking for accuracy. The corollary is that anything interesting or different is immediately attended to until it is incorporated into the map or identified as unimportant. The dominant motivation is therefore intrinsic. We are seeking to make sense of what is happening in our world.

6. Locale or spatial memory is enhanced through sensory acuity, or enhanced awareness of smell, taste, touch, sound, and so on. Some people seem to have unusually well-developed sensory systems, as Margaret Mead apparently did (Houston 1981). Many ancient cultures, such as those of Native Americans, have highly developed sensory acuity; but most of us can improve with practice.

7. Although maps for specific places are relatively instant, some large, intricate maps may take a considerable amount of time to be formed. They are the consequences of many experiences that only gradually come together.

CREATING THEMATIC MAPS

We have primarily focused on maps relating to physical space, but locale memory is not limited to maps in physical space. There are also mental maps of information, which exist as part of an interconnected pattern. That is, they exist in "mental space." We call these *thematic maps*, as do O'Keefe and Nadel. Thematic maps are critical for establishing more sophisticated links that aid in the transfer of knowledge. Thus there may be significant themes in our life, such as the need for a personal relationship or a political ideology, that operate to organize and shape much of our behavior. According to O'Keefe and Nadel, these themes serve as mental representations of the type of fluid, complex, and interactive relationships found in maps representing physical space. Our natural mental maps, therefore, seem to be at the heart of *thematic teaching*. That same memory system is engaged when we use stories, metaphors, celebrations, imagery, and music, all of which are powerful tools for brain-based learning.

How the Systems Interact

The locale system registers a continuous "story" of life experience. The taxon systems house the "parts" out of which the story is constructed. In other words, the locale system makes use of the contents of taxon systems. In effect, both systems naturally interact to generate meaning. The locale system must clearly be able to deal with rapid shifts in context and must register an "entire" context at a glance. One of its key features, therefore, is its indexing function. It can "call up" relevant items stored in the taxon systems, such as faces, trees, cars, and behaviors that were once new and meaningless. In fact, indexing is essential to the formation of our spatial maps.

If indexing is to be quick and effective, there must be many strong connections. If the strength and complexity of the connections are inadequate, information can only be called up in limited ways and is very inflexible. For example, we might learn some communication responses by rote and then find that when we need them, they are either difficult to remember or are so rigid that they cannot be applied appropriately in context. Similarly, a student may memorize some math rules but find it impossible to use them when operating a cash register. That, in effect, is the difference between memorization and understanding. A preliminary definition of meaningful learning, therefore, refers to storage of items that have so many connections, and are of such quality, that they can be accessed appropriately in unexpected contexts.

How do we develop the appropriate connections? We do it in the normal course of events by learning from significant experience. The new information that we acquire daily is always embedded in meaningful or important life events. Some new items are processed unconsciously. Some are deliberately analyzed and explored. Either way, they become meaningful quickly, by virtue of their being packaged in relevant, complex, and highly socially interactive experiences. This is the thrust of Vygotsky's theory of social learning (1978). It is also at the heart of the "whole language" theories of writers such as Goodman (1986) and Smith (1986).

Routes and Maps

Taxon memories may consist of single words, specific behaviors, or even complex information that has been memorized. Locale memories are of events or mental/emotional maps that occur in "relationship" and are continually changing or being updated. These systems are always interacting in the course of everyday events—it is a matter of degrees.

The best way to understand the difference between the two memory systems as they can be used in teaching is to understand the difference between using a route (taxon systems) or a map (locale memory) to go somewhere. Let us suppose, by way of illustration, that a group of teachers is attending a conference and decide to have dinner one night at a highly recommended restaurant in the suburbs. The point of this exercise is to demonstrate how teaching specific facts and skills to predetermined outcomes, largely relying on the taxon system, is different from developing understanding by maximizing the use of the locale system.

Following a Route. It is early in their stay, and not knowing the city, they ask for the quickest route to the restaurant. They could memorize the instructions by heart or simply record them on paper. Either way, they set out in their rented car and make a point of closely following the instructions, noting the correct streets and turns. They arrive at the restaurant in good time without once getting lost. If they had been called on to make a major detour, they would probably have been quite lost and would have had to seek further directions. They also tended to concentrate heavily on their route, checking road signs for accuracy and ignoring the larger context, including sights, along the way.

Establishing a Map. Contrast this event with what transpires as they have a few days to explore the convention city. In addition to using a few specific routes, they will be forming short-term, instant maps all the time—whenever they change location. However, something else is happening in the longer term. Our teachers have begun to get a sense of buildings and how streets are organized and relate to each other. They discover theaters and laundries, shopping areas and residential districts. They now have so much personal knowledge of the city that even without a printed map and even without seeking specific directions, they can find their way to the airport and to the restaurant they went to on the first night. They may even make detours to see a local attraction, buy gifts, and so on. They have thus developed a complex larger map as they acquired their general "sense" of the city. It is this internal map they use to solve any problem relating to alternate routes.

RELATIVE ADVANTAGES OF ROUTES AND MAPS

When our teachers learned a specific route to get to the restaurant, it was useful because it helped them to meet a specific objective. Although they had almost no knowledge of the city, the route was acquired fairly quickly, was relatively easy to follow, and was based almost entirely on what someone else told them. It was convenient and may have been appropriate if they had no interest in acquiring more information.

But the route was also limited. Without the assistance of a map or other linking procedures, once their route failed them, the teachers would have been lost. Developing their map was interesting and enjoyable. They did it because they wanted to. It took a significant amount of time, but it contained an enormous amount of information. And when the time came to call upon it, not only could they find their own specific route, but they also had extensive resources to fall back on if the first route failed.

It is pretty clear that we need both routes and maps. In fact we often develop a complex map by beginning with one or two routes, such as the route between the teachers' hotel and the convention center. In the long term and for creative responses in any complex context, maps are much more valuable. Routes are useful in the short term and as steps along the way in building maps.

ROUTE AND MAP LEARNING IN SCHOOLS

Translating the previous example to teaching, we can see that route learning is the model underlying behavioral objectives and performance-outcome models. Like the route to the restaurant, we have a beginning, a middle, and an end that is prespecified and lends itself readily to multiple-choice and other common forms of testing. Contrast this with inquiry learning, critical thinking and analysis, and creative and group processes, where outcomes and learning are open ended, personally meaningful, and unique.

A great deal of education is route learning and not map learning. Even if this is not intentional, it occurs for many reasons. First, methods used often predispose the brain to rely heavily on taxon systems. Teachers also lack sufficient control because outcomes and procedures tend to be both limited and predetermined, whether for educational, policy, or test-taking reasons. This actually shuts down map-building functions because maps are always complex and personal. Maps constitute an internal organization of information and always contain much more than the information packaged in a lesson or textbook. When every step is predetermined, students simply do not have the opportunity to organize information adequately. Moreover, they frequently fail to see the relevance of such information or a direct need for it. Hence they tend to memorize rather than think.

A second reason is that intrinsic motivation is often sabotaged by the imposition of a strong extrinsic system of motivation. Curiosity is replaced by rewards and punishments provided by the teacher. These include the use of tests, grades, token economies, smiley stickers, and getting out of school early (a very strange reward, which presumably confirms a consensus that schools are places one would not want to spend any time in). In ways ranging from offering extra credit to imaginative "begging," teachers have attempted to coerce children to solve more math problems per minute, answer the questions at the back of the page, write the report, or copy the sentences on the board. All of this is predominantly route learning, relying almost exclusively on taxon systems.

Third, in schools, the short-term advantages of route learning are obvious. Route learning gives quick, recognizable results, which can be measured readily. Thus route learning lends itself much more readily to testing. Formal testing, as it exists now, tests primarily for what Hart (1978) calls "symbol specific" learning. To raise test scores, thousands of schools across the nation have instructed teachers to "teach to the test." Moreover, route learning is teacher controlled and hence fairly simple to deliver.

"The crisis in education, part of which is the students' inability to think and reason, may be more easily understood when we recognize the abandonment by educators of rich map learning for goal-directed, route or symbol specific learning" (Nummela and Rosengren 1988). Maps are frames of reference. In them, a student must find a way to relate new information to other information. This is a creative and messy process. The problem is that teachers often have not been exposed to creative map-teaching models or forfeit map learning to accommodate the mandate for higher test scores. Students are drilled to remember the necessary information (routes), rarely understanding the meaning or implications of facts learned. The somewhat frightening result is that students frequently learn how to complete required work for external rewards and approval without ever experiencing the sheer joy of creative, unique, debated, and thought-out solutions that take them beyond the obvious. And what they learn, when they learn it, are specific routes that can be called on in predetermined situations, but not more sophisticated maps that can be used to develop the additional solutions that may be needed if the routes do not work.

THE SOLUTION: USE ROUTES WHEN NECESSARY, BUT FOCUS ON EXPERIENTIAL AND THEMATIC MAPPING

Route learning is useful at times. We need our store of procedures and categories; they are what the locale system uses to build maps. Moreover, people must be motivated externally to learn some things that are not initially meaningful or for which it is too time consuming or trivial to develop meaning. Children who have not developed more complex reasoning powers often need taxon memorization or skills learning to execute necessary and appropriate social behavior. The point is that if they are not learned in relationship to some context, they remain as relatively isolated, inert procedures and pieces of information. We do not automatically pull them together in maps simply because they have been memorized in some way.

Our dominant objective must be to teach for map learning. In other words, we must help students relate the material they need to know to what they already know. Doing so will capitalize on a natural process with which they are already equipped. That is the ability to learn from experience. The solution, which we explore in Part III of this book, is to deliberately embed new taxon content in rich, lifelike, and well-orchestrated experiences that require genuine interactions. In effect, we need to give students real experiences, engaging all their systems and their innate curiosity and involving them in appropriate physical movement, social interactions, practical projects, uses of language, and creative enterprises.

To teach everything so that it becomes a habit is foolish. It is rather like saying that we can help people become Einsteins and Mozarts by teaching them in the way that the military trains its troops. Yet that is what we have done.

> Although Einstein wrote little of his life and work, what he did record contains a recurrent theme: His interest in science and, presumably, his creativity, were undermined by forces that exerted external control over his work. As a youth, he attended a regimented, militaristic school in Germany where the pressures of exam period so overwhelmed him that he temporarily lost his interest in science which was, even at that time, quite substantial. [In 1949, Einstein recalled the deleterious effects of this school:] "This coercion had such a determining effect upon me that, after I had passed the final examination, I found the consideration of any scientific problems distasteful to me for an entire year" (Amabile 1983, p. 7).

One solution has been the introduction of discovery learning. Unfortunately, even this often fails to work because discovery is used as a trick or device to get students to remember the facts that the teacher wants them to remember. That is very different from discovery as Einstein experienced it.

Our experiences provide the background against which we check incoming information and in that sense determine who we are and how we see the world. Learners who both live in a democracy and experience democratic schools and classrooms are different from learners living in autocratic, controlled environments while they learn about democracy (Hartshorn and May 1928, White 1967). The former are much more likely to understand and practice democracy. This is true regardless of how well they do on the test and is particularly true when learners have had the opportunity to question and reflect on their learning.

When we expand learning from what the child knows already, then we can readily include new facts, ideas, and skills. Ignoring the child's natural memory is to ignore what that child can bring to the learning. Without a better use of our locale memory system in learning, most teaching becomes meaningless and segmented. In the case of many minorities, such as Native Americans, we do particular harm. Locale memory is especially emphasized and honored in many ancient cultures. A learning environment that ignores this is foreign to them, and our definition of "learning" can be seen as useless or, at the very least, confusing.

Schools that fail to acknowledge the student's ability to learn from experience, fail students.

COMPARISON OF ROUTE AND MAP APPROACHES TO A LESSON

Let us look at two ways of conducting a lesson built around the lowly potato. It may be that some specific information is to be learned. A science student, for instance, might need to know that there are more than 1,000 varieties of potato and be familiar with the position of the potato in the vegetable kingdom. Another issue might be the chemical composition of the potato, including starch, protein, minerals, and water.

ROUTE LEARNING, EMPHASIZING TAXON SYSTEMS

The Lesson Plan. We would have a predetermined lesson plan complete with specified outcomes all relating to the potato. Relevant facts about the potato would be identified through lecture and textbook information. The teacher acts as the primary authority, judging right and wrong responses. By and large, information from other subject areas would be considered irrelevant. A variety of memory strategies might be employed that focus on practice and rehearsal, but the object would remain memorization of facts. Testing would likely be in a formal, standardized mode.

Motivation. Motivation would be primarily extrinsic for all students who do not have some interest in or internal purpose or reason for knowing about potatoes. In general, desire for a high grade or fear of getting a low grade are the primary motivators.

Brain Activation. Activation of the brain would be fairly specific. What we mean by this is that, in addition to its normal global operation, for the purposes of memorization a relatively small number of neurons is firing repeatedly. Such specific effort results in rapid and substantial fatigue. Hence regular rest breaks must be taken between trials, and the process is unlikely to be enjoyable or stimulating unless part of a larger pattern invoking intrinsic motivation.

Results. Many students will remember some information in the short term, but forget it soon after the test. A few will remember a significant amount for longer periods. Testing for specific memories will be easy and relatively simple minded. However, the tests will reveal very little about what else students learned. And, in fact, the students will learn very little that they could apply in a broader or practical context or in a creative way.

MAP LEARNING, BASED ON THE LOCALE SYSTEM

The Lesson Plan. Some of the facts to be learned would still be specified, but the lesson plan would be different because the objective would be to use the information to build maps. That can only be possible if there are additional objectives being met, basically aimed at helping a student build internal relationships. Thus subject boundaries would be crossed and the potato could be used for explorations in history, geography, science, literature, music, sociology, art, and so on. But this is not just a memorization strategy. One purpose would be to actually use the potato to help students understand those other areas.

For example, the teacher might begin by bringing to class a rather interesting looking and generously sprouting potato, accompanied by a story from history about a war or incident of extreme prejudice that involved the potato. It could become apparent that the history of the potato really is fascinating. Did students know it was the vegetable of the poor until a famine hit England and the wealthy were forced to eat it? The class could study the famine and the historical and social implications, including the relevance of prejudice and social class distinctions. Relationships would be drawn between the past, our own society, and actual student experiences. This could lead to a study of the effect of economic realities on societies both past and present. Even the laws of supply and demand could be better understood. Geographic features of different countries could be tied to a scientific exploration of soil needs and the consequential effect on nutrition. Ecology issues can be introduced. All of this will be enriched by the use of art, music, literature, field trips, visits from those actively working in relevant areas in the community, and creative projects that directly relate content to life. Thus many subjects could be integrated around the potato—and in a way that would allow the brain to tie all the facts together.

Motivation. The student's personal curiosity is invoked. This is not always easy to do, but it is at the heart of locale learning. The teacher has a much better chance to engage the student because personal interests can be incorporated through the provision of choices and personal experience can be invoked. In many respects, this motivation is similar to the curiosity associated with mastering a hobby and the complexity of the experiences that relate to the hobby.

Brain Activation. The global operations of the brain are more directly engaged in learning because many areas of learning, including the senses and emotions, are brought into play. This type of learning disperses learning throughout the brain, and there is much less stress on specific brain cells. Hence students can participate in this type of learning for much longer periods of time. They will be more deeply involved and more excited.

Results. Most students will remember some information in the short term. Many more will recall a significant amount of information in the long term and will also be able to invoke it in different contexts and for different purposes. They will also have developed some understanding of many other issues than those of the original subject. Thus mapping also means that the subject itself can subsequently be used by the student automatically in the development of further maps. There will be a small amount of formal and standardized testing, but most evaluation will be complex and will be integrated into the instructional process in a challenging but nonthreatening way (see Chapters 8 and 11).

We have used the potato as one example, but thematic teaching of this kind can be done around any object, appropriate picture, or metaphor.

* * *

Whatever we set out to teach will be enveloped in a complex experience, irrespective of what we intend. That is because the learner's locale system is always monitoring the entire environment. Hence the challenge for a teacher is to integrate new content into that experience. Real-life experience therefore becomes the organizer for education.

Educators need to pay attention to all the dimensions and layers of stimuli that go into the makeup of experience. The peripheral sensory environment must be addressed. The ongoing social relationships must be appreciated and enhanced. The inner concerns and personal objectives of learners must be engaged because that is the key to invoking their curiosity and sense of novelty. They are biologically driven to make sense of their world. Because much processing is done beneath the level of awareness and after a lesson is over, an effective atmosphere must be maintained throughout a school on an ongoing basis. And while specific strategies to aid in the memorization of some routes and procedures are important, the focus of education *must* be on the generation, by the learner, of more and more useful, sophisticated, and personally meaningful interconnections characteristic of flexible maps.

5

THE TRIUNE BRAIN

*Particularly today, when so many difficult and complex
problems face the human species, the development of
broad and powerful thinking is desperately needed. There
should be a way, consistent with the democratic ideals
espoused by all of these countries, to encourage, in a
humane and caring context, the intellectual development
of especially promising youngsters. Instead we find, in
the instructional and examination systems of most of
these countries, an almost reptilian ritualization of the
educational process. I sometimes wonder whether the
appeal of sex and aggression in contemporary American
television and film offerings reflects the fact that the
R-complex is well developed in all of us, while many
neocortical functions are, partly because of the repressive
nature of schools and societies, more rarely expressed,
less familiar and insufficiently treasured.*

Carl Sagan, *The Dragons of Eden,* 1977,
pp. 202–203

Carl Sagan's comments are challenging. We have made impressive
strides in science and technology. Why is it then, with all our accumulated knowledge and technology, that defense of territory; hierarchies of dominance, power and suppression; and intense displays of
ego still play such a critical part in the way we interact with one
another? And how might this difficulty in changing the way we go
about our business be related to the question of why it continues to
be so difficult to change the way that schools are run?

One explanation is offered by Paul MacLean (1969, 1978),
the former director of the Laboratory of the Brain and Behavior at the
U.S. National Institute of Mental Health. MacLean's theory is popularly
referred to as the "triune brain theory" because he suggests that the
human brain is actually three brains in one. He further suggests that

one predominant explanation for the propensities mentioned by Sagan is the existence of ancient survival patterns lodged in the most primitive of the three brains. He adds that the development of human beings whose behavior is motivated by compassion, concern for the future, the ability to plan ahead, and empathy for other living forms is possible, but requires greater use of the most recent addition to the brain—the prefrontal lobes.

There are, of course, other models of the brain based on its evolutionary development (see, e.g., Ornstein and Thompson, *The Amazing Brain*, 1984). Nevertheless, the triune brain theory is significant for educators because it provides us with a different and useful way of looking at behavior, is compatible with relevant psychological and sociological theories, and provides some coherent direction for what it will take to generate change.

BRAIN RESEARCH AS ARCHAEOLOGY

MacLean compares his work to that of an archaeologist searching back in time through layers of the brain's evolutionary development. He has identified three major layers or "brains," which were established successively in response to evolutionary need. They are the reptilian system or *R-complex*, the *limbic system*, and the *neocortex*. Each layer is geared toward more or less separate functions, but all three layers interact substantially. In some respects, MacLean's theory is reminiscent of Freud's division of consciousness into id, ego, and superego, Plato's structure of the soul into three layers or levels, and Socrates' three layers of soul-life, and other tripartite theories.

THE BROTHERS TRIUNE

A preliminary way of looking at this is to compare the three layers with three brothers living under one roof. The oldest brother, the R-complex, is in charge of maintenance. This includes providing food and waste disposal and attending to general security and comfort. Most of his behaviors are automatic and ritualistic, and he strongly resists change. He does not use language, though in some ways he can respond to it.

The second brother, representing the limbic system, feels deeply. He monitors emotion and plays a significant role in remembering new information and organizing events. He is concerned to some extent with self-defense through fight or flight. He also tries to maintain balance between the oldest and the youngest by keeping the oldest brother from totally dominating the family and by serving as a conscience.

The youngest and largest of the brothers is the neocortex. He is creative, can use language, compose music, and engage in very complex analysis. He is capable of formal operational or abstract thought, can anticipate and plan for the future, and is, in general, very intelligent.

Each brother is involved to some extent in the behavior and decisions of the other. They can be supportive of each other. They can also be in conflict. The oldest brothers are most likely to dominate when threat is perceived, because then the top priority is safety and survival. Working together, however, they can successfully deal with quite extraordinary challenges.

OUR ANCESTRAL BRAIN—THE REPTILIAN COMPLEX

The reptilian brain (or R-complex) consists largely of the brain stem. Its purpose is closely related to actual physical survival and overall maintenance of the body. Digestion, reproduction, circulation, breathing, and the execution of the "fight or flight" response in stress are all primarily located in this system. Because the reptilian brain is basically concerned with physical survival, the behaviors it governs have much in common with the survival behaviors of animals. It plays a crucial role in establishing home territory, reproduction, and social dominance. The overriding characteristics of R-complex behaviors are that they are automatic, have a ritualistic quality, and are highly resistant to change.

MacLean (1978) takes exception to John Locke's proposition that we are born like a "tabula rasa" or a blank slate and that all human behavior, with the exception of simple survival mechanisms such as breathing, is learned. He has found too many similarities between the human and animal worlds, such as display behavior:

> If all human behavior is learned, why is it that in spite of all our intelligence and culturally determined behavior, we continue to do all the ordinary things that animals do? Social hierarchies among lizards are maintained by the repeated performance of signature and challenge displays. Components of such display are also used in the so-called signature display and in courtship. Teachers are used to seeing such displays, both inside and outside the classroom. It is of interest that once the dominant lizard has others bowing to him, they will nevertheless join him in attacking a strange lizard entering their domain. Lizards caged together will gang up on a stranger. Mindful of the claim that all human behavior is learned, one might ask, "Do schoolboys and collegians learn to haze and bully by reading accounts of the ganging up of lizards on a newcomer?" (pp. 319–320).

MacLean contends that there are identifiable categories of reptilian behaviors evident in human beings. Here are some examples.

TERRITORIALITY

We defend our property both in the physical and abstract sense of ownership, as evidenced by the terms "my house," "my family," "my country," "my room," and "my chair" (exemplified by the Archie Bunker chair). Supervisors of student teachers have to remind the students to be aware of where they sit in the lunchroom or teacher's lounge. Veteran teachers can be impatient when they find that their favorite place in the room has been "taken" by a newcomer. Equally obvious is the way that college students will pick a seat on the first day of class and automatically sit in that seat for the remainder of the term.

"PREENING" OR RITUALISTIC DISPLAY

We do what makes us "stand out" and attract attention, characterized by the sense of "look at me, I am unique." We may even believe it ourselves when we finally purchase that red Porsche.

NESTING BEHAVIORS

These are often revealed in the way we fix up the house, decorate it, prepare it for our personal use, and so on. It is, for instance, the place in which we rear our young, so we attach importance to having enough space (a room), storage and supplies (cupboards), appropriate colors, and so on.

MAINTAINING SOCIAL HIERARCHIES

Despite ostensible commitment to democratic processes, most organizations are based on what have been called "dominance hierarchies" (Eisler 1987). The dominance derives from such factors as perceived biological, intellectual, social, or physical superiority.

MATING RITUALS

Adolescents and adults both engage in these in their own ways. Flirting is a mating ritual in any language.

FLOCKING BEHAVIOR

Flocking is closely linked to social conformity and is found everywhere. In schools we can observe it in groups of students socializing together, perhaps being identified by common hairstyles, clothing, acceptable behaviors determined by "in group" standards, and so forth.

OTHER GROUP BEHAVIORS

The R-complex can act as a very useful lens through which to view gang and other group membership. Gangs typically stake out and defend their territory, sometimes violently. Membership often requires ritual initiation. Dominance hierarchies are reflected, among other things, in the selection and power of leaders and in the relative obeisance of followers. A uniform of some type is the norm, as is the tendency of gang members to spend time together and behave in ways that are approved by the group.

Isopraxic Behaviors. MacLean (1978) posits another interesting way of cross-categorizing the biologically driven behaviors. These definitions also shed some light on group behavior. He defines isopraxic behaviors as those in which two or more members of a group communicate by doing the same thing. These behaviors rely heavily on the members' ability to imitate. Because these are common to a particular group, they help to maintain its identity. An example might be the particular salutation given to a team member who succeeds in scoring a touchdown in football. Another example might be a secret sign or the wearing of some insignia such as Greek letters.

Perseverative and Reenactment Behaviors. These behaviors are marked by strict adherence to inflexible routine, ritual, and strict conformity to precedent. Once something works, it is very likely to be repeated even if circumstances have changed to a large degree. This is where some specific superstitions have their origin.

> The constitutional part of us that reinforces routine has a powerful means of making it known when there has been a break in routine. As anyone knows who has suggested a change in curriculum, there is hardly anything more sure to upset the emotional and rational minds than the alteration of long established routine. It was as though the whole sky would fall. In like vein, anything that reinforces routines may have a reassuring, calming effect (MacLean 1978, p. 322).

Much of the behavior of fraternities, sororities, and other groups of all types (including teachers), which harbor rules about membership or a multitude of rituals highly resistant to change, might be explained in this way.

Tropistic Behaviors. These are of particular interest to educators because they relate to different receptive periods in a child's or student's development. The most obvious period is the one linked with an emerging sexual identification; but all periods are marked by specific fetishes, fads, and fashions, often shown in hairstyles and "designer" clothes.

Deceptive Behaviors. Animals deceive to forestall or confuse their enemy or prey. In human beings, these behaviors take the form of subverted direct aggression such as faking, lying, or pretending. MacLean points out:

No mention can be made of deceptive behavior without being reminded that white-collar criminality has never been so much in the news as during the last few years. If we have learned through culture that "honesty is the best policy," why is it that people are willing to take enormous risks to practice deception? Why do the games we teach our young place such a premium on deceptive tactics and terminology of deception? How can pupils be expected to come off the playing fields and not use the same principles in the competition and struggle for survival in the classroom? (MacLean 1978, p. 234).

THE GUARDIAN AT THE GATE—THE LIMBIC SYSTEM

The limbic system, the second brain to evolve, houses the primary centers of emotion. It includes the *amygdala*, which is important in the association of events with emotion, and the *hippocampus*, which is the critical part of the brain dealing with locale memory, referred to in Chapter 4. MacLean, like O'Keefe and Nadel, sees the role of the hippocampus as linked to contextual memories. The hippocampus appears to receive internally generated information from the septal and other areas and externally generated information "from sensory systems projecting to nearby transitional cortical areas" (Isaacson 1982). Contextual memories, therefore, are a composite of our inner and outer worlds. The limbic system is also involved in primal activities related to food and sex, particularly having to do with our sense of smell and bonding needs, and activities related to expression and mediation of emotions and feelings, including emotions linked to attachment and bringing up our young. These protective, loving feelings become increasingly complex as the limbic system and the neocortex or "third brain" link up.

The limbic system is the first of the more "human" systems in that it is thought to be what Isaacson (1982) calls "nature's tentative first step towards providing self-awareness, especially awareness of the internal conditions of the body" and how we "feel." Some speculate that the beginnings of altruistic behavior are located there (Sagan 1977). Because the limbic system is capable of combining messages from our inner and outer experiences, it serves to inhibit the R-complex and its preference for ritualistic, habitual ways of responding. In that sense, the limbic system offers us our first opportunity to "rewrite" our ancestral responses.

OUR "THINKING" BRAIN—THE NEOCORTEX

Also called the *neomammalian* brain, the neocortex constitutes five-sixths of the human brain. It is the outer portion of our brain and is approximately the size of a newspaper page crumpled together. The neocortex makes language, including speech and writing, possible; in that sense, it is different from the other two "brains." Much of the processing of sensory data occurs in the neocortex. It renders logical and formal operational thinking possible and allows us to see ahead and plan for the future. Its capacities are at the heart of science and art, and it is so rich and complex that we cannot begin to do it justice here.

INTERCONNECTEDNESS OF THOUGHT AND FEELING

We have mentioned that all three layers of the brain interact. This means more than that they just influence each other. It means that none of the ingredients that we deal with in education, such as "concepts" and "emotions" and "behaviors," is separate. They influence and shape each other. The full extent of this interconnectedness is unclear, of course. Even the range of possible emotions is unknown. Thus both Ekman (1985) and Clynes (1977) suggest that all people have a set of primary emotions, but the two writers identify slightly different primary sets.

The interconnectedness of concepts and emotions, however, should be expected, given the fact that the limbic system mediates both emotion and memory. Examples are all around us. They include the happy memories of family and success; the memories associated with grief and loss; the phobias that we pick up about, say, math and computers, and from close encounters of unpleasant kinds; and the enormous amounts that we remember about the hobbies and subjects that enthrall us.

According to MacLean, subjectively "something doesn't exist unless it's tied up with an emotion" (Holden 1979). Emotions give a sense of reality to what we do and think. Rosenfield (1988) also contends that memory is impossible without emotion of some kind, that emotion energizes memory. The practical consequence is that the enthusiastic involvement of students is essential to most learning.

There is more, however. Concepts are actually "shaped" by emotions; and as Lakoff demonstrates in *Women, Fire and Dangerous Things* (1987), emotions themselves are rich conceptually. Lakoff establishes his case through the use of metaphor. He shows, for example, that when we deal with anger we often use such phrases as:

- Those are inflammatory remarks.
- She was doing a slow burn.
- He was breathing fire . . .
- He was consumed by his anger (p. 388).

Here the metaphor of fire shows that anger has many faces. And in fact there are many other metaphors for anger, as there are for other emotions. Thus I might feel a bubble or burst of happiness. What this means is that the emotional depth and range that students have must affect their actual capacity to grasp ideas and procedures. Similarly, content that is emotionally sterile is made more difficult to understand. A brief self-exploration of the personal meaning of many concepts, such as "friend," "companion," "enemy," "burden," and "challenge," reveals how value and emotion laden they are.

To teach someone any subject adequately, *the subject must be embedded in all the elements that give it meaning.* People must have a way to relate to the subject in terms of what is personally important, and this means acknowledging both the emotional impact and their deeply held needs and drives. Our emotions are integral to learning. When we ignore the emotional components of any subject we teach, we actually deprive students of meaningfulness.

FURTHER INFERENCES FOR EDUCATION

MacLean's theory is intuitively appealing and appears to make sense of much that everyone, including teachers, experiences. It can be used to help us understand what is actually happening in schools, in institutions, and on the streets. It can also be applied to make some basic but sound recommendations for education, as we show in this book. However, it is also critical not to reduce MacLean's theory to the obvious and hence to what we already know and do. As the research on the brain reveals, all regions of the brain interact in complex ways. It is entirely incorrect to assume that in any situation one of our three "brains" is working and the others are not. What we can do, perhaps tentatively, is assume that at times one particular focus may be dominant while the rest of the brain acts in support and that education and in fact all of society can influence which focus dominates.

In practice, we frequently use the immense intellectual capabilities of the neocortex in the pursuit of basic objectives, such as mating behavior and the defense of territory. Students do this. Parents do it. Teachers do it. Society does it. That is because the three brains are operating simultaneously, whether or not we are aware of it.

We have used our neocortex, for example, to develop complex perfumes to attract the opposite sex and have developed knowledge of the chemical makeup of hair so that we can enhance its attractiveness through thickness, health, and color. As Olympia Dukakis says in the movie *Steel Magnolias*, "the difference between us and the animals is that we can accessorize." Our knowledge about textiles, plastic surgery, and dentistry are used to enhance our sex appeal and embellish our courtship rituals. We also employ all the power and grace of language, the arts, and our symbol systems in this venture. Using the neocortex for this type of embellishment of R-com-

58

plex rituals gives us the feeling of progress even while we maintain and safeguard our ritualistic survival patterns.

ACKNOWLEDGING THE TRIUNE BRAIN IN TEACHING

RITUALISTIC BEHAVIORS NEED TO BE "PLAYED OUT" IN POSITIVE WAYS.

Sports and physical games fulfill basic instinctual drives. They are also the natural vehicles to begin more sophisticated learning. All types of games are natural to children and adults. Exploring language, formulas, and new information through games can bind one of our basic R-complex needs to learning.

SOCIAL INTERACTIONS AND EMOTIONAL WELL-BEING ARE CRITICAL TO OUR SURVIVAL, PLAY A CRUCIAL ROLE IN UNDERSTANDING, AND ARE DEEPLY MOTIVATING.

Cooperative learning, communication skills, and learning how to live in a complex society with people of similar and conflicting needs and emotions should receive as much attention as "cognitive development." Our deep need for interconnectedness with others, which is often played out negatively in the form of gangs or exclusive groups, can also be a vehicle for expanding knowledge. Participating in debates, telling stories, role-playing historical figures, reenacting historical events, and generating "expert panel" solutions to social and medical or other scientific problems are only a few of the intellectually challenging behaviors that involve our need for social belonging and interaction. Such methods can also address the need to "stand out" (preening) and develop our own talents or expertise.

SCHOOLS NEED TO REDIRECT R-COMPLEX PREFERENCES.

Much of the energy of the secondary school day is currently devoted to social activities—deciding how to dress, what shampoo to use, and where and how to engage in preening or mating rituals. It is extremely important that students do not come away with the belief that social rituals and emotional highs devoid of intellectual challenge are the limits of the joy and fulfillment that they can experience.

The alternative is to help students experience the genuine excitement inherent in any subject through, say, research in science or the expression of their creative abilities. It is also a matter of helping students reflect on their own ritualistic behaviors and search for more sophisticated and challenging ways of living and learning. One issue, of course, is whether this redirection is possible.

HOPE FOR THE FUTURE—OUR PREFRONTAL CORTEX

Though compassion and concern for others long preceded the 20th century, they are extremely important. Teaching becomes critical because it can help students appreciate complex issues in order to make better choices. But so far we know of no test for compassion, empathy, and other related qualities that is given with the same enthusiasm as IQ tests are. Why are we so enamored of cognitive and mechanistic notions of learning and artificial intelligence while our higher human functions remain uninvestigated? In our society, we do not yet appear to value accomplishments that can be attributed to the intelligence of our motives and values.

Acknowledging emotional factors and the power of ritualistic, reptilian behaviors may not, by itself, lead to the enhancement of education because the "locus of control" may still be in the more primitive parts of the brain. Our ability to sense beauty, experience compassion, and gain appreciation for life also needs to be enhanced in the classroom. To that end, MacLean, among others, sees the prefrontal cortex as one part of the brain that provides hope for our survival as a species.

The prefrontal cortex is that region of the neocortex inside our foreheads. Even though the removal of the prefrontal cortex results in no apparent change in IQ as we now measure it, it appears to be largely responsible for a wide range of abilities that neuropsychologists call "adaptive behaviors." These include planning, analysis, sequencing, and learning from errors, as well as the inhibition of inappropriate responses and the capacity for abstraction. Thus increased compassion and empathy become possible because we can acquire the cognitive capacity to "put ourselves in another's shoes."

Until recently, survival has meant physical victory against "the enemy" and such obvious foes as disease, hunger, and natural disasters. There are new threats that are much more subtle and less well understood. They involve our understanding of ecological issues that tie our existence to the survival of the rain forests and to the capacity to see common interests and overlapping concerns. They require an appreciation of the problems for all of us posed by such facts as that the United States alone, with 4 percent of the world's population, uses 60 percent of the world's resources; that 1,000 children are born each day to drug-dependent mothers; and that 27 percent of Native American children are born with fetal alcohol syndrome.

Interrelational thinking and action require, among other things, the ability to delay gratification and to act on the basis of complex understanding and with compassion and empathy, for all of which the prefrontal cortex is necessary. MacLean believes that these qualities may well be critical new survival features. He states:

> Have you seen the fish squirm and wiggle in the heron's crop as it is swept along to be slowly peeled away by burning juices? Have you heard birds cough themselves to death from air-saccultitis? Have you risen in the night to give them cough syrup? Have you seen the cat play with a mouse? Have you seen cancer slowly eat away or strangle another human being? The misery piles up like stellar gases tortured by a burning sun. Then why, slowly, progressively, did nature add something to the neocortex that for the first time brings a heart and a sense of compassion into the world? Altruism, empathy—these are almost new words. Altruism—"to the other." Empathy—"compassionate identification with another individual." . . . In designing for the first time a creature that shows a concern for suffering of other living things, nature seems to have attempted a 180 degree turnabout from what had been a reptile-eat-reptile and dog-eat-dog world (pp. 340–449).

LEARNING AS THE NEW SURVIVAL PRINCIPLE

MacLean is largely concerned with survival. The thrust of his theory is that when our survival is threatened, we tend to invoke basic patterns of behavior. This point is also supported by O'Keefe and Nadel (1978).

The promise of the theory is that there is an entirely new survival process available to us. The primitive approach to survival is "fight or flight." The potential of the neocortex is that it can find new ways to survive because it is capable of profound learning. And that, we will see, requires us to use our brains in ways that have never been done before on a large scale.

With the three brains operating appropriately together, we have the capacity to significantly reprogram and redirect old brain propensities. Survival will always be important, but *we have at our disposal the capacity to totally rethink what it means to survive and to implement the solutions.* In *Foundation,* Isaac Asimov (1983) has one of his characters say that "violence is the last refuge of the incompetent." We agree.

The challenge is to make the rethinking sufficiently powerful and meaningful so as to transcend the narrow meanings of the R-complex and the limbic system. That, we suggest, is the proper role of art, literature, the humanities, the sciences, and all the other grand achievements of the human soul. They are not fodder for the memory machine. In fact, approaching them as "stuff" to be memorized is probably worse than useless. They are expressions of what people *are* capable of doing. But they have to be adequately experienced to be fully appreciated.

Once more, Carl Sagan (1977) says it elegantly:

As a consequence of the enormous social and technological changes of the last few centuries, the world is not working well. We do not live in traditional and static societies. But our governments, in resisting change, act as if we did. Unless we destroy ourselves utterly, the future belongs to those societies that, while not ignoring the reptilian and mammalian parts of our being, enable the characteristically human components of our nature to flourish: to those societies that encourage diversity rather than conformity; to those societies willing to invest resources in a variety of social, political, economic and cultural experiments, and prepared to sacrifice short-term advantage for long-term benefit; to those societies that treat new ideas as delicate, fragile and immensely valuable pathways to the future (pp. 203–204).

6

THREAT AND THE BRAIN

You've been afraid about Ina. But you needn't be. The
worst of this kind of shock is that it puts your thinking
out of action and hands you over to your emotions. Now
just pull yourself together and think!

Patricia Wentworth, *Through the Wall*,
1950, p. 172

At one time, a compartmentalized view of the human
body was generally accepted. Recent knowledge of the
anatomical and functional links between brain and body
point in a different direction. Brain researchers
now believe that what happens in the body can affect
the brain, and what happens in the brain can
affect the body. Hope, purpose, and determination are
not merely mental states. They have electrochemical
connections that play a large part in the workings of the
immune system and indeed, in the entire economy of
the total human organism.

Norman Cousins, *Head First—The Biology of*
Hope, 1989, p. 73

Watching someone become red with embarrassment or feeling our
hands become icy before a public talk is so common to us that we
do not see it as a significant event. But what we are observing are
actually indicators of subtle changes occurring in the rest of the physiology, including the brain, as the result of perceived threat. The brain
appears to be very much like a camera lens: the brain's "lens" opens
to receive information when challenged, when interested, or when in
an "innocent," childlike mode and closes when it perceives threat that
triggers a sense of helplessness.

Evidence from different fields strongly suggests that some
types of learning are positively affected by relaxation and challenge

and inhibited by perceived threat. For example, perceptual psychologists have long been aware of the "narrowing of the perceptual field" (Combs and Snygg 1949), which occurs when an individual perceives an experience as threatening. Leslie Hart (1983) calls such perceptual narrowing "downshifting." When we downshift, we revert to the tried and true—and follow old beliefs and behaviors regardless of what information the "roadsigns" provide. Our responses become more automatic and limited. We are less able to access all that we know or see what is really "there." Our ability to take into consideration subtle environmental and internal cues is reduced (Gruneberg and Morris 1979). We also seem less able to engage in complex intellectual tasks, those requiring creativity and the ability to engage in open-ended thinking and questioning. Indeed, much behavior and thinking become phobic in the sense that specific stimuli trigger instant, potentially inappropriate, and usually exaggerated, responses. Anyone who has ever been a new teacher walking into a classroom—or has seen one—will know what this means. Interns often take weeks before they step out from behind the podium or desk, or begin to see students as individuals.

Downshifting, then, appears to affect many higher-order cognitive functions of the brain and thus can prevent us from learning and generating solutions for new problems. It also appears to reduce our ability to see the interconnectedness or interrelationships required by thematic or ecological thought processes. Because it also affects our frontal lobes, it may well keep us from fully developing the strictly "human" qualities that MacLean (1978) sees as the essence of a whole new survival principle.

Downshifting, in large part, is the reason students fail to apply the higher levels of Bloom's Taxonomy (Bloom, Englehart, Furst, Hill, and Krathwohl 1956). Making maximum connections in the brain requires a state we describe as "relaxed alertness." This is a combination of low threat and high challenge (explored in more detail in Chapter 10). Our objective here is to identify some of the characteristics and consequences of downshifting and to show how it occurs as the response of the brain to perceived threat. We begin by referring to a related topic that has been in the public domain for many years—the notion of stress.

WHAT DOES STRESS THEORY TELL US ABOUT THE OPTIMAL USE OF THE BRAIN?

Stress is a phenomenon that is familiar to all of us. It "is an arousal reaction to some stimulus—be it an event, object, or person. This stress reaction is characterized by heightened arousal of physiological and psychological processes" (Girdano and Everly 1986).

Not all stress is harmful. Indeed, life without stress is not possible. Hans Selye (1978) distinguished between two types of stress, as follows:

> We must, however, differentiate within the general concept of stress between the unpleasant or harmful variety, called *"distress"* (from the Latin *dis* = bad, as in dissonance, disagreement), and *"eustress"* (from the Greek *eu* = good, as in euphoria). During both eustress and distress the body undergoes virtually the same nonspecific responses to the various positive or negative stimuli acting upon it (p. 74).

Selye goes on to say that "the fact that eustress causes much less damage than distress graphically demonstrates that it is 'how you take it' that determines, ultimately, whether one can adapt successfully to change" (p. 74).

The underlying message is that our mental and emotional responses affect the functioning and operating of the body. *Body and mind, therefore, influence each other.* More specifically, in one set of stressful circumstances, the person becomes dysfunctional and the body is damaged; in another set of stressful circumstances, the person functions effectively, and the body, though fatigued, is much less affected. This has been dramatically illustrated in ways that are interesting for educators. University students going through exams, for example, were shown to have lowered levels of helper T cells, which are a part of the immune system and protect the body from invasions such as cancer and cold or flu viruses (Borysenko 1987). Examinations, in other words, adversely affected the immune system of some students (threat related to ego issues was highly implicated). Relaxation techniques, on the other hand, have been shown to reverse such immune suppression.

There is now a substantial body of information about the actual physiological processes at work. For example, the body creates the hormone cortisol in direct response to certain types of stresses; and chronic stress is associated with high levels of cortisol in the body. The hippocampus, the region of the brain associated by O'Keefe and Nadel with the locale memory system, is also the region most sensitive to cortisol and is negatively affected by high levels of this hormone. As we discuss later in this chapter, one inference (Jacobs and Nadel 1985, O'Keefe and Nadel 1978) is that *under stress the indexing capacities of the brain are reduced, and the brain's short-term memory and ability to form permanent new memories are inhibited.*

Other recent evidence further differentiates specific biochemical responses to stress. For example, Richard Dienstbier (1989) reports on what may well represent the physiological proof that eustress and distress affect the body and the brain differently. His research confirms that one type of arousal (stress response) is associated with high levels of cortisol, mediated by the pituitary adrenal-cortical system, and another type of arousal is stimulated by the sympathetic nervous system in the form of adrenalin and noradrenaline. Dienstbier agrees that cortisol is associated with situations of unavoidable or chronic stress when we are prevented from fleeing from a stressor or fighting it directly to resolve the sources of stress. In humans and animals alike, these hormones abound when we find ourselves in situations where other individuals or events control us and we feel helpless. Cortisol is produced in excessive amounts in the body under conditions of distress. "In chronic stress, the role and presence in the blood of corticoids, hormones from the adrenal cortex, increase and assume more importance" (Pelletier 1977, p. 71). High levels of cortisol are associated with depression, immune disorders, and heart disease.

Dienstbier adds that levels of adrenalin and noradrenalin, on the other hand, tend to increase when we react to difficult situations as "challenges." He says further that the adrenaline and noradrenaline type of arousal actually strengthens us to handle further challenges if we have a sufficient break between challenges and they are not continuous. *The deciding factor, therefore, appears to be whether we see a solution to a problem and see ourselves as capable of resolving it.* In behavioral terms, it depends on who is in charge of the contingencies. Am I helpless or do I have some control?

This characterization of two types of stress—one accompanied by a sense of pervasive threat related to a sense of helplessness and one accompanied by a sense of resolution or challenge—is crucial. Distress interferes with our health and our emotions. Moreover, there appear to be two different kinds of effects: an ongoing weakening of the system under continuous threat and the sudden debilitation that occurs in times of crisis. The solution also involves two processes. One is a continuing and appropriate degree of relaxation that maintains the system in a state of well-being generally (and maintains general low levels of cortisol). (We document this further in this chapter and in Chapter 10.) The other is the eustress, or excitement, that accompanies an appropriate degree of personal challenge.

There is a large industry devoted to the reduction of distress. What has been largely ignored, however, is that distress not only interferes with health and physiological functioning, but also inhibits cognitive functioning. It impedes our capacity to think, solve problems, and perceive patterns because of the inseparability of body, emotion, and intellect. *Downshifting, in fact, is actually one aspect of distress.*

The notion of distress in its guise as downshifting finds further voice in the two major theories of brain functioning discussed in this book. In particular, we also begin to see how and why cognitive functions are affected.

THE TRIUNE BRAIN AND DOWNSHIFTING

FROM NEOCORTEX TO LIMBIC AND R-COMPLEX

Hart (1983) refers to the constriction of brain functioning as "downshifting" because, in terms of MacLean's model of the triune brain, we are literally shifting "down" from the neocortex into the older, more automatic limbic system and reptilian complex. The R-complex does not reason, it reacts. Hart states, "Downshifting is always to more traditional, more familiar, cruder behavior—to what we would do if we had much less brain" (p. 128).

Lozanov (1978b), the Bulgarian psychologist/educator, comes to a similar conclusion. He writes:

> The archaic parts of the brain are gradually being covered with cortical layers which are being incessantly perfected [the neocortex]. Besides this, the new functional and structural areas filtrate and modify the pressure of the old ones, but at the same time they [cortical layers] are more liable to get hurt and become inhibited in shock situations. Then more often than not the archaic forms of information processing, algorithmization [habitual function] and reprogramming push their way through. Thus they show quite clearly that they have not ceased to exist and exert their influence on the new functional formations (p. 21).

Both writers are making the same point. When we perceive a threat, the more primitive parts of the brain begin to dominate. Both writers, therefore, have a philosophy of education that is built on reducing threat.

IMPLICATIONS FOR EDUCATORS

In terms of MacLean's theory, then, the more threatened and helpless students feel, the more we would expect to see behavior that we could characterize as "reptilian." Deeply entrenched programming relating to territory and identity become so important that group conflicts might degenerate into more primitive or aggressive behaviors. The need to belong to a group may lead to peer pressure that becomes overwhelming. This need will reveal itself, for instance, in the ways in which students act in accordance with the expectations of their peers in class. We might also expect social activities and attitudes to intrude into every aspect of the school and after-school life. Moreover, the actual activities, ranging from dress to codes of behavior, will be significantly influenced by those in the community who are seen as role models, because dependency on models and extrinsic reinforcement increases (Spielberger 1972). A simple but telling example is the power of film stars and athletes to influence the attitudes of students—even to what shoes and clothes they wear.

We might also expect students to have trouble grasping, or be unwilling to explore, patterns that conflict with what they already know, that require them to think in totally new and therefore potentially threatening ways, and that involve the delay of gratification and implementation of the ritualistic behaviors that currently give life meaning. Why should discussions of complex issues prevail in student elections, for instance, if adult politicians who are highly influential as role models appeal only to our most basic primitive drives in their election campaigns?

We suspect, in fact, that inability to delay gratification and inability to tolerate ambiguity and uncertainty are among the most important and devastating of all consequences. There is evidence that success correlates highly with ability to delay gratification. For example, the British sociologist Elliot Jaques (1986) suggests that cognitive power is positively correlated with what he calls "time horizons," or the length of time during which one can be practically engaged. George Leonard (Whitten 1990) also argues that we must gain a feel for the rhythm of long-term learning. This could prove difficult if downshifting interferes with our capacity to access our frontal lobes—the region of the neocortex largely responsible for long-term planning and the capacity to deal realistically with the future.

We should remember, incidentally, that adults involved with schools are equally affected. Our territory, behavior, security, groups, and rituals are also being challenged. We could therefore expect adults to downshift and respond to problems in ways that are also deeply ingrained. This is often how adults in schools deal with "maintaining discipline." In other words, much of the "inappropriate" behavior of students, whether it takes the form of talk, dress, or action, when automatically construed by adults as threatening, will appear to be disrespectful, irrespective of what motivates it. Thus behaviors that are meaningful and could be better understood if adequately reflected upon or communicated, are instantly interpreted as discipline problems. Such behaviors could quite conceivably be reinterpreted at a more complex level. For example, they might be recognized as indicators of the fact that those same students are really anxious or need lessons that are more challenging and creative.

DOWNSHIFTING AND THE LOCALE MEMORY SYSTEM

FROM LOCALE TO TAXON MEMORY

O'Keefe and Nadel examined the behavior of rats learning complex tasks. Some of the rats had hippocampal lesions. The researchers also found changes in brain functioning similar to those described in the previous section, but explained the process in a different way. As pointed out in Chapter 3, the hippocampus and related regions of the brain coordinate, or index, signals from the outside (the environment) with what is in the brain (cognition and emotion). Threat appears to affect this indexing process. Downshifting, in their view, results from a deterioration of the indexing function of the brain.

Nadel and others argue that the downshifting is not "down" but refers rather to a shifting to the automatic activation of strongly entrenched thoughts or behaviors in the taxon systems (Nadel and Wilmer 1980; Nadel, Wilmer, and Kurz 1984; Gruneberg and Morris 1979). We have already discussed the difference between taxon and locale memory. Taxon memories are relatively context free. They are fixed, or set, as stable and predictable entities. The locale system, however, is highly flexible and is making and testing maps all the time. In times of perceived threat, much of this flexibility is lost; and the individual becomes dependent on specific routes or taxon memories.

THE HIPPOCAMPUS AND STRESS

Jacobs and Nadel (1985) further point out that the hippocampus is extraordinarily susceptible to stress hormones. "We postulate that stress disrupts the function of the hippocampally based locale system and its context-specific learning capacities while potentiating taxon systems and their context-free associations" (p. 518). They go on to say:

Stress elicits the release of ACTH from the pituitary gland, which in turn stimulates the secretion of corticosterone (or cortisol) from the adrenal glands [produced by the adrenal cortex]. There are corticosterone receptors distributed throughout the brain, but they are found most prominently in the hippocampus. . . . Stress in adults has been shown to regulate the number of corticosterone receptors in the hippocampus (and frontal cortex) (p. 518).

For the sake of accuracy, we must add that the idea that spatial memory is exclusively located in the hippocampus is highly controversial. Regardless of such details, however, the general thrust of the theory lends credence to the overall evidence that downshifting is an identifiable and critical phenomenon.

RESULTS AND RELEVANCE TO EDUCATORS

O'Keefe and Nadel (1978) reported that the rats with hippocampal lesions showed "stereotyped behavior patterns which are often quite difficult to alter" and that "a similar effect is produced in insoluble or highly stressful situations. Here, *behavior becomes quite stereotyped*, even in the face of non-reward." And finally, "This extreme *rigidity of behavior*, based on the *repeated use of particular responses*, is a regular feature of hippocampal behavior in general and normal behavior in those situations completely eliminating the participation of the locale system." The general term they use is *"response perseveration"* (emphasis added).

Spielberger's (1972) observations of the way in which humans deal with anxiety so closely parallels O'Keefe and Nadel's (1978) description of their rats, that the similarities are unlikely to be accidental. Spielberger (1972) reports that anxious humans appear to experience many of the following: an increase in "cautiousness, perseveration, rigidity, [and] stereotyped thinking" and behavior, as well as reduced responsiveness to the environment. In addition, human subjects experiencing anxiety were also unable to perform "complex intellectual, problem solving, achievement and learning activities." They also become much more attentive to reinforcement by others through rewards and punishment. In effect, they *prefer* external forms of motivation and lose sight of intrinsic motivation. Anxious individuals were generally more susceptible to persuasion and modeling by significant others. This translates, for instance, into fulfilling goals formulated by others, as opposed to looking for connections that are personally meaningful. This may also explain why those with generally low abilities appear to prefer—in fact, report learning more from—skills approaches. If negative stress is closely related to a feeling of helplessness, then it makes sense that students experiencing a degree of general uncertainty prefer tasks that reduce such uncertainty. Individuals experiencing anxiety also became more preoccupied with themselves instead of what they were attempting to learn. This also resulted in their being less aware of possibilities that could help them in their learning. And even though anxiety leads to a greater need for emotional and social support, anxious people tend to withdraw from others.

When expressed in terms of the possible responses of students in times of threat, most learning is extremely difficult. Old behaviors are maintained; but peer group modeling is highly persuasive, and some modes of survival are mastered quickly. In short, from the perspective of the triune brain, the implications for educators remain the same, as does the general cause—the perception of ongoing threat. Moreover, because the very attempt to change those behaviors is itself perceived as threatening, it may well be that much classroom time actually serves to strengthen both entrenched behaviors and resistance to change.

DOWNSHIFTING AND CREATIVITY

If downshifting is accompanied by a loss of flexibility, we would expect to find further support for the notion in research on creativity, and that is precisely the case. In fact, this work is even more valuable because it also provides persuasive evidence in support of the taxon/ locale model of memory.

Without seeking to define creativity in detail, we know that it includes boundary breaking or the ability to go beyond standard frames of reference. It therefore includes both the perception and generation of new patterns (Jelen and Urban 1988, Rogers 1962). Creativity is facilitated by "autonomy, greater interest, less pressure and tension, more positive emotional tone, higher self-esteem, more trust, greater persistence of behavior change, and better physical and psychological health" (Deci and Ryan 1987). In other words, as Amabile (1985, 1986) states, "Intrinsic motivation is conducive to creativity and extrinsic motivation is detrimental." Deci (1980) also shows us that intrinsic motivation plays a critical role in reflective creative learning and that extrinsic motivation, on the other hand, is closely related to work involving noncreative, memorized skills and tasks. This difference apparently holds across different research methods, subject populations, and assessment procedures.

These findings closely parallel the characteristics of the taxon and locale memory systems. Taxon learning involves the acquisition of relatively fixed routes and is motivated, in general, by extrinsic rewards and punishments. Locale learning involves the generation of personal maps through an individual's creation of personal/intellectual meanings; and locale learning is motivated by an innate need to make sense of experience.

An even more important point has begun to emerge from such research: in some circumstances, extrinsic motivation inhibits intrinsic motivation. In other words, *a system of rewards and punishments can be selectively demotivating in the long term*, particularly where others have control over the system. It reduces the desire as well as the capacity of learners to engage in original thought. " 'Rewards,' says Amabile, have this destructive effect primarily with creative tasks, including higher-level problem solving: 'The more complex the activity, the more it's hurt by extrinsic reward.' The task, however, need not be too complex" (Kohn 1989, quoting Amabile).

Why does this happen? Several factors seem to be involved. Rewards for specific outcomes encourage people to focus narrowly on a task, to do it as quickly as possible, ignore other information, and take few risks. People respond as if being controlled by the reward. They tend to feel less autonomous and experience conditions associated with chronic stress or a sense of not having control or potency, resulting in Selye's "distress." Educators also need to be aware that people may grow to be dependent on rewards. Of course, not all rewards have the same effect. The issue seems to be how rewards are experienced. There are ways to buffer the effects of reward so that they do not preclude creative work.

* * *

After a decade of teaching focused on rewards, punishment, and narrow outcomes, it is easy to concur with educators, researchers, and the general public who lament the fact that our students can't *think*. One central issue is that rewards and punishments can never be separated. Every explicit reward under the control of an external agency may be accompanied by an implicit threat and sense of helplessness. Thus each of the factors referred to previously has a built-in component of fear of some sort of loss. We know that perceived threat inhibits the functioning of the locale memory system. Hence a system of education that is built almost exclusively on a system of rewards and punishment, from smiley stickers to grades for specific outcomes, innately reduces the capacity of a person to engage in creative learning. It is also clear that creativity is exciting in itself. Creativity, therefore, is the source of much intrinsic motivation.

In Figure 6.1 we have summarized the predisposition of the brain to rely on entrenched taxon memories or to invoke the more creative, interconnected locale system.

What Is a Threat?

We have glossed over the definition of "threat" so far because it is such a complex phenomenon. For practical purposes, *a threat is anything that triggers a sense of helplessness*. What constitutes a threat, therefore, may vary from person to person. This is not a simple concept.

Figure 6.1   Taxon and Locale Memory Systems

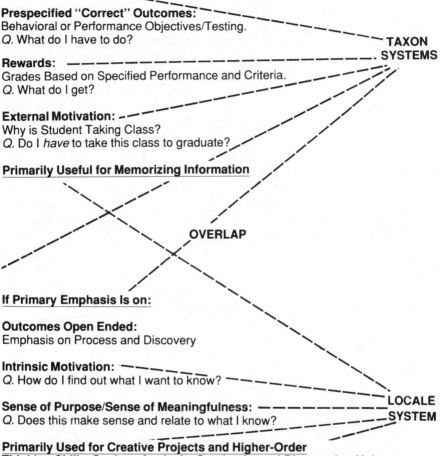

If Primary Emphasis Is on:

Prespecified "Correct" Outcomes:
Behavioral or Performance Objectives/Testing.
Q. What do I have to do?

Rewards:
Grades Based on Specified Performance and Criteria.
Q. What do I get?

External Motivation:
Why is Student Taking Class?
Q. Do I *have* to take this class to graduate?

Primarily Useful for Memorizing Information

TAXON SYSTEMS

OVERLAP

If Primary Emphasis Is on:

Outcomes Open Ended:
Emphasis on Process and Discovery

Intrinsic Motivation:
Q. How do I find out what I want to know?

Sense of Purpose/Sense of Meaningfulness:
Q. Does this make sense and relate to what I know?

LOCALE SYSTEM

Primarily Used for Creative Projects and Higher-Order Thinking Skills, Such as Analysis, Synthesis, and Discovering Unique Outcomes

The person may perceive threat anywhere survival is felt to be at risk. Downshifting is therefore not limited to children in school, but also plays a crucial role in the adult world and society as a whole. It is also appropriate to speak of degrees of downshifting because all threat is not equal in force. This is by no means a simple phenomenon that can be corrected by removing potential obstacles or simply making children feel secure. Real learning involves challenge and excitement and the ability to transform threat into challenge.

Here is an example that is familiar to most of us. From the very beginning, students want to be acknowledged by those who have the power to make them feel good or bad by their approval or disapproval. Rewards, grades, recognition, and the like contribute to their sense of identity. In the long run, it is this need to maintain and enhance a positive view of themselves that is central to their survival and is, therefore, a focus of potential threat. Of course, we are all in the same boat to some degree whenever recognition by others is essential to our self-esteem. The need to be first, to be best, to succeed, to be liked, to excel, to win, to enjoy, and to gain attention all relate to this sense of identity. Ego needs are highly implicated in and susceptible to downshifting and distress.

Lozanov (1978a, b) has developed a helpful organizing concept for educators that may bring some order to the notion of threat. He suggests that we are all shaped by what he calls "social suggestive norms." These constitute beliefs we hold about our own capabilities and what is appropriate, correct, and generally true. They are at once barriers to learning and the horizons beyond which we need to go. When these norms are adversely affected we "raise" our barriers. In other words, we both protect ourselves and downshift. We may do so by directly engaging in hostilities of some kind. We may also internalize and repress our concern and then rebel indirectly in some way.

There are three barriers to learning, which all interact. One is the critical/logical barrier. It deals with our sense of logical consistency. We feel threatened or violated, from this perspective, whenever we are asked to believe something that logically conflicts with a prior belief. This barrier tends to be raised when a teacher or speaker, especially one with prestige, misquotes or gives information which we interpret as incorrect. A second barrier, the intuitive/affective barrier, is violated whenever we "feel" or "sense" that an action is hurtful or emotionally inappropriate. Children, of course, feel this way when publicly embarrassed or when they are identified as "different," as often happens with minority children or children with special needs. The third barrier is the moral/ethical barrier. This barrier is activated when our beliefs about right and wrong are challenged or questioned. Anyone who has ever engaged in an argument on religion will understand this barrier and the resultant polarization in rigid thinking for all concerned.

In practice, many of the demands that we impose on students, ranging from placing unreasonable time limits on learning and restraints on individual thinking to excessive competition and motivation by means of shame and guilt, will cause all but the most resilient of students to downshift. In fact, by this definition we suggest that *most schools maintain most students in a downshifted state* and prevent them from engaging in the complex learning that we profess to desire and need.

The dilemma, of course, is that learning is impossible without having students transcend their own social suggestive norms. The solution, which we go into in more depth in Chapter 10, is for teachers to begin by harmonizing *with* the barriers of students. When we respect their current views and provide them with the appropriate degree of safety and opportunity to creatively explore, then we can take them beyond their immediate limitations. That is the nature of the challenge that good teachers provide.

Is Learning Motivated by Threat Possible?

Every educator and parent knows that rewards and punishments work in many situations to ensure that a fact or procedure is memorized, often to the point when it will not be questioned. There are times when this is actually important. Young children must have some safety routines installed, such as knowing how to cross a street safely, in much the same way as a computer is programmed. These are essential for survival. Similarly, people who deal with some sorts of emergencies, ranging from military personnel to fire fighters, must be able to respond appropriately and without hesitation in times of extreme threat. The consequence is that they are often exposed to stress and threat in the course of their training. It is a good way to ensure that the appropriate behavior will occur under battlefield or high-threat conditions. Such training is directed toward ensuring that a predictable response occurs, regardless of the circumstances.

Programming, therefore, can take place under threat. Some critical thinking, problem solving, intellectual explorations, and innovative and creative thinking are also possible. Thus, a frightened soldier can sometimes devise an innovative way to blow up a bridge. What is usually difficult in times of threat is the ability to question the general frames of reference. People under threat can thus find creative ways of implementing preestablished programs. They can vary the theme, but not reinvent it.

In practice, therefore, we could say that some types of training succeed in threatening circumstances, but education—of the sort that induces complex and innovative questioning and thinking—is unlikely to result. Yet much of the teaching that we do occurs under threat to students of low grades or failed tests and focuses on automatic recall as a critical measure of success. This approach can induce some memorization. If we want students to know what the information means, to expand on and to question it, and to make as many connections as possible with the rest of what they know, then we must challenge intrinsically motivated students within richly stimulating, low-threat environments. Using the military or factory model for most classroom teaching, therefore, makes little sense.

Hart (1983) puts it this way:

> While rote learning can be accomplished under a good deal of threat, . . . pattern discrimination and the more subtle choices . . . suffer severe inhibition. So does the use of oral or written language and any form of symbol manipulation. The valuable learning that is built through any kind of play, of course, comes to a full halt; threat forestalls play—play implies absence of threat! The inescapable point emerges, *cerebral learning and threat conflict directly and completely.*

Our goal must be to create low-threat conditions for learning.

WHAT IS THE ALTERNATIVE?

What we need is a grasp of the state of mind that allows for optimal brain functioning. Jerome Singer (1977), in *Alternate States of Consciousness*, suggests that "optimal stimulation is stimulation that is sufficiently novel that it can be gradually assimilated and thus holds our interest, keeps us exploring, but does not frighten or dismay us" (p. 99). We would like to build on this definition. The optimal state for learning is roughly equivalent to that of a top athlete who is performing at the peak while maintaining a deep sense of relaxation, allowing the body to perform without inappropriate tension. We call this state "relaxed alertness" (for further discussion, see Chapter 10). We suggest that this state of mind will emerge if at least two conditions are met:

1. *A degree of general relaxation*

There are two aspects of general relaxation. First, students and teachers need to have a generally relaxed nervous system. This is the "deep physiological rest" that we referred to in Chapter 3. It is essential for the continuously effective functioning of both body and mind. Research on meditation appears to support this. For example,

Murphy and Donavan (1988) report that although meditation appears to be instrumental in lowering cortisol levels in the blood over time, it actually appears to enhance sympathetic activity, which includes the production of adrenalin and noradrenaline. This may mean that meditation reduces the hormones associated with threat, but not with challenge.

Second, students and teachers alike must feel safe enough to take risks. This is a specific kind of safety and is not the equivalent of being comfortable. As we discuss in Chapter 10, it is more akin to the safety that children feel when they are playfully experimenting.

2. Intrinsic motivation

The evidence indicates that learning is fostered by creativity and challenge. These factors together constitute intrinsic motivation. What matters, then, is that we master the ability to elicit intrinsic motivation in students. In part, of course, it will stem from assisting them to relate what is being studied to what is meaningful to them. In part, it is a matter of assisting them to be creative.

Many factors, to be dealt with in later chapters, are involved in some way. These factors include the student's ownership and sense of control over the learning, positive social bonding, hope and positive expectancy, a world that makes sense, playfulness, joy, respect of students and teachers for themselves and each other, self-discipline and the capacity to delay gratification, and a sense of cohesion or connectedness.

IS THERE MORE?

As we mentioned earlier, some types of creative thought are possible in a person who feels threatened. A case in point is the refugee who is inventive at finding ways to avoid being caught. One student equivalent is creativity in finding excuses. It is also clear that low threat and high challenge are not precise states, nor are they mutually exclusive. People often experience elements of both, sometimes without knowing it. Moreover, these states fluctuate. Because we will always have to deal with some threat in life, reverting to some automatic survival mode is sometimes both inevitable and essential. In fact, students must learn how to deal with threat, not simply be protected from it. A business and political world that is constantly changing may be a source of threat, even when a person has a more relaxed nervous system and the ability to transform much threat into challenge. In modern life, people are exposed to deadlines, information overload, competition for jobs, and a host of other factors. It is a mistake, however, to assume that the best way to teach people how to succeed in that environment is only through programming and replicating it in schools.

*   *   *

The key is to build success, confidence, and practical intelligence and to keep students stretching so that the range of situations in which they can function effectively continually increases. They will have crisis enough in their lives. In general, therefore, schools should be safe. Beyond the obvious point that stress associated with excessive control by others and a feeling of helplessness contributes to more restricted mental functioning, relaxation and relaxation techniques need to be studied and understood by educators. Educators also must have a grasp of the general conditions that create distress and need to be able to orchestrate an environment in which a relaxed and challenging atmosphere is maintained.

Although literature, the arts, and our own experiences and research indicate that downshifting is an everyday phenomenon, more research is needed from the neurosciences and physiology. In particular, there is a need to understand the physiological differences between threat and challenge. The fact is, however, that we know enough already to take the first steps and to make the decisions about changing education that have to be made. We are not arguing that learning will only take place in some sort of ideal or perfect atmosphere. What we advocate is an atmosphere that consistently and predominantly offers low threat and medium or high challenge.

7

PRINCIPLES OF BRAIN-BASED LEARNING

*We underrate our brains and our intelligence. Formal
education has become such a complicated, self-conscious
and overregulated activity that learning is widely
regarded as something difficult that the brain would
rather not do. . . . But reluctance to learn cannot be
attributed to the brain. Learning is the brain's primary
function, its constant concern, and we become restless
and frustrated if there is no learning to be done. We are
all capable of huge and unsuspected learning
accomplishments without effort.*

Frank Smith, *Insult to Intelligence*, 1986, p. 18

The previous chapters have presented a number of perspectives on
how the human brain appears to work. Our objective here is to
summarize the accumulated insights of the research dealt with thus
far in a form that is of practical benefit to educators. The summary
and consolidation takes the form of 12 principles that can serve as a
general theoretical foundation for brain-based learning (see Caine,
R.N., and Caine 1990). The principles also provide guidelines for defining and selecting programs and methodologies.

EDUCATION AS AN OPEN QUEST

If these principles are as sound as we believe they are, then they
provide us with a framework for learning and teaching that moves
us irrevocably away from the methods and models that have dominated education for more than a century. The behavioral model, particularly as practiced in education, must be put to rest. What replaces

it is an open quest, bound primarily by the limitations we choose and place on ourselves and the dictates of the human brain itself. If we become overwhelmed by the lack of the right answer or procedure as we let go of certainty, we can perhaps seek comfort in the thought that above all else, brain-based learning opens doors. It is time that we moved on.

1. THE BRAIN IS A PARALLEL PROCESSOR.

The human brain is always doing many things at one time (Ornstein and Sobel 1987). Thoughts, emotions, imagination, and predispositions operate simultaneously and interact with other modes of information processing and with the expansion of general social and cultural knowledge.

Implications for Education. Good teaching so "orchestrates" the learner's experience that all these aspects of brain operation are addressed. Teaching must, therefore, be based on theories and methodologies that guide the teacher to make orchestration possible. No one method or technique can adequately encompass the variations of the human brain. However, teachers need a frame of reference that enables them to select from the vast repertoire of methods and approaches that are available.

2. LEARNING ENGAGES THE ENTIRE PHYSIOLOGY.

The interaction of the different parts of the triune brain attest, for instance, to the importance of a person's entire physiology. The brain is a physiological organ functioning according to physiological rules. Learning is as natural as breathing, but it can be either inhibited or facilitated. Neuron growth, nourishment, and interactions are integrally related to the perception and interpretation of experiences (Diamond 1985). Stress and threat affect the brain differently from peace, challenge, boredom, happiness, and contentment (see Ornstein and Sobel 1987). In fact, some aspects of the actual "wiring" of the brain are affected by school and life experiences.

Implications for Education. Everything that affects our physiological functioning affects our capacity to learn. Stress management, nutrition, exercise, and relaxation, as well as other facets of health management, must be fully incorporated into the learning process. Because many drugs, both prescribed and "recreational," inhibit learning, their use should also be curtailed and their effects understood. Habits and beliefs are also physiologically entrenched and therefore resistant or slow to change once they become a part of the personality.

In addition, the timing of learning is influenced by the natural development of both body and brain, as well as by individual and natural rhythms and cycles. There can be a five-year difference in maturation between any two children of the same age. Expecting equal achievement on the basis of chronological age is therefore inappropriate.

3. THE SEARCH FOR MEANING IS INNATE.

The search for meaning (making sense of our experiences) and the consequential need to act on our environment are automatic. The search for meaning is survival oriented and basic to the human brain. The brain needs and automatically registers the familiar while simultaneously searching for and responding to novel stimuli (O'Keefe and Nadel 1978). This dual process is taking place every waking moment (and, some contend, while sleeping). Other research confirms the notion that people are meaning makers (see Chapter 8). The search for meaning cannot be stopped, only channelled and focused.

Implications for Education. The learning environment needs to provide stability and familiarity; this is part of the function of routine classroom behaviors and procedures. At the same time, provision must be made to satisfy our curiosity and hunger for novelty, discovery, and challenge. Lessons need to be generally exciting and meaningful and offer students an abundance of choices. The more positively lifelike such learning, the better. Many programs for gifted children take these implications for granted by combining a rich environment with complex and meaningful challenges. In our view, most of the creative methods used for teaching gifted students should be applied to all students.

4. THE SEARCH FOR MEANING OCCURS THROUGH "PATTERNING."

Patterning (Nummela and Rosengren 1986) refers to the meaningful organization and categorization of information. In a way, the brain is both artist and scientist, attempting to discern and understand patterns as they occur and giving expression to unique and creative patterns of its own (Hart 1983, Lakoff 1987, Nummela and Rosengren 1986, Rosenfield 1988). The brain is designed to perceive and generate patterns, and it resists having meaningless patterns imposed on it. "Meaningless" patterns are isolated pieces of information unrelated to what makes sense to a student. When the brain's natural capacity to integrate information is acknowledged and invoked in teaching, then vast amounts of initially unrelated or seemingly random information and activities can be presented and assimilated. (The construction of meaning is discussed in depth in Chapter 8.)

Implications for Education. Learners are patterning, or perceiving and creating meanings, all the time in one way or another. We cannot stop them, but can influence the direction. Daydreaming is a way of patterning, as are problem solving and critical thinking. Although we choose much of what students are to learn, the ideal process is to present the information in a way that allows brains to extract patterns, rather than attempt to impose them. "Time on task" does not ensure appropriate patterning because the student may actually be engaged in "busy work" while the mind is somewhere else. For teaching to be really effective, a learner must be able to create meaningful and personally relevant patterns. This type of teaching is most clearly recognized by those advocating a whole-language approach to reading (Altweger, Edelsky, and Flores 1987; Goodman 1986), thematic teaching (Kovalik 1986), integration of the curriculum (Shalley 1987), and life-relevant approaches to learning.

5. EMOTIONS ARE CRITICAL TO PATTERNING.

We do not simply learn things. What we learn is influenced and organized by emotions and mind sets based on expectancy, personal biases and prejudices, degree of self-esteem, and the need for social interaction. Emotions and cognition cannot be separated (Halgren, Wilson, Squires, Engel, Walter, and Crandall 1983; Ornstein and Sobel 1987; Lakoff 1987; McGuinness and Pribram 1980). Emotions are also crucial to memory because they facilitate the storage and recall of information (Rosenfield 1988). Moreover, many emotions cannot be simply switched on and off. They operate on many levels, somewhat like the weather. They are ongoing, and the emotional impact of any lesson or life experience may continue to reverberate long after the specific event.

Implications for Education. Teachers need to understand that students' feelings and attitudes will be involved and will determine future learning. Because it is impossible to isolate the cognitive from the affective domain, the emotional climate in the school and classroom must be monitored on a consistent basis, using effective communication strategies and allowing for student and teacher reflection and metacognitive processes. In general, the entire environment needs to be supportive and marked by mutual respect and acceptance both within and beyond the classroom. Some of the most significant experiences in a student's life are fleeting "moments of truth," such as a chance encounter in a corridor with a relatively unknown teacher or, possibly, a "distant" administrator. These brief communications are often instinctive. Their emotional color depends on how "real" and profound the support of teachers, administrators, and students is for one another.

6. THE BRAIN PROCESSES PARTS AND WHOLES SIMULTANEOUSLY.

There is evidence of brain laterality, meaning that there are significant differences between left and right hemispheres of the brain (Springer and Deutsch 1985). In a healthy person, however, the two hemispheres are inextricably interactive, whether a person is dealing with words, mathematics, music, or art (Hand 1984; Hart 1975; Levy, J. 1985). The "two brain" doctrine is most valuable as a metaphor that helps educators acknowledge two separate but simultaneous tendencies in the brain for organizing information. One is to reduce information into parts; the other is to perceive and work with it as a whole or series of wholes.

Implications for Education. People have enormous difficulty in learning when either parts or wholes are overlooked. Good teaching necessarily builds understanding and skills over time because learning is cumulative and developmental. However, parts and wholes are conceptually interactive. They derive meaning from and give it to each other. Thus vocabulary and grammar are best understood and mastered when incorporated in genuine, whole-language experiences. Similarly, equations and scientific principles should be dealt with in the context of living science.

7. LEARNING INVOLVES BOTH FOCUSED ATTENTION AND PERIPHERAL PERCEPTION.

The brain absorbs information of which it is directly aware and to which it is paying attention. It also directly absorbs information and signals that lie beyond the field of attention. These may be stimuli that one perceives "out of the side of the eyes," such as grey and unattractive walls in a classroom. Peripheral stimuli also include the "light" or subtle signals that are within the field of attention but are still not consciously noticed (such as a hint of a smile or slight changes in body posture). This means that the brain responds to the entire sensory context in which teaching or communication occurs (O'Keefe and Nadel 1978).

One of Lozanov's fundamental principles is that every stimulus is coded, associated, and symbolized (Lozanov 1978a, b). Thus every sound, from a word to a siren, and every visual signal, from a blank screen to a raised finger, is packed full of complex meanings. For example, a simple knock on the door engages attention and is processed for possible meaning by reference both to much of a learner's prior knowledge and experience and to whatever is happening at the moment. Peripheral information can therefore be purposely "organized" to facilitate learning.

Implications for Education. The teacher can and should organize materials that will be outside the focus of the learner's attention. In addition to traditional concerns with noise, temperature, and so on, peripherals include visuals such as charts, illustrations, set designs, and art, including great works of art. Barzakov (1988) recommends that art exhibits be changed frequently to reflect changes in learning focus. The use of music has also become important as a way to enhance and influence more natural acquisition of information. And the subtle signals that emanate from a teacher have a significant impact. Our inner state shows in skin color, muscular tension and posture, rate of breathing, and eye movements. Teachers need to engage the interests and enthusiasm of students through their own enthusiasm, coaching, and modeling, so that the unconscious signals appropriately relate to the importance and value of what is being learned. One reason that it is important to practice what we preach and, for example, to be genuinely compassionate rather than to fake compassion, is that our actual inner state is always signaled and discerned at some level by learners. Lozanov (1978b) coined the term "double planeness" to describe this internal and external congruence in a person. In the same way, the design and administration of a school send messages to students that shape what is learned. In effect, every aspect of a student's life, including community, family, and technology, affects student learning.

8. LEARNING ALWAYS INVOLVES CONSCIOUS AND UNCONSCIOUS PROCESSES.

We learn much more than we ever consciously understand. "What we are discovering . . . is that beneath the surface of awareness, an enormous amount of unconscious processing is going on" (Campbell 1989, p. 203). Most signals that are peripherally perceived enter the brain without the learner's awareness and interact at unconscious levels. "Having reached the brain, this information emerges in the consciousness with some delay, or it influences the motives and decisions" (Lozanov 1978b, p. 18). Thus we become our experiences and remember what we experience, not just what we are told. For example, a student can learn to sing on key and learn to hate singing at the same time. Teaching therefore needs to be designed in such a way as to help students benefit maximally from unconscious processing. In part, this is done by addressing the peripheral context (as described previously). In part, it is done through instruction.

Implications for Education. Much of the effort put into teaching and studying is wasted because students do not adequately process their experiences. What we call "active processing" allows students to review how and what they learned so that they begin to take charge of learning and the development of personal meanings. In part, active processing refers to reflection and metacognitive activities. One example might be students' becoming aware of their preferred learning style. Another might be the creative elaboration of procedures and theories by exploring metaphors and analogies to help in the reorganization of material in a way that makes it personally meaningful and valuable.

9. WE HAVE AT LEAST TWO DIFFERENT TYPES OF MEMORY: A SPATIAL MEMORY SYSTEM AND A SET OF SYSTEMS FOR ROTE LEARNING.

We have a natural, spatial memory system that does not need rehearsal and allows for "instant" memory of experiences (Bransford and Johnson 1972; Nadel and Wilmer 1980; Nadel, Wilmer, and Kurz 1984). Remembering where and what we had for dinner last night does not require the use of memorization techniques. We have at least one memory system actually designed for registering our experiences in ordinary three-dimensional space (O'Keefe and Nadel 1978). The system is always engaged and is inexhaustible. It is possessed by people of both sexes and all nationalities and ethnic backgrounds. It is enriched over time as we increase the items, categories, and procedures that we take for granted. Thus there was a time when we did not know what a tree or a television was. The system is motivated by novelty. In fact, this is one of the systems that drives the search for meaning mentioned previously.

Facts and skills that are dealt with in isolation are organized differently by the brain and need much more practice and rehearsal. The counterpart of the spatial memory system is a set of systems specifically designed for storing relatively unrelated information. Nonsense syllables are an extreme case. The more separated information and skills are from prior knowledge and actual experience, the more dependence there needs to be on rote memory and repetition. We can compare this memory system to the inventory of an automobile shop. The more items are available, the more the shop can repair, build, and even design cars. It can also do so with greater ease and speed and less stress. At the same time, if management becomes too enamored of the stocking of inventory, and mechanics and designers fail to see how to use the materials available, then an imbalance has been created. In the same way, emphasizing the storage and recall of unconnected facts is an inefficient use of the brain.

Implications for Education. Educators are adept at the type of teaching that focuses on memorization. Common examples include multiplication tables, spelling words, and unfamiliar vocabulary at the lower levels, and abstract concepts and sets of principles in different subjects for older students and adults. Sometimes memorization is important and useful. In general, however, teaching devoted to memorization does not facilitate the transfer of learning and probably interferes with the subsequent development of understanding. By ignoring the personal world of the learner, educators actually inhibit the effective functioning of the brain.

10. We Understand and Remember Best When Facts and Skills Are Embedded in Natural, Spatial Memory.

Our native language is learned through multiple interactive experiences involving vocabulary and grammar. It is shaped both by internal processes and by social interaction (Vygotsky 1978). That is an example of how specific "items" are given meaning when embedded in ordinary experiences. All education can be enhanced when this type of embedding is adopted. That is the single most important element that the new brain-based theories of learning have in common.

Implications for Education. The embedding process is complex because it depends on all the other principles discussed here. Spatial memory is generally best invoked through experiential learning, an approach that is valued more highly in some cultures than in others. Teachers need to use a great deal of real-life activity, including classroom demonstrations, projects, field trips, visual imagery of certain experiences and best performances, stories, metaphor, drama, and interaction of different subjects. Vocabulary can be experienced through skits. Grammar can be learned in process, through stories or writing. Mathematics, science, and history can be integrated so that much more information is understood and absorbed than is currently the norm. Success depends on using all of the senses and immersing the learner in a multitude of complex and interactive experiences. Lectures and analysis are not excluded, but they should be part of a larger experience.

11. Learning Is Enhanced by Challenge and Inhibited by Threat.

The brain downshifts under perceived threat and learns optimally when appropriately challenged. The brain will downshift under threat (Hart 1983). The central feature of downshifting is a sense of helplessness. As we mention in Chapter 6, it is accompanied by a narrowing of the perceptual field (Combs and Snygg 1949). The learner becomes less flexible and reverts to automatic and often more primitive routine behaviors. Downshifting is roughly like a camera lens that has a reduced focus. The hippocampus, a part of the limbic system, which appears to function partially as a relay center to the rest of the brain, is the region of the brain most sensitive to stress (Jacobs and Nadel 1985). Under perceived threat, portions of our brain function suboptimally.

Implications for Education. Teachers and administrators need to create a state of relaxed alertness in students. This combines general relaxation with an atmosphere that is low in threat and high in challenge. This state must continuously pervade the lesson, and must be present in the teacher. All the methodologies that are used to orchestrate the learning context influence the state of relaxed alertness.

12. EACH BRAIN IS UNIQUE.

Although we all have the same set of systems, including our senses and basic emotions, they are integrated differently in every brain. In addition, because learning actually changes the structure of the brain, the more we learn, the more unique we become.

Implications for Education. Teaching should be multifaceted to allow all students to express visual, tactile, emotional, and auditory preferences. There are other individual differences that also need to be considered. Providing choices that are variable enough to attract individual interests may require the reshaping of schools so that they exhibit the complexity found in life. In sum, education needs to facilitate optimal brain functioning.

DISCARDING OUTMODED ASSUMPTIONS

There are several general implications of the 12 principles. One is that the brain is a social brain (Gazzaniga 1985). Not only do all the regions interact, but we become what we are through our interactions with the community and the environment. This "becoming" is partly receptive and partly generative—we discover and we create. One of our fundamental tasks as educators, therefore, is to better appreciate the social construction of knowledge (see, e.g., Vygotsky 1978).

Another implication is that we are moved inexorably beyond the information-processing model of memory as the predominant paradigm for learning. For instance, as we mention in Chapter 4, an essential aspect of that model is the suggestion that we all have an information bottleneck. Of the wealth of information in the environment, the model suggests that we can place only a small amount in short-term memory at any one time. We are further advised that long-term memory depends on the processing and working of the contents of short-term memory. To the extent that we have limited learning to such a scenario, we have actually precluded ourselves from taking advantage of the greater capacities of the human brain.

Clearly, we do have a limited capacity to focus attention. However, we indirectly perceive and respond to much that is happening in our total environment. Moreover, we process much of that information unconsciously. The consequence is that our focus of attention becomes a tool, like a spotlight, but it is not nearly as limiting as we have been led to believe. Students are capable of much more because everything is always operating in relationship to a much larger context.

WHAT EDUCATORS NEED TO DO

Determining how to implement these principles is not a matter of preferring one specific methodology over another. In a recent ASCD yearbook, Madeline Hunter (1990) states:

> There are no teacher or student behaviors that have to be in every lesson. . . . We are . . . becoming sensitized to the appropriateness, artistry, and outcomes of what is occurring in the classroom. . . . This necessitates skill in selecting from a pharmacy of educational alternatives, not being committed to one "best way" (p. xiv).

We all have access to an extensive societal repertoire of strategies and methods. We need a way of selecting the methodologies that will maximize learning and make teaching more effective and fulfilling. The first task is to reconceptualize learning outcomes to deal with the primary importance of meaningfulness. We do that in the next chapter. It is an approach to education that recognizes the primacy of complex experience and regards learning as the art of capitalizing on experience. The three interactive elements of the process are spelled out in Chapters 9–11.

III

BRAIN-BASED SCHOOLING

8

EXPLORING THE MYSTERY OF MEANING

Two stonecutters . . . were engaged in similar activity.
Asked what they were doing, one answered, "I'm
squaring up this block of stone." The other replied, "I'm
building a cathedral." The first may have been
underemployed; the second was not. Clearly what counts
is not so much what work a person does, but what he
perceives he is doing it for.

Willis Harman, *Global Mind Change*,
1988, p. 144

FROM INFORMATION TO MEANING

One thrust of the brain principles (see Chapter 7) is that the brain responds differently to meaningless and meaningful information and situations. If we want students to use their brains more fully, we have to teach for meaningfulness. This issue is not new, of course. Psychologists have known for a long time that one of the most important elements in learning is meaning (Cermack and Craik 1979) and that meaning is related to depth of information processing (Craik and Lockhart 1975). Moreover, meaningfulness is clearly an important ingredient in the development of skills and in job satisfaction (see Applegate et al. 1988).

Many problems in education stem from the fact that meaningfulness is disregarded or misunderstood. This occurs in several different ways. For example, many outcomes are spelled out in purely behavioral terms that emphasize memory and ignore meaningfulness for the learner. It may be an objective, for example, for a student to be able to define and recognize nouns and verbs, to recite the multiplication tables, or to grow crystals in a test tube. The knowledge embodied in these outcomes constitutes the mechanics of any subject. From this perspective, some of the traditional distinctions made between types of knowledge do not matter. For example, we tend to differentiate between *declarative* knowledge (knowing that something is the case) and *procedural* knowledge (knowing how to do something) (Squire 1986). Both of these can be what we call "surface knowledge" if all that is required is programming and memorization.

In considering outcomes and objectives of learning, educators must appreciate and reexamine the difference between memorization and meaningful learning. We must get beyond the notion that learning is determined by preconceived outcomes. As already mentioned, even "discovery learning" is often just a guise for having students arrive at predigested understandings. Meaningful learning, on the other hand, is essentially creative. All students must, therefore, be given permission to transcend the insights of their teachers. We must also reject a definition of "meaningfulness" that is restricted to some notion of intellectual understanding devoid of an emotional connection that is experienced as a "felt" sense for an idea or procedure. In fact, we argue that "felt meaning" is what we have when we perceive a pattern or make the connections that matter to us. That felt sense is at the heart of genuine expertise in every domain, and it must be incorporated into the teaching of every subject. Moreover, this sense of interconnectedness, which occurs when emotions and cognition come together, is a key to the appreciation of life and learning and to overcoming the downshifting that so often precludes us from functioning compassionately and effectively.

MEANING AS MOTIVATION

We contend in Chapter 7 (see Principle 3) that the search for meaning and the consequential need to act on our environment are automatic, survival oriented, and basic to the human brain. The mind/brain innately seeks to make connections. We are, therefore, born to learn.

This follows in part from the work of O'Keefe and Nadel (1978), who demonstrated that the locale memory system is motivated by novelty and curiosity. We are literally driven to make sense of unfamiliar and, in many instances, incomplete stimuli. Other examinations of the brain have led to related conclusions. Springer and Deutsch (1985) stated: "It is very common for the verbal left hemisphere to try to make sense of what has occurred in testing situations where information is presented to the right hemisphere" (p. 33). In fact, the entire brain process of working with parts and wholes is directed at organizing input and experiences to make sense of them.

Other research confirms that the search for meaning is at the heart of intrinsic motivation and that much of the energy and drive to pursue goals and engage in essential tasks comes from the search for meaning. The central thrust of Piaget's work, for instance, is that children are always engaged in the process of making sense of things. "Like detectives, they investigate, reason, question, fantasize, and experiment in an attempt to understand what people do and how things work" (Cowan 1978, p. 11). Similarly, Postman and Weingartner (1969) assert that all students are essentially "meaning makers." The philosopher Susan Langer "posited a basic and pervasive human need to invent meanings, and to invest meaning in one's world. It was a property of the human mind to search for and to find significance everywhere, to transform experience constantly to uncover new meanings" (Gardner 1982, p. 50). P.E. Morris notes, "The main activities of the cognitive system are directed to making sense of and dealing with the ongoing interactions between the individual and the world" (Gruneberg and Morris 1979, p. 30). And an extensive body of work on reading supports the conclusion that reading is not a matter of decoding words but of extracting meaning from a text (see, e.g., Adams and Collins 1977, p. 1).

WHAT ARE WE REALLY TRYING TO ACHIEVE?

What we are searching for is a way of dealing with meaningfulness that opens the way to a more powerful, effective, and satisfying type of education. We need to appreciate Doll's point: "Learning occurs on a number of levels and in a variety of manners—this is the nature of complexity" (Doll 1989, p. 69). Thus he refers to the distinction between "technical" and "grounded" knowing (Oliver and Gershman 1989).

We would like to make a similar but slightly different distinction. What we have in education today is an extreme emphasis on what we call *surface knowledge*, which is basically content devoid of significance to the learner. What is needed, we suggest, is the expansion of *natural knowledge*. Every individual brings to every learning situation a font of knowledge that is personally meaningful. Technically it is perceptual knowledge—it is what people use to organize their grasp of the world in which they live. Every school subject is potentially a way of enhancing the capacity of students to "read" their world. It can, and should, become part of their natural knowledge. To appreciate what is involved, we need to explore the character of surface knowledge in a little more depth and then introduce the dimensions of meaningfulness that are at the heart of the acquisition of natural knowledge.

SURFACE KNOWLEDGE

As we point out in Chapter 1, surface knowledge is anything that a robot can be programmed to "know." Surface knowledge has very little meaning. There is very little connectedness with other knowledge, with social and emotional issues, or with other aspects of the learner's psyche. In Whitehead's (1979) terms, surface knowledge is "inert knowledge." It embraces the mechanics of any subject—all those facts, procedures, and behaviors that can be acquired by memorization. It consists of the information that is stored almost exclusively in the taxon systems, irrespective of how elaborate those programs are. It is the outcome of rote memorization and is the predominant product of education today.

We are not suggesting that we eliminate memorization, which is important in some contexts. We have already discussed the need for people to have some behaviors instilled. Before we mature, for instance, some types of social behavior need to be internalized, regardless of how meaningful they seem. It is also essential to sufficiently master the mechanics of any discipline or physical activity. Thus vocabulary is an essential ingredient of any language, and laboratory procedures are indispensable in the study of most sciences. What is critical, however, is that *memorization should usually take place in the course of acquiring understanding.* All memorization, in fact, occurs in a complex context; and that context must be actively invoked. Understanding should be part of what is taught and should not be left to chance.

The exercise in Figure 8.1 illustrates teaching for surface knowledge. We ask the reader to attempt to memorize the symbols and relationships.

Figure 8.1

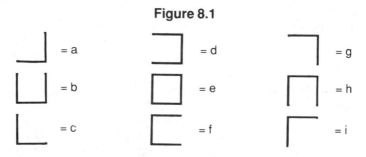

The list in Figure 8.1 can represent anything a teacher might ask students to memorize. Unless the student can invent a meaning, the information gleaned is surface knowledge; and the exercise is basically quite meaningless. Yet such information often constitutes the makeup of a lesson and examinations and can span all subject areas.

There is clearly something missing.

THE MISSING LINKS: TWO DIMENSIONS OF MEANING

Two crucial dimensions of meaning are missing from most education. The first is creative insight and a "sense" of what is meant. With Gendlin (1962), we call that *felt meaning.* The other is purpose, which is at the heart of *deep meaning.* Both are indispensable to the acquisition of natural knowledge.

FELT MEANING—THE "AHA" SENSATION

Insight is much more important in education than is memorization. Felt meaning begins as an unarticulated general sense of relationship and culminates in the "aha" experience that accompanies insight. We might experience felt meaning when a poem that we are reading begins to make sense. We might also feel this way when a lesson plan falls into place or we find a way to solve a complex administrative problem. A frequently remarked-on experience is the sense of relief and energy that often accompanies this type of insight. Sometimes the sensation is slight. Other insights evoke emotions ranging from awe and an almost mystical sense of oneness to joy and delight. In phenomenological terms, it occurs when we perceive a "gestalt" or a coming together of parts in a way that "fits." This is classically illustrated by those perceptual puzzles or collections of dots that "suddenly" turn into recognizable pictures. It occurs in many circumstances and with varying degrees of intensity. In speech, for instance, "one is 'surer' that one has identified a word correctly if the word fits the context of what has gone before" (Bruner, Goodnow, and Austin 1967, p. 18). This seems to include what has been called a "test by affective congruence" (Bruner et al. 1967, p. 20).

In Chapter 3, for example, we stated that the brain is a parallel processor. Simply memorized, this fact would not mean a great deal. By linking the definition to something complex but familiar, like the makeup of a city, the reader may have been barely conscious of a sense of "aha" or "That makes sense." When that happens, we have created a felt meaning for what is being discussed. This, in fact, is a central feature of the brain's more sophisticated forms of patterning that we spell out in Principle 4 (see Chapter 7). It is the experience we have when those "vast amounts of initially unrelated or seemingly random information and activities" are assimilated. New information is thus connected to what we already know and grasp.

By way of example, we return to our previous exercise. In Figure 8.2 we join the symbols with something familiar to the reader— knowledge that is based on many past, personal experiences—the tic-tac-toe diagram.

The interesting thing is that not only do the symbols instantly fall into place, but by accessing our locale memory we also experience one-trial learning. Few readers will ever forget this diagram. In the truest sense, felt meaning expands our frames of reference and provides a road map of how the new information might fit.

We use the term *felt* for two reasons. First, that is how people tend to describe this sense. Thus it is illustrated in the person who has a "feel" for finance or business. Similarly, Greg Norman, the Australian golfer, has said that a good golfer needs to have a "feel" for the shot.

95

Figure 8.2

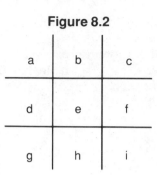

In an article on the future of U.S. industrial design, Michael Schrage says, "It's certainly not something that comes out of the mouth of a business school professor. Great design isn't taught; it's felt" (Schrage 1989). Though we contest the notion that it cannot be taught, we agree wholeheartedly with the notion that what is learned is a "sense."

Second, as we have shown, every system participates in the coming together of this sensed meaning. It requires the concurrent participation of senses, emotions, motor systems, respiration, and thought. Emotions are extremely important because, as we conclude in Principle 5, emotions and cognition cannot be separated and the conjunction of the two is at the heart of learning.

Felt meaning has been largely overlooked. One reason is that the notion of "insight" is frequently reserved for momentous events. However, people have insights in all knowledge domains and in all walks of life. The problem, perhaps, is that most insights occur in such a matter-of-fact way that they are taken for granted and are not appreciated. For example, it is impossible to use language effectively without having a grasp of, and feeling for, how language works. However, we rarely stop to appreciate our own use of language. Another problem is that traditional learning theory, with its emphasis on memory, tends to divorce creativity from learning. When that happens, the insightful aspect of learning is lost. This is tragic because the brain needs to create its own meanings. Meaningful learning is built on creativity. It is also the source of much of the joy that students could experience in education.

Implications for Education. Among the critical issues in education are motivation, discipline, and student retention. It seems to us that they are related and that educators who have a grasp of felt meaning have a tool for dealing with all those issues. *Creativity is inherently joyful, challenging, and absorbing.* It introduces laughter into what would otherwise be tedium. It engages attention and imagination; and when skillfully facilitated, it enhances communication and group processes. The regular experience of practical creativity, we suggest, in and of itself makes schooling more attractive to students. It induces more participation in their own education. In addition, students who have the opportunity to create have an opportunity to make sense of what they are doing. That helps them to appreciate the role that formal education plays in their lives and reduces the urge to rebel and flee. There is, fortunately, a growing body of evidence that links creativity and the arts with health (Coughlin 1990); and there are some signs of an emerging interest in art education (Ames 1990).

DEEP MEANING—WHAT WE LIVE FOR

Deep meaning refers to whatever drives us and governs our sense of purpose. It includes all the instincts embedded in our reptilian brains, from survival and territoriality to nesting and flocking. It includes our needs for social relationships and an emotionally rich life. And it includes our intellectual and spiritual needs. Maslow (1968) expressed something of the range of deep meanings with his hierarchy of needs. And because there are so many factors competing for expression and because people are so different, George Kelly (1955) suggested that we simply talk of individual "constructs."

These drives are sources of individual meaning. They are what people live for. And they are meaningful, regardless of whether they are articulated and whether they are conscious. We therefore prefer a less mechanistic term than Kelly's and have chosen the term *deep meanings. People access passion when deep meanings are engaged*; deep meanings, therefore, are at the core of intrinsic motivation. In the words of physicist David Bohm, "only meaning arouses energy" (1987, p. 97). In part, deep meanings provide a sense of direction because they govern what people look for and what they are willing to do, whether in sports, computing, music, finance, or writing poetry. And, in part, deep meanings are a source of the energy that people are capable of bringing to bear on a task or activity.

We refer once more to the tic-tac-toe diagram. Even though the learner learned the symbols by placing them in a familiar diagram, the all-important question is still, What does this mean? How will you use it and of what use is it? There is a gestalt, but it remains on the surface. Thus felt meaning can become merely a trick to acquire more surface knowledge if we ignore the learner's desire or need to know. We therefore expand on our model with an example provided by Bill Atkinson, the inventor of Hypercard. He had been searching for a way to memorize the Morse code. He had limited success until he discovered the following diagram, shown in Figure 8.3.

It was his desire and need to know, combined with felt meaning, that transformed the Morse code into natural knowledge for him—something he could now use and remember at will.

Figure 8.3

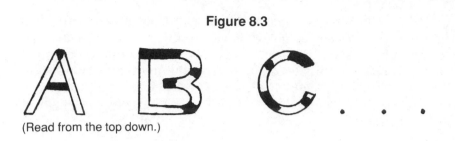

(Read from the top down.)

Our tic-tac-toe diagram is extremely simple; but in teaching and learning, concepts can become immensely complex and require teachers to have a great deal of creativity and insight. Because deep meanings vary from person to person, students must be given choices and be given permission to explore their need to understand.

It is the power of these personal and often hidden meanings, in fact, that legitimizes psychotherapy, much of which is specifically designed to help people "talk things out" and recognize poorly understood drives and behaviors. Language is useful because it can act as a mediator between our deep meanings and our awareness. We therefore subscribe to the view that there must be some sorts of deep structure that contribute to the organization of language below the level of awareness.

One of the more dramatic conclusions that flow from the brain theories is that threat affects those deep meanings that are dominant. When we are threatened, we downshift into more automatic beliefs and practices. Threat, therefore, may activate primitive, inflexible behaviors related to territoriality, tribal clustering, preening and flocking, and so on; and these often become the forces that drive and direct the behavior of students as well as teachers, parents, and the community at large.

Another issue is the importance of the spiritual urges that people have. Regardless of what the "truth" is, it is often those spiritual notions that most give meaning to life. Moreover, these urges operate in the minds and brains of people irrespective of the constitutional separation of church and state. Both adults and children need a cosmology that helps them see interconnectedness. Deprivation of that cosmology is itself deeply threatening and may, in fact, simply trigger the type of religious belief that does not make room for complexity and disagreement.

Implications for Education. Educators have often avoided dealing with deep meanings because they involve passion and the apparent absence of logic. However, there is obviously more to life and to understanding than what has traditionally been regarded as rational.

What educators and the community need to acknowledge is that these meanings are operating constantly, in students, parents, teachers, administrators, and other people who influence education. We do not consider them mysterious. The process of uncovering such meanings is not fraught with danger, nor can it be programmed. On the contrary, our individual deep meanings contribute to our interpretation of events and experiences regardless of what others intend. The danger lies in ignoring them. We must, therefore, learn how to deal with them productively and effectively. That is part of the teaching process and must be appreciated if learning is to be significantly improved and connections in the brain maximized.

This notion has significant implications for the field of counseling, particularly counseling in schools. Allowing students to discover and understand what drives them and that their behaviors lead to specific consequences seems to be an appropriate ingredient in much classroom activity. Moreover, there is no reason why awareness of our innate drives should be limited to the counselor's office. In all healthy individuals, particularly if they are in a safe, challenging environment, there will be times when meanings need to be acknowledged and processed. In the type of education we describe, old meanings surface at unpredictable times because they are challenged by new ones. Although such times should be heralded as welcome chances to rewrite our "scripts," they may be accompanied by some confusion and the need to clarify or solidify the new perception. This is part of self-reorganization. Usually this can be dealt with effectively in a classroom if the teacher is caring and practical, has appropriate communication skills, and recognizes the process. If there is severe stress, however, or when meanings are closely linked with trauma, then counselors must be available to create alternative perceptions and experiences.

"Talking through" alone, however, will not automatically lead to appropriate change. The new awareness must be linked to the way individuals experience themselves; therefore, all changes must be carried through in behavior.

MEANINGFUL KNOWLEDGE IS NATURAL KNOWLEDGE

Natural knowledge is what we have come to call "second nature." It is what results when information, felt meaning, and deep meaning come together. The learner has acquired a felt meaning for the subject or concept or procedure so that new information and procedures fit together. In addition, there is a sufficient connection with the learner's interests or deep meanings so that the information and procedures are personally relevant.

An example might be a young child who masters computers easily. The information consists of the parts, the hardware and software, together with a wide range of procedures. For many children, all those ingredients are like any other game that has to be mastered; there is a frame of reference (a technological game played with friends) that enables them to rapidly acquire a sense—or felt meaning—for how everything is connected. And underlying the entire process is a set of drives, ranging from competitiveness to the desire to be part of a group, that gives purpose and a deeper degree of organization to what is being done.

In practice, natural knowledge is acquired by increasing the number and quality of interconnections in the brain. The question is, how does this work?

We note in Principle 4 that the brain is designed to perceive and generate patterns. We are born with the capacity to recognize many patterns almost instantly. Among the features that we can detect are lines and edges, light and dark, color, frequency and pitch of sounds, and other basic sensory qualities. We have innate capacities to respond to ritual and many types of communication. And there are basic-level categories, derived from our experience of our own bodies operating in the world, such as the notions of inside and outside (Lakoff 1987).

NATURAL CATEGORIES

The term we like for these feature and pattern detectors is "natural categories." As we mature and learn, we create, build on, and add to our natural categories. This occurs when the contents of our taxon memory systems become sufficiently interconnected and indexed by the locale system. Thus we begin to recognize trees, cars, buildings, compassion, computers, shops, ritualistic greetings, and so on without having to think about them. These categories are the organizers of our perceptions. In essence, they are not what we think about but what we perceive and think with. We expand and build collections of categories, which are then used in pattern perception. In the context of reading, for instance, it has been said that "more important than structures which are in some sense 'in' the text are knowledge structures the reader brings to the text" (Anderson, R.C., et al. 1976). Other terms that have been used for these knowledge structures are "schemata" (see, e.g., Anderson, R.C., et al. 1976; Rumelhart 1980), "frames" (Minsky 1975), and "scripts" (Schank and Abelson 1975). Our message to educators is that we should teach new information and procedures by taking advantage of what students already know.

Natural knowledge, therefore, consists primarily of all those categories and other structures that organize our actual perception.

CHARACTERISTICS OF EXPERTS

Experts are those who have translated the elements of their field into their own natural categories.

The expert has acquired a felt meaning for the domain so that new information and procedures *fit into place*. In addition, there is a sufficient connection with the expert's interests or deep meanings so that the information and procedures are personally relevant.

One example is the musician who may perceive the key in which a song is played without having to think about it. And an experienced teacher will see classrooms, parents, timetables, discipline issues, and so on quite automatically. In fact, it is quite common for people in a profession to take on the "frame of mind" of that profession. Thus we say that a person thinks like a lawyer or teacher or nurse. For example, an attorney will (or should) know what a contract involves and will be able to read and understand one better than most nonlawyers.

There are three quite noticeable characteristics of experts who acquire perceptual mastery of a field. One has been remarked on many times. It is the fact that the expert sees "larger" patterns or "larger" and more complex chunks (see Chi 1976). Traditionally, the distinction is made between the chess novice and the grand master. Each can think several moves ahead, but the grand master recognizes and thinks in much more sophisticated patterns and moves. Similarly, a master teacher will see a pattern in a student's behavior that may look like a series of unconnected events to a novice.

A second characteristic of experts is their grasp of context. R.C. Anderson and others (1976) argue that "the meaning of a communication depends in a fundamental way on a person's knowledge of the world and his/her analysis of the context as well as the characteristics of the message" (p. 3). An expert can read the important patterns in the external world. That is why what appears to a new teacher to be chaos and disorder in a classroom often has purpose and meaning to the experienced teacher.

Our observations suggest that there is a third characteristic, which is less often noted but equally important. *The way* in which experts remember information in their domains is different from the way in which novices remember. A novice tends to deliberately memorize, whereas an expert stores new information in roughly the same way as we use our locale system to record the information in our daily experiences, such as the details of our meal last night or comments made by a gossip columnist about a film star. For example, a computer expert can read a computer magazine once and remember the new products; a golf commentator can remember and understand the implications of specific shots on specific holes in tournaments; and a financier can quickly grasp the implications of new methods of financing.

Natural knowledge is very much like expertise, in that natural knowledge frames the way in which we observe and perceive the world. That is why the objective of education *must* be the expansion of natural knowledge.

THE OBJECTIVE OF EDUCATION IS THE EXPANSION OF NATURAL KNOWLEDGE

A major source of confusion in educational debates has concerned learning outcomes. It seems to us that almost all learning objectives are, in fact, specified in terms of memorization or the acquisition of surface knowledge. If people are to be genuinely competent in their fields in complex and unpredictable situations, then what they need is an expansion of natural knowledge. We must teach as though teaching for genuine expertise. This is not the same as mastery. Mastery usually refers to memorization of a skill to the point of automaticity, but not to the point of complex understanding. A person may "master" some math equations but still be totally unable to apply them in a real-life problem. One of our goals must be to have students who can carry out procedures on demand *and* who understand what they are doing.

Of course, there can be levels of natural knowledge in any field. A person may be at home with some types of computer software and be a novice with others. We may all be good communicators in some respects and yet have a great deal to learn about communication. The same notion applies to any subject or skill. Thus a student may be able to read simple stories very well but have a great deal of difficulty with more complex material. But a student is often like an expert at some level, even though still a novice by reference to other criteria. Educators must grasp the notion of degrees of expertise and teach for them. Moreover, because natural knowledge is not intrinsically limited, educators must refrain from interrupting its acquisition simply because their own expectations have or have not been met.

Natural knowledge is not the equivalent of absolute truth. People may organize their perceptions in bigoted, prejudiced, and limited ways and can have very different conceptual systems. Hence it is important for educators to continually push for an expansion of students' frames of reference. We may wish them to become competent in fields ranging from economics and history to art and science so that they can interpret events in many different ways. Moreover, we need to take advantage of cultural diversity. This, indeed, is also what business is beginning to seek. In addition, people may become competent in a domain at a basic level. It is extremely important that students be capable of thinking in more demanding ways, both conceptually and contextually. On the one hand, students need to grasp formal operations, without which some types of abstract thought are impossible. On the other, they need to become sensitive to the human and ecological issues inherent in any issue because there is always more involved than meets the eye. Put more simply, students need to be able to think and to care.

Finally, we need to foster in students a predisposition toward expansion. The more they are internally motivated to explore, the easier it is to teach for the generation of natural knowledge. We have shown that the desire to understand is inherent in the human brain. Perhaps the most devastating consequence of disregarding meaningfulness is the ensuing demotivation of students. Our task, then, is to capitalize on and encourage their innate need to know.

How Do We Teach for the Expansion of Natural Knowledge?

You are never given a wish without also being given the power to make it true. You may have to work for it, however (Bach 1977, p. 92).

All I ever needed to know about how to live and what to do and how to be I learned in Kindergarten (Fulghum 1988, p. 4).

Teaching for memory is fundamentally different from teaching for the expansion of natural knowledge. The former tends to be like laying bricks, in the hope that in due course those bricks will turn into a wall or a building. The latter begins with the notion of a building— such as the stonecutter's cathedral mentioned at the beginning of this chapter. The former is an accumulation of parts. The latter is an expansion and refinement of wholeness and interconnectedness. As we mentioned in the preceding section, this is the difference between a novice and an expert. The question, then, is *how to teach for expertise from the very beginning, when a person is still a novice.*

Prietula and Simon pointed out:

Expertise . . . involves much more than knowing a myriad of facts. Expertise is based on a deep knowledge of the problems that continually arise on a particular job. It is accumulated over years of experience tackling these problems and is organized in the expert's mind in ways that allow him or her to overcome the limits of reasoning (1989, p. 120).

What has been very little understood is that we are teaching *all* learners for expertise. The general answer to our question, therefore, is that we need to provide all students with *a sufficient accumulation of appropriate experiences.*

The notion that much of what we learn is gathered from experience is not new. It is part of what links many prominent writers and educators, such as John Dewey (1962, 1965, 1966), Alfred North Whitehead (1979), and Maria Montessori (1965). Unfortunately, their message and the phrase "learn from experience" have a great deal of hidden depth that is almost invariably ignored. In particular, many educators subscribe to the notion that learning from experience is only one type of learning. This is illustrated by those who differentiate between lectures and experiential learning, and who equate experience with some sort of participative activity closely linked to vocational training. As is perhaps abundantly clear at this point, our definition of *experience* far surpasses such a narrow conceptualization.

We have established that we are all immersed in complex, global experiences every moment of our lives, much as a fish is surrounded by water. The locale system constantly monitors our movement in space; our sensory and motor systems are engaged in every life activity; we explore every event for meaning in a way that involves our emotions and thoughts and visceral body. One of the most important lessons to derive from the brain research is that, in a very important sense, *all* learning is experiential. What we learn depends on the global experience, not just on the manner of presentation. Dewey fully realized this. He wrote:

> We never educate directly, but indirectly by means of the environment. Whether we permit chance environments to do the work, or whether we design environments for the purpose makes a great deal of difference. And any environment is a chance environment so far as its educative influence is concerned unless it has been deliberately regulated with reference to its educative effect (Dewey 1966, p. 19).

We do not, however, automatically learn enough from our experience. What matters is how experience is used. Our conclusion is that in deliberately teaching for the expansion of natural knowledge, we need both to help students have appropriate experiences and to help them capitalize on the experiences. Three interactive elements are essential to this process, and all three are implicit in the previous quote by Prietula and Simon (1989).

1. Teachers need to *orchestrate the immersion of the learner in complex, interactive experiences* that are both rich and real. A good example is the use of immersion in the teaching of a second language (Dolson 1984).

2. There must be a personally meaningful challenge. This is the intrinsic motivation that is part of the state of mind that we identify as *relaxed alertness*.

3. There must be intensive analysis so that the learner gains insight about the problem, about the ways in which it could be approached and about learning generally. We call this the *active processing of experience*.

This is not, we should add, a linear model. Each element contributes to the other two, and the three are constantly interacting. They are the subjects of Chapters 9–11.

INDICATORS OF UNDERSTANDING: EVALUATION

As educators, we have to be able to *see* that a learner understands. It is appropriate, of course, to use some formal tests and measures of performance in the assessment program. We suggest, however, that most formal testing simply measures limited aspects of the acquisition of surface knowledge. This is particularly true of multiple-choice questions. The use of such testing must be limited because it often forecloses on the options available to learners and changes the conditions of the performance. It has been said, for instance, that "behaviorally stated objectives reduce wasted time in temporary diversions, ephemeral entertainment, or other irrelevancies" (Popham 1968, quoted in Jenkins and Deno 1971). Our point is that those "irrelevancies" often include both the context and the creative insights that are indispensable for meaningful learning.

A solution that we find extremely practical is to evaluate our students by combining *measures of complex performance* with *indicators of understanding*. These emerge quite readily if we look at the acquisition of felt meaning and the development of natural knowledge in the workplace and elsewhere. We are asking exactly the same question when we seek to discover whether our child is learning to speak, whether a person has mastered a hobby, or whether someone really is an expert in a particular domain. What we use at work and at home are indicators of complex performance in real and often unplanned tasks. An expert, for example, is a person who can react appropriately in both predictable and unpredictable situations. A superb example is the capacity to engage in a conversation that unexpectedly calls one's knowledge into play. This happens all the time in the workplace and in social gatherings, whether we are talking about computers, changes in Eastern Europe, art, or finance. We use similar indicators of unexpected competence to tell us that a child has genuinely begun to speak. At other times, a problem will be presented for which there is no known answer. The expert is the person who can be reliably called on to work on and solve the problem.

We can translate such evaluations into educational applications by developing complex contexts that call for competent performance and for both predictable and unpredictable, but appropriate, behaviors. Our task is to know when and how to look for evidence of understanding. It can be done. This contextual assessment is discussed further in Chapter 11.

9

ORCHESTRATED IMMERSION

Upon this gifted age, in its dark hour,
Falls from the sky a meteoric shower
Of facts . . . they lie unquestioned, uncombined.
Wisdom enough to leech us of our ill
Is daily spun; but there exists no loom
To weave it into fabric . . .

Edna St. Vincent Millay

Education and the process of educating is a total
integral, contextual situation which includes students,
teachers, parents, administration and environment.

Jean Houston, *Millennium: Glimpses into the*
21st Century, 1981, p. 159

We have concluded, on the bases of the 12 brain principles and other research, that all the ingredients of complex experience are already operative in life and always color the content of any learning environment. Students are perceiving, feeling, relating, and processing all the time. All of those ingredients must be engaged in the educational venture.

The thrust of orchestrated immersion, specifically, is to *take information off the page and the blackboard and bring it to life in the minds of students*. Immersion focuses on how students are exposed to content. When wholeness and interconnectedness cannot be avoided, students are obliged to employ their locale memory system in the exploration of content.

The objective, therefore, is to immerse students in what Kristina Hooper calls "compelling experiences" (1988). These may be brief or may span weeks or months. By definition, they are immensely varied and contain both unpredictable and predictable elements. They are powerfully evocative, challenging, meaningful, and coherent environments for the brain. Educators, therefore, need to identify and appreciate the various elements of such experience and need to know how to bring them together effectively. That "bringing together" through practical skill and artistry is what we call "orchestration."

WHAT DOES IMMERSION LOOK LIKE?

Video games, although often not working in support of the goals of education, constitute one excellent example of immersion. They work because the player enters into the video world of time and space and becomes a character engaged in a quest that is both familiar and new. The student's locale memory system has been activated in the context of the game: vocabulary and details as well as skills stored in the taxon systems separately are invoked, and new vocabulary and skills are "picked up" almost automatically. This further illustrates what we mean by embedding taxon information in the experiences registered in locale memory.

Another example is the experience of being in a foreign country or culture. Every issue or need, whether we ask for something, look around as tourists, search for a place, or engage in any other action, is packaged in a multiplicity of verbal and nonverbal signals. The visitor is totally immersed in the content and context to be learned. Of course, at times this will be threatening—and the visitor might resist learning. Other elements that contribute to a feeling of safety and willingness to take a risk are, therefore, important.

One of the authors, Renate, used this approach in high school German classes. On entering the class, for all intents and purposes, students were *in Germany*. They had German names, and from Day 1 they were invited to speak only German. English became the foreign language. The physical environment included all types of German artifacts and posters of places in Germany. Students rewrote their dialogues for presentation in front of class. They translated fairy tales and acted them out, and they sang German songs. The result was that in one year, students from these classes won 1st, 2nd, 4th, and 6th places in the state language contest.

Total immersion in multiple overlapping experiences is also at the heart of the way we each learn our native language. As children, we listened, we watched, we were involved, we mimicked and gestured and participated in language at ever more complex levels. The development of whole-language learning is predicated on this process (Flores, Garcia, Gonzalez, Hidalgo, Kaczmarek, and Romero 1986; Goodman 1986). Reading, writing, speaking, and acting cannot be separated from each other. All interact as we learn to use language and to perceive and communicate meaningfully.

One of the strengths of "Brain-Compatible Learning," developed by Hart, is the appreciation of rich experiences. Hart (1983) suggests that most classrooms should be at least *ten times* richer than they currently are. We saw this implemented at Drew Elementary School in New Jersey. Lynn Dhority (1982) employs a related notion. His objective is to introduce so many new items into the first lesson that student limitations are overwhelmed. In effect, he induces them to process globally and not in a purely segmented, brick-building fashion.

Similarly, for great thinkers, immersion in a field in rich, complex, practical, and imaginative ways is usually indispensable to subsequent creative insight. Einstein, for example, combined extensive theoretical work with a rich imagination. Indeed, he once imagined actually riding a beam of light as a prelude to his insight into the nature of relativity. And Hindle (1982) quotes Robert Fulton as saying, "The mechanic should sit down among levers, screws, wedges, wheels, etc., like a poet among the letters of the alphabet, considering them as the exhibition of his thoughts, in which a new arrangement transmits a new Idea to the world."

All too often, students do not participate in the more exciting aspects of learning. The objective of brain-based learning is to find ways to help the student have experiences that are similar in complexity, challenge, and creativity to those of creative experts. Learning this way will always involve a combination of information that is given with a restructuring that is both creative and personally meaningful. Creating these rich maps takes time. In part, that is because the experiences need to be processed or digested, as we discuss in Chapter 11. Yet the number of connections ultimately formed ensures much more in-depth understanding and preparation for future learning than any symbol-specific or taxon memorization can achieve.

THE TEACHER AS A DESIGNER OF EXPERIENCE

Orchestration involves the development of an approach to teaching that combines planning with opportunity for spontaneity—by both teacher and students. A young teacher, for example, told the following story. She had been working with a group of 2nd graders identified as slow learners. She was trying to teach them what commas and periods and exclamation marks represented. After several explanations focusing on the fact that commas meant slow down, periods meant stop or pause, and exclamation marks meant emphasis, she had them read aloud. There was no change. They read without paying any attention to what she had told them. Finally, exasperated, she had them put on their coats and follow her outside. She told them, "I am going to read to you and I want you to walk around in a circle. When I say 'comma'

I want you to slooow down, whenever I say 'period' I want you to stop dead in your tracks, and when I say 'exclamation mark' I want you to jump up and down. Do you understand?" She tried this for five minutes with perfect success. When they went back inside and read, all of them slowed down at the commas, paused at periods, and used emphasis at exclamation marks.

This is a good example of a teacher's creatively involving students in an experience that was both complex and made sense because it tied the new information to their own natural knowledge of walking and jumping. Although her actions were spontaneous, they evolved out of the context, including the teacher's own frustration, and tapped her own creative talents. Such spontaneous creativity is often the result of an inner confidence as a communicator and a focus on making sense rather than rote learning. People in all walks of life have this creativity. By the way, the teacher in this example attributed her reaction to her experiences as a mother.

Such spontaneous teaching events are critical in brain-based learning. They introduce novelty in a way that enhances complex mapping. However, they must be part of a larger mastery of planning and design that teachers must have if they are to effectively orchestrate experiences for learners. Brooke Hindle (1982) defines design as "the relation of things in space." In effect, educators must be able to relate events, people, places, and objects in time and space.

A person who can orchestrate experience well has what Donald Schön calls artistry:

> • Inherent in the practice of the professionals we recognize as unusually competent is a core of artistry.
> • Artistry is an exercise of intelligence, a kind of knowing, though different in crucial respects from our standard model of professional knowledge (1990, p. 13).

Like all professionals, teachers must assimilate basic procedures and strategies and then implement them in a way that reveals personal artistry. One of the reasons some methodologies work very well for some teachers and not for others, we suspect, has to do with the sense of artistry of different teachers and their innate but often unrecognized ability to integrate different elements of experience.

DYNAMIC GESTALTS: CREATING A SENSE OF LIVING WHOLENESS

Knowledge becomes natural when it is sufficiently connected with what else is already known. These patterns of interconnectedness are what we call "maps." To help students create sophisticated maps in the brain, teachers must not present subject matter in isolated, meaningless pieces. Rather, the student needs to experience a sense of wholeness. Crowell (1989) calls it "dynamic unity." As Houston (1981) says, "Why is it that Johnny cannot read, spell, or balance his checkbook? How could he, when his education was so fragmented?" (p. 159).

Many opportunities for making connections must be provided for students, from which they can extract meaningful patterns and global relationships. To do this, we need to diverge from our heavy emphasis on specific outcomes. Rather, we need to invoke frames of reference that allow for creativity within understood parameters. They are the elements that contribute to a sense of wholeness and, at the same time, contain and permit *flexibility, change,* and *excitement.* We have coined the term *dynamic gestalts* to describe them.

For example, consider the plot of a mystery novel written by a favorite author. As readers, we make an often unconscious agreement with the writer about the nature of the plot. The author has a great deal of latitude, but the reader has a basic sense of how the book will unfold and a sense of the beginning, middle, and end. We can then tolerate an enormous amount of frustration or anxiety relating to the characters. We feel violated, however, if the author toys with our "agreement" about how romance builds, crime develops, and people are rewarded and punished.

At a more abstract level, religion provides a similar sense of agreement. As long as we have a grasp of a greater purpose and a sense of continuity and connectedness, day-to-day events make sense. These larger "plots," "belief systems," and "agreements" are dynamic gestalts because they provide overall patterns that make sense. These patterns tie together bits and pieces of information and give a cohesive meaning and purpose to our daily learning. Educators must provide students with dynamic gestalts within which to examine and explore every subject. A major task of educators, therefore, is to perceive dynamic gestalts and learn how to use them. Here are some examples.

ESTABLISHING CURRICULAR THEMES

The focus should be on themes around which a curriculum can be organized, encompassing the subject matter to be studied. Almost all educators have to begin with a curriculum that incorporates content specified, to a large extent, by others. State curriculum frameworks, for example, are frequently developed by legislatively empowered committees. The content often is spelled out in a way that is fragmented and largely meaningless when translated to individual teachers and classrooms.

Themes allow for the organization of seemingly fragmented topics. They are essential tools in the educator's kit because they invoke universal ideas and concepts that almost everyone can identify with independently of subject mastery. The general theme is not merely a catchy title, but is the central organizer for the subject to be studied. It lets us know where we are going.

Appropriate themes invoke emotions, provide a personal challenge, and stir the imagination. Leo Wood (Wood and Odell 1989) chose "Life Is a Miracle" as his theme for teaching chemistry. General themes go beyond the concrete and beyond a specific subject. "Chemistry Is a Miraculous Subject" would not achieve the same effect. Subthemes are identified and explored; for example, a subtheme in chemistry might be "bonding." Chemical bonding is then examined in the light of human bonding in friendship, marriage, and parenting. General themes open the way to the use of powerful and appropriate analogies and metaphors, which can serve as a bridge to understanding new and unfamiliar information.

ENCOURAGING COMPLEX, REAL PROJECTS OF PERSONAL INTEREST TO STUDENTS

Students must be exposed to subject matter in many different ways, a great number of which must be complex, real projects. These projects should be developmental in nature and link work over time. They should assist in connecting content to the world in which the student actually lives. They can generate the sort of communication and group interaction upon which many people thrive. And they can be vehicles for teaching much more than the specific content of any one course.

Teachers often seem to fear that the use of real-life activities and large-scale projects will interfere with the coverage of the prescribed materials. In effect, they often feel that invoking locale memory will jeopardize the treatment of taxon information. Our experience is directly to the contrary. The proper use of complex activities makes it possible to deal with substantially *more* material than would otherwise be the case. The teacher or students may model or demonstrate the subject, bring in experts, engage in genuine problem solving, interview authorities, and create learning games.

If the topic to be studied is the eagle, for example, students deal with it in many different ways. They may explore nesting, feeding, and reproductive patterns and the eagle's ecological requirements, together with relevant information spanning several subject areas. They listen to recordings of the live eagle as it moves through the air, and they read literature featuring eagles. They study the eagle as a political symbol and its role in the arts. Students develop areas of expertise or experts are brought to class or are recorded or videotaped. Computer simulations and tracking programs are made available to students to help them identify where eagles are located and whether they are thriving. The mood that should prevail is that of a team of researchers or explorers engaged in a meaningful, exciting adventure.

PROVIDING MULTISENSORY REPRESENTATIONS

One of the benefits from the interest in individual differences has been a recent emphasis on engaging all the senses. We agree that some learners prefer information to be written; others prefer it to be spoken. Some need touching and physical manipulation; others are less concrete. However, we all have senses—and they all operate all the time. A safe general rule, therefore, is to ensure that all senses be engaged in the design of experiences for students and that students need to have deep and rich sensory experiences of whatever is to be learned.

The notion of multisensory representations can be expanded to include the combination of feeling and thought. George Brown (1971) built on this concept to develop what he calls "confluent education." Others have emphasized the importance of more fully bringing the body into education. This is at the heart of Asher's "Total Physical Response" approach to the teaching of language (Asher 1982). Multisensory experiences are even more fully expressed by George Leonard (1987), who has suggested that dance, drama, and music be introduced to assist in linking the body and the senses and giving meaning to what would otherwise be unconnected data.

TELLING STORIES AND EXPLORING MYTHS

Stories and myths help tie content together and aid natural memory. "Once upon a time" there was more of an appreciation for stories than there is now. Testimony to their power is offered by the news and entertainment media. Stories are powerful because they "bind" information and understanding over time. In fact, there is strong reason to believe that the organization of information in story form is a natural brain process. Remember that the locale system records our ongoing life experience from moment to moment. It does not do this totally randomly, but is constantly sifting through that experience for meaning. At a minimum, a story is a sequence of experiences with a meaningful theme. Lynn Nadel said, in fact, that the locale system "records the story of each individual life" (personal communication 1987). In essence, each of us is living a story, and one way in which we relate to others is through empathizing with *their* stories. There is evidence from other sources to support the importance of schemata and context as aids to memory (Anderson, R.C., Reynolds, Schallert, and Goetz 1976; Anderson, R.C., Spiro, and Anderson 1977;

Pichert and Anderson 1976). We suggest that the brain research confirms that evidence and begins to explain why stories are so important.

Integrating Great Literature. Teachers acknowledge the power of stories when they introduce a new subject by recounting some background history. The problem is that a straight historical narrative often misses the power of a story because it tends to be presented as additional inert surface knowledge. Our experiences are dramatic. They include emotion, mystery, tension, and climaxes. They may be fantastical or real. The key is to learn the art of using stories. In practice, this becomes a sound reason for integrating great literature into the teaching of almost any subject. For example, Barbara Caine (personal communication 1989) uses the novels of George Eliot in college-level history courses as a basis for exploring 19th century England. We previously mentioned another college-level example provided by the Colorado School of Mines, which uses Mary Shelley's *Frankenstein* in its introductory course on chemical engineering.

Engaging Learners' Dreams. A *quest* is a personal story in which we embed our personal challenges and our own deep meanings. People who wish to win at Wimbledon, fly in the space shuttle, write a great novel, develop a major new computer program, or perform at Carnegie Hall are living a personal dream. They combine and personally organize their life experiences around their deeply held drives, very much like a general theme. This can be tapped in school by using projects that in some way engage students' dreams. The keys are to make the projects manageable and real, as well as exciting. A superb illustration is the ongoing competition among science students in school to design experiments that could be performed on the space shuttle [Student Space Science Involvement Program, administered through the National Science Teachers Association (NSTA)]. The approach, however, can be adopted at any community level and in any context. The essential point is that these are ways of "binding" information and understanding over time.

USING METAPHORS

Metaphors are intrinsic to the construction of new knowledge and are at the heart of the acquisition of felt meaning. Metaphor has interested philosophers for a long time and is of more and more interest to educators (see, for example, Ortony 1980, Winner 1988). It has been used as an instructional framework in such processes as Synectics™ (Gordon, W. 1961). George Lakoff (1987) suggests that metaphor works on at least two levels. Our basic experience provides us with what we have been calling "natural categories." These derive in part from how we move in physical space; this idea is supported by the work of O'Keefe and Nadel (1978). Thus we have basic notions for "up" and "down," and for containers with an "inside" and "outside." These experiences encompass much more than the actual physical events that describe them. They become metaphors that explain emotional states or social events. For example, we "move up" in the hierarchy, or we may be "down-and-out." We then construct new knowledge on the basis of these and other metaphors. As we have written elsewhere, "metaphors bring with them preestablished sets of relationships as well as positive emotional experiences and rich sensory memories in which new knowledge can be embedded. They therefore become means to coherently engage all the systems of the brain/mind" (Caine, G., and Caine 1990, p. 30).

The educational implication is clear. We must use metaphors intentionally in every subject, though the evidence suggests that they operate very differently for different age groups (Gardner 1982); and these differences must be addressed. We must make a deliberate attempt to articulate and make better use of those complex relationships that underlie mapping. A superb example of this in teacher education is provided by Sam Crowell (1989), who uses the theme "Teacher as Artist" with student teachers. Their purpose is to explore a different aspect of the nature of art each week, and Crowell invites them to explore the connection between art and teaching. The course is also a marvelous way for teachers to gain insight into themselves as artists or designers. A teacher as artist thinks and designs the classroom differently from a teacher as researcher or teacher as administrator. Teachers benefit by being able to access numerous roles; and "living" the metaphor opens the door to discovering one's ability to perceive and act more broadly. The course may therefore deal with preparation, persistence of themes, the artist's need for creative expression, and seeing life in different ways. Teachers then begin to notice possible parallels between how they approach teaching and how artists approach their craft.

CONSIDERING THE ENTIRE PHYSICAL CONTEXT

> What we have seen in education is exactly the same pattern of breakdown that we have seen in every arena of society. . . . Innovation has to be worked in relation to the whole educational system. Unless something grows as part of the organism as a whole, there will be nothing but fragments (Houston 1981, p. 159).

A major theme in this book is the power and importance of the entire physical and perceptual context in which we work and live. In effect, the entire sensory environment is "packaging" for any specific issue or content with which we are faced. Our context is meaningful and affects us, whether or not we are consciously aware of the consequences. That is why part of the solution is to create what George

115

Leonard (1987) calls a "total environment." As an example, the Montessori method invites parents and educators to take advantage of everything in the child' environment (Hainstock 1971).

Complex Environmental Factors. We pay only nominal attention to the sensory environment in the design of schools. Why else are most classrooms above the kindergarten level so sterile? The message we send is that this is a "serious" place where people "work." We do not advocate any one specific environment, but we do recommend giving attention to how the physical context complements what both teacher and students expect to happen. In general, schools try to avoid temperatures that are too hot or cold, and they pay some attention to noise control. Schools occasionally use illustrations and paintings to give a place more "life." The reason for doing this is often poorly defined or understood. Our point is that the environmental factors that influence learning are vastly more complex and subtle than has previously been realized. Teachers and administrators can make use of such physical stimuli to help students learn better. We do not propose to discuss subliminal perception, though there is some evidence that people respond to signals that are below the threshold of awareness (Gregory 1987, p. 753). However, we suspect that even within the range of what can be directly perceived, very "light" or barely perceptible signals wield significant influence.

Perhaps we can illustrate the power of the context by examining the care with which we arrange the decor in our own homes. The colors we choose, the art, the music, the design of the furniture, the layout of the kitchen, the type of garden, and the neighborhood where we choose to live are all important, even though we may pay very little direct attention to most of these items once they have been selected. All of these factors are equally important in the school and the classroom. Hence some of the skill in good teaching lies in the capacity to orchestrate the sensory context of the class. Educators must pay attention to the meanings implicit in the design of schools and in the organization of classrooms. In particular, teachers can make even more extensive use of peripherals (Lozanov 1978a). These include copies of great works of art, posters, and classical and other forms of music that emphasize particular themes or subjects.

Peripherals and Immersion. Peripherals also set the tone for the school. Immersion cannot be limited to the classroom. Students who feel comfortable doing or learning about art in the classroom but would never "talk" art with friends are dichotomizing learning and life and lose opportunities for further immersion. In most schools, the class content and social life outside of class have little to do with each other—except for "homework." A school that wishes to maximize on immersion must make the entire school a learning environment. When projects and subjects overlap, when teachers discuss subject matter with each other, when respect for learning is reflected in the physical environment of the school, and when we encourage interactions and experiences to focus on class activities or subject matter outside of class, then we are truly immersing students in an environment that capitalizes on learning.

PROVIDING SOCIAL RELATIONSHIPS AND A SENSE OF COMMUNITY

The human brain is a social brain (Gazzaniga 1985). It is clear that we have a brain-based drive to belong to a group and to relate to others. Hence educators need to support and consolidate social relationships and a sense of community. Friendship and companionship are both intrinsically important to us and contribute to safety, security, and relaxed alertness because a genuinely supportive group helps to reduce threat. The Carnegie Foundation's study, *An Imperiled Generation* (1988), supports this notion: "The successful schools we visited were true communities of learning and places where students were known and have ongoing contact with their teacher" (p. 22).

The Power of Groups. The Peninsula School in California (Fadiman 1988) beautifully illustrates the power of community that is developed by supportive relationships within the classroom, between different age groups, among the teachers, and with parents and the local community (see Chapter 12). Others have established that involving parents in schooling helps to build a larger sense of community that is extremely valuable. One example is the Comer process of reform of urban schools (Comer 1987; Haynes, Comer, and Hamilton-Lee 1989). The Comer process involves four centers of focus, one being a team of parents. The other centers are a school governance and management team, a mental health team, and a team (also involving parents) responsible for social projects.

Although a high degree of interaction is not always possible, particularly with transient school populations, it is extremely useful for teachers to use small and large groups in their classes. Complex learning, for example, a method developed at Stanford University, uses group interaction (in elementary schools) to help students develop problem-solving skills. In complex learning, students in small groups engage in research and development. This model thus provides a structure, but also allows for the natural self-organization of the group. The Stanford research on "Complex Instruction" (Cohen 1984; Cohen and Lotan 1990; Cohen, Lotan, and Leechor 1989) demonstrates that learning increases when students are jointly engaged in problem solving. Indeed, learning often actually decreases when teachers interfere excessively (Harste 1989).

There are many reasons for the power of groups. Working through a project with a group is often perceived to be a more "real" experience; such work certainly engages the various mind/brain systems. The research on Complex Instruction referred to above demonstrates a positive and critical link between verbal interaction and learning, and groups can trigger multiple ways of interacting. Discussion in a group is also an effective way of processing experience. It provides learners with rehearsals and the opportunity to reconstruct knowledge on an individual basis.

Multiple Statuses of Participants. Groups do not automatically enhance learning for all students. We suggest that groups must be engaged in generally challenging activities while attention is paid to social and emotional interactions. The Stanford University research emphasizes the importance of multiple statuses among participants within heterogenous groups (Cohen 1984; Cohen, Lotan, and Catanzarite 1990). If interactions are limited to only a few high-status individuals, then the immersion effect is minimized. Ideal social relationships are complex. They are those in which *everyone is a learner and everyone is a teacher.* In other words, there must be a genuine "atmosphere" of learning. Students teach each other. Students teach the teacher. And the teacher, parents, and members of the community all help to teach as called on. There are an infinite number of ways that this can be done. What must be present are a sufficient degree of respect, a grasp of reality, and freedom to engage in complex interactions. Students are not "talked down to"—they are invited to learn about something that affects the value and quality of life.

The corollary is that teachers' personalities and social qualities are exceptionally important, in addition to their knowledge and skill. Teachers need to facilitate bonding, encourage student leadership, communicate on different levels and in different ways, and respect cultural differences. And they must genuinely appreciate and feel a sense of the community that they seek to establish for students. This is why we emphasize that the teacher, as a total person, is so critical to the learning process. The training of teachers takes time and, along with imparting content and techniques, must include the development of personal growth and reflection.

BRAIN-BASED EDUCATIONAL METHODOLOGIES

We all have at our disposal a large societal repertoire of educational methodologies. We describe some of what is currently available by way of illustration. They do not have to be reinvented. Nor are they mutually exclusive. What matters is the way that we select and use them. In all instances, the objective is to engage the learner in more than the memorization of surface information.

The Integrated Curriculum

Integration of the curriculum is an excellent way to increase richness and contribute to meaningfulness. Possibly the simplest way to begin to integrate the curriculum is to combine the content of two classes, such as history and literature. This can be done by one teacher. The next step is to have two teachers, each representing a different discipline, team teach. This is not simply a matter of having two subjects presented side by side. It is a cooperative endeavor, in which teachers demonstrate the ways in which the subjects are integrated. This type of teaching is easily sabotaged by interpersonal conflict and lack of communication skills. We saw an excellent example of an integrated curriculum in the humanities department of the Hightstown High School in New Jersey (see Shalley 1987). Because much of this type of teaching requires flexibility in terms of student contact time, there must also be flexibility in assigning teaching time. The curriculum can be further integrated with art and music. What it takes is an appropriate theme or frame of reference, such as a period in history, around which to organize the contributions from other subjects. If history is the organizing subject, and the 19th century has been selected, for example, then students are fully immersed in the 19th century from historical events to literary writings, to art, music, discoveries in science, and geographical changes. Teachers help students to see how these various aspects historically interacted and affected each other.

There has been a strong move in some schools toward the combination of subjects. The issue has been examined recently by Heidi Jacobs (1989) in *Interdisciplinary Curriculum*. We have observed it at every level, from elementary school, where it is quite common, to high schools and college, where it is comparatively rare.

There are several reasons why interdisciplinary teaching is important:

1. *The brain searches for common patterns and connections.* Thus history, properly enlivened by relevant literature, becomes a way of making meaning out of other content.

2. *Every experience actually contains within it the seeds of many, and possibly all, disciplines.* Thus recent developments in Eastern Europe involve history, geography, politics, comparative religion, economics, and social science, as well as provide fertile soil for dealing with music, math, and information technology, to name a few disciplines.

3. *One of the keys to understanding is what is technically called redundancy.* In other words, if the same message can be packaged in several ways, the receiver has a much better chance of grasping what is actually happening. This lies at the heart of recent developments in information theory (Campbell 1982) and reinforces the importance of immersion.

THEMATIC TEACHING

Geared to the self-contained classroom, thematic teaching is more compatible with the way elementary schools are organized. The approach can also be used at the secondary level—with slight modifications. The idea, which educators such as Susan Kovalik (1986) and her associates are implementing, is to adopt some event or topic that allows for inclusion of many topics, such as "communication," "growth," or "cycles," out of which an entire year's or semester's program can be built. The reasoning behind this approach is that the central theme or set of themes helps students relate all the information. A thematic map based on the notion of "family," for example, shows what the content of such an integrated curriculum might involve (Figure 9.1).

Figure 9.1 Thematic Map of "Family"

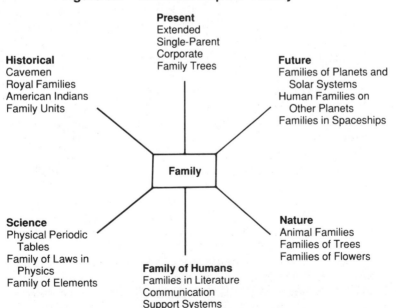

Present
Extended
Single-Parent
Corporate
Family Trees

Historical
Cavemen
Royal Families
American Indians
Family Units

Future
Families of Planets and
    Solar Systems
Human Families on
    Other Planets
Families in Spaceships

Family

Science
Physical Periodic
    Tables
Family of Laws in
    Physics
Family of Elements

Family of Humans
Families in Literature
Communication
Support Systems

Nature
Animal Families
Families of Trees
Families of Flowers

The various subtopics always relate back to the central theme so that every component of the course is connected. It is important to remember that the teacher does not do all the teaching. The students do the discovering, and the parents and community often are involved. Computers are also valuable elements in such teaching.

THEMATICAL ORCHESTRATION

Ivan Barzakov (1988) has developed an even more sophisticated approach than that of thematic teaching. He uses what he calls "global themes" as organizers of meaning. These are based on archetypes that have some sort of universal application, such as "war and peace" or "order and chaos." In practice, therefore, the universals are always larger than the scope of any particular course.

The idea is that we should always use at least two universals. In the global theme, there is a "tension" between them. Thus one example of a global theme is "conflict versus resolution," another is "finality and eternity," and a third is "order out of chaos." The subject matter of the course is then organized around the theme. Thus a course on computing can have subthemes on hardware, software, and applications. But all of these can be explained in terms of how they help to generate order out of chaos. For example, we can see how a computing system helps in the management of a complex business. We might also see how computers lead to even more chaos in other ways—for example, by creating information overload. We have found teachers who are personally interested in issues such as "harmony and tension" or "individuality and community" and who thoroughly enjoy using these as organizers for their courses.

Having organized the course around global themes that allow the teacher to introduce material from many other subject areas, Barzakov then orchestrates the peripheral environment, using art and music, to give expression to these themes. Thus he might lead into the history of computing with a piece of music that is highly suggestive of order emerging out of chaos. And he will use art, such as the work of some of the impressionists, to reinforce the message. He will then change these paintings and reposition them, so that they are constantly shedding additional light on the subject being discussed. We appreciate that such teaching presents logistical difficulties in most schools as they are now organized.

COOPERATIVE LEARNING

Cooperative learning builds on and enhances the capacities of people to communicate and collaborate (Johnson, Murayama, Johnson, Nelson, and Skon 1981; Kohn 1986). It is a process of generating group relationships so that the group can support all of its members. Specific attention is paid to developing communication and group skills. Different roles are allocated, such as those of timekeeper and recorder, and these are rotated so that everybody participates in each role. The ideal, in fact, is for the group to share the responsibility for the learning of each student in such a way that members want to help each other.

Of course, cooperative learning can become overstructured and a veneer for excessive control. How it is implemented is a matter of the personality and style of individual teachers. The key is to be true to the spirit of the process.

INNOVATIVE USES OF TRADITIONAL METHODS

Using Language Extensively. Language is powerful. There is much that cannot be expressed in language; yet, with rare exceptions, the people who are best in their field are also people who can talk about it in many different ways. We learn our native language by a partially random and a partially orchestrated immersion in a variety of interactive experiences. Speaking and writing are ways of making those experiences understandable. That is one reason why it is so useful for a student to explain to a receptive parent what she did in a course, even if she doesn't feel confident about what she learned.

Every subject has a language of its own that needs to be mastered. At another level, language is a way of obtaining feedback from the environment. And at a still deeper level, language is a mediator between our different systems and between our own conscious and unconscious mind. As Gazzaniga (1985) says, "Language reports the cognitive computations of other mental modules" (p. 93). We acquire deeper insights in part as we find clearer ways to talk about and describe what we experience and what it means to us. It is not just a matter of getting the right answer. As we talk about a subject or skill in complex and appropriate ways—and that includes making jokes and playing games—we actually begin to feel better about the subject and master it. That is why the everyday use of relevant terms and the appropriate use of language should be incorporated in every course from the beginning.

Providing for Practice, Rehearsal—and Re-creation. We are not excluding practice, but we do question the extraordinary overemphasis on rote memorization. There are many challenging and stimulating ways to explore and rehearse. We have available to us a wealth of resources and techniques in such forms as games, simulations, multimedia technologies, and the various arts. Laughter and fun

122

are not out of place when they are the result of immersion, as in the case of "fun drills" put together by students or a song written by the teacher. Leo Wood's song of "The 5 Essential Chemical Reactions" sung to the tune of "I've Been Working on the Railroad" is only one such example (Wood and Odell 1989).

FREEDOM AND CONTROL

There is a tension in orchestration between freedom and control. On the one hand, the school and the classroom must have a sufficient degree of orderliness. On the other, students must have choice and variety. Teachers must relax their control, to provide for individual differences and intrinsic motivation. If students are to be predominantly self-motivated, they must be given the opportunity to focus on their areas of interest and to participate in activities they find interesting.

For example, some students will enjoy interviewing an expert or searching out great art. Other students can read or develop computer programs or study legends. The range of relevant information and possible modes of expression is endless. The teacher ensures that these projects are of high caliber, are challenging, and extend the student's knowledge and understanding. The teacher also strives to have all the students exposed to all the information gathered so that they have the opportunity to integrate their knowledge. Their contributions must be valued. This is part of what is meant by challenge.

Individuality goes hand in glove with complexity of experience. Teachers must *not* overspecify what students are exposed to. Because what teachers emphasize shapes what students are permitted to grasp, excessive control may actually inhibit learning. Harste (1989), for example, confirms this with respect to reading and language. Children who have a teacher who uses a phonics approach learn to do phonics. Children with a teacher who uses a skills approach to teaching reading learn to do the skills approach. Children who are given a personally meaningful prompt to write their own complex stories, on the other hand, use more sophisticated grammar and content than those who experience the directly controlled skills or phonics approach. That is not to say that children never benefit from skills or phonics. These approaches may actually be helpful in the absence of appropriate immersion. Children lose when they restrict themselves to what was taught and ignore their own natural abilities and knowledge.

There are several ways of maintaining orderliness within the scope of freedom allowed. Just as in the larger society, orderliness is based in large part on accepted customs, courtesy, and mutual respect.

Equally important is the element of playfulness. We have a tendency to employ all the methods described in this chapter with an attitude of deadly seriousness. The spirit of brain-based learning is somewhat different. Creativity, connectedness, spontaneity, and other qualities are frequently light and playful in nature. By taking the task too seriously, both teacher and student may downshift to some degree and then become less capable of optimal performance. Relaxed alertness, the alternative to downshifting, is an essential state of mind for these procedures and approaches to be effective. It is, therefore, the subject of the next chapter.

* * *

The model in Figure 9.2 may serve to summarize the difference between traditional and brain-based teaching.

When our intent is to immerse learners in complex and real experiences, we need to make major changes in how we go about

Figure 9.2 Comparison of Teaching Models		
Elements of Orchestration	Traditional Teaching	Brain-Based Teaching
Source of Information	Simple. Two-way, from teacher to book, worksheet, or film to student.	Complex. Social interactions, group discovery, individual search and reflection, role playing, integrated subject matter.
Classroom Organization	Linear. Individual work or teacher directed.	Complex. Thematic, integrative, cooperative, workstations, individualized projects.
Classroom Management	Hierarchical. Teacher controlled.	Complex. Designated status and responsibilities delegated to students and monitored by teacher.
Outcomes	Specified and convergent. Emphasis on memorized concepts, vocabulary, and skills.	Complex. Emphasis on reorganization of information in unique ways, with both predictable outcomes, divergent and convergent, increase in natural knowledge demonstrated through ability to use learned skills in variable contexts.

teaching. All of the methods and models described, and more, are options available to educators. They are models for orchestration, not memorization. They come in formal and less formal models. What matters is how we use them. The teacher's job is to invite and encourage students to experience and recreate the appropriate information in as many ways as possible. The key to being a more effective educator, therefore, is not simply to find a specific methodology or technique. It is to grasp what actually happens in the brain during learning and to appreciate how all the different components of experience work together to help the brain do its job. That understanding enables us to select intelligently from all the methodologies at our disposal and to orchestrate them in a way that is appropriate for the situations in which we find ourselves.

We must not forget that much of what happens in the school is in the context of a larger society in action. The media, politicians, local businesses, traffic, the weather, pollution and clean-ups, the entertainment industry, clubs, the behavior of parents, and so on all contribute to students' experiences. The impact of the world beyond the school cannot be underestimated. In terms of immersion and how the brain learns, therefore, all of society participates in education. We need to begin to think in new, global ways about education generally.

10

RELAXED ALERTNESS

Her hands trembled and she pressed them together to
make them stop, for Kapugen had taught her that fear
can so cripple a person that he couldn't think or act.
Already she was too scared to crawl.
"Change your ways when fear seizes," he had said, "for
it usually means you are doing something wrong."

Jean Craighead George, *Julie of the Wolves*,
1972, p. 42

Research shows that children learn language best in a
low-risk environment in which they are permitted and
encouraged to test hypotheses of interest to them.

Jerome Harste, *New Policy Guidelines for*
Reading, 1989, p. 51

LEARNING ENGAGES THE ENTIRE SELF

In his workshops, William Purkey (1970), the author of *Self-Concept and School Achievement*, refers to information as "cards" for the brain, with each card color coded. The color refers to the emotional tone associated with the incoming information. This is one approach to the fact that meaningful learning both engages, and leads to adjustments in, every mind/body system that we have, including our emotions. There is nothing in the brain that would give validity to the belief that emotions and cognition are processed separately. As educators, we must come to terms with what this means.

Cognitive psychology and much recent educational research have focused on the way individuals interact with information to reorganize and expand knowledge. This learning process has been likened to the way computers learn. All sorts of models, from "program formation" to "information processing" and "schema theory," help us understand how knowledge is formed; but these models largely ignore the fundamental and powerful role that emotions play in learning except, perhaps, as energizers or constraints. Emotions are more important. One theme of the brain principles (see Chapter 7) is that emotions and thoughts actually interpenetrate and shape each other.

In Chapter 3, we suggest that the child's brain can be likened to a sponge that absorbs experiences, which literally shape the brain. Early experiences include everything from social rituals like toilet training to learning to read and write. All such learning is packed with "feeling tones." Children learn early that people can hurt, that people can make us happy, that food in our stomachs feels good, and that empty stomachs do not. Children come equipped with a sense of what feels good and what doesn't. This is built into all organisms; and as Combs and Snygg (1949) pointed out more than 40 years ago, even the lowly amoeba knows enough to move toward food and away from danger.

Context and Content

Put very simply, as children learn, they always absorb the entire experience, including feelings. Thus the entire context, as well as the content, is learned. The context includes "facts" about who the child is, based on how significant others respond to expectations, behaviors, and needs. In time, *good* and *bad* become highly complex and individualized notions, inextricably meshing feelings and information. It is this process that forms what is then referred to as the *self*.

According to self-concept theorists (e.g., Combs 1962; Combs, Richards, and Richards 1976; Marsh and Shavelson 1985; Purkey 1970), the self is a uniquely organized system made up of beliefs, biases, memories, predispositions, expectations, knowledge, fears, reactions, behaviors, talents, and meanings. Shifting our understanding of "things" and ideas also means shifting our organization of "self." We suggest that all new learning, at other than surface levels of meaning, automatically results in major interaction with both "cognition" and "self-perception." *Self-concept cannot be divorced from learning.*

Cognition and Emotion

The importance of self-concept and academic achievement has been discussed by many educators. We must point out, however, that just as emotions are critical to learning, learning and the expansion of knowledge are critical in forming positive emotions. Focusing on feelings without regard to performance, creativity, and intellectual understanding is inefficient and as cumbersome from the point of view of the brain as ignoring the emotional impact of the learning experience. This is one of the major fallacies underlying self-concept improvement programs that focus heavily on making children feel better about themselves without tying such feelings to performance and genuine shifts in knowledge. For one thing, self-concept, once formed, is lodged in so many areas of the brain that a genuine "shift" in self-esteem cannot be achieved without shifting hundreds and perhaps thousands of environmental triggers that support the negative beliefs about the self. This is why taking people totally out of their environment is so effective in helping them act and see themselves differently. It is also why putting them back in the same environment brings back most of the old behaviors and perceptions.

As we acknowledge the intricate relationship between cognition and emotion, we part company with the computer as a model for human learning. The answer to using the full capacity of the human brain is not a simple one of reprogramming. A person has an infinite capacity to differentiate between what enhances the self and what does not. The human brain moderates its own programming and has access to the enormous capacity of the emotions in that venture.

Acquiring new natural knowledge fundamentally changes the way our self is organized, including the way in which we perceive ourselves. In meaningful learning, the brain itself is reorganized, and that has consequences for the perceived self.

LEARNING AS SELF-REORGANIZATION

It is important to recall the distinction between memorization of surface knowledge and the expansion of natural knowledge. Memorization can be likened to storage. There usually is no provision made for a fundamental shift or development of higher order inside the learner. If it does occur, it is rare and left to chance. The acquisition of natural knowledge through immersion is different. There are many fundamental shifts, large and small, generated within the learner as new knowledge links with what is familiar or meaningful. Moreover, these shifts are neither directed nor controlled by the learner. Acquisition of natural knowledge is the result of the entire process. When immersion is orchestrated properly, including the fact that the learner is intrinsically motivated, the learner will have spontaneous and often unnoticeable shifts or flashes of insight—those "aha's" that represent felt meaning. The emergence of the "aha" is frequently preceded by periods of uncertainty or ambiguity and hard, intrinsically motivated work requiring delay of other forms of gratification. The uncertainty is natural because the relationship between the information gleaned and parts of the self

128

are constantly being rearranged, enlarged, and reorganized. Karl Pribram (1987) calls this aspect of learning "active uncertainty." We suggest that this process is absolutely critical to helping the brain make maximum connections and that it can proceed smoothly only in an atmosphere of general safety and sufficient challenge.

SELF-REORGANIZATION AND DISEQUILIBRIUM

This model of learning is consistent with the emerging theory of self-organization in science. As already mentioned, Prigogine and Stengers (1984) have demonstrated that in systems that are in a state of disequilibrium, provided some other conditions are met, there comes a time when there is a sudden and spontaneous shift into a higher (or, in some circumstance, lower) degree of orderliness. Arthur Koestler (1972) calls this process the "integrative principle." That higher order, we suggest, is reorganization that involves *felt meaning*. It is a largely self-generated reconstruction or reorganization that brings items together in a coherent and meaningful way. This, of course, is at the heart of Piaget's notion of development. When the original state of equilibrium is disturbed, the resultant disequilibrium must be reconciled because it registers as a disturbance. It is reconciled when the learner moves to a broader or more inclusive notion—a more sophisticated schema or map (Cowan 1978, Doll 1986).

William Doll describes an experiment in teaching mathematics based on these concepts:

> The concept of self-organization through disequilibrium meant we had to organize the Friday curriculum and our presentation of it in such a manner that we had enough of a "burr" to stimulate the students into rethinking their habitual methods but not so much of a burr that reorganization would fall apart or not be attempted. *Maintaining this dynamic tension between challenge and comfort was one of the skills we had to perfect* [emphasis added] (1989, pp. 67–68).

The fundamental task of the teacher is to facilitate the self-reorganization of the student. That is partly accomplished through orchestrated immersion, which involves the creation of a context that contains new information in a useful and coherent form. What students do, however, depends on what goes on in their own minds.

SELF-REORGANIZATION AND DOWNSHIFTING

Once formed, the self is both fluid and capable of change, yet change does not always come easily. The self, in fact, is highly resistant to change, particularly if such change is interpreted as being unsafe. "Safety" does not refer only to physical safety. It includes the safety of my ego or who I think I am. Anything that can conceivably diminish me in my eyes or in the eyes of those I value, acts as a threat to my own survival as a person. This is basically what is behind downshifting.

Dealing with Barriers. This entire process is elegantly outlined by the Bulgarian Georgi Lozanov (1978a, b). He describes the shift in what he terms the *social suggestive norm*, which must occur if learners are to go beyond their own boundaries and truly redefine themselves in terms of their new understanding. His notion of barriers, which we introduce in Chapter 6, helps define how this process works in the learning environment. Barriers include the affective/intuitive barrier, the critical/logical barrier, and the moral/ethical barrier. If any of these are violated in the classroom, downshifting in some form occurs. The consequence is that students revert to more automatic, deeply entrenched modes of thinking—and their thoughts are far removed from the topic being taught. In practice, this is often seen when students are no longer paying attention.

We raise our barriers when we feel threatened or violated. For example, sudden changes in plans may raise barriers, and learners need time to adapt to the changes. Miscommunications and disagreements can raise barriers, which must be resolved in some fashion. Barriers are raised for self-protection against uncertainty, including "incorrect" answers and publicly displayed outcomes. Older learners probably become more sensitive to intellectual content affecting the critical/logical barrier, whereas young learners are sensitive to the "feeling tone," or violations of their feelings. Barriers are natural. Dealing with them is an essential part of learning and teaching. Lozanov (1978a, b) points out, therefore, that teachers must take time to address barriers and *harmonize* with them. That involves such factors as teacher congruence, which we discuss later in this chapter.

Understanding Threats and Reinforcements. Threat and downshifting are directly tied to the evaluation process as well as to status, roles, and messages of one's intrinsic worth within a social group. In the home and the community, threat can also be generated by demeaning messages. Most devastatingly, the home can threaten children with turmoil or other experiences closely linked to abandonment. In addition, children who arrive at school with already well-formed, rich "maps" and natural knowledge that parallel the cultural expectations of the teacher, have an enormous advantage over children with more impoverished maps or ones from a culture or with language unfamiliar to the teacher and significant others (Moraes 1986). The children with appropriate maps are much less likely to be threatened. Schools mirror society by reinforcing many of those differences, rather then being places for developing richer maps through the engagement of children in meaningful learning.

We have suggested, through brain Principle 11, that students who are under threat downshift, with the general consequence that they find it difficult, if not impossible, to be the authors of, and take charge of, their own learning. Under threat, students' capacity to perceive and generate new meanings is reduced. Creativity and constructive imagination are reduced. Downshifted students prefer tried-and-true procedures and thinking patterns. They do not like uncertainty or ambiguity and want "the answer" now. They become dependent on extrinsic rewards and punishments. And there is even strong evidence to suggest that teaching that emphasizes extrinsic rewards or punishment automatically reinforces further downshifting.

Nourishing the Self. Empowering the self requires an increase in the intellect, as well as the engagement of the emotions. We do not mean to suggest that genuine kindness and caring are ever out of place, nor that such positive interactions do not have a cumulative effect. On the contrary, brain-based teaching considers the protection of feelings to be a top priority. This is one of the reasons why a brain-based classroom must allow for questioning, open discussion, and communication strategies, such as active listening and "I messages" proposed by Thomas Gordon in *T.E.T.: Teacher Effectiveness Training* (1974). It is simply that kindness and caring must not be separated from the other ways of nourishing the self. It is true that *perhaps the most important asset a person can have is being able to learn.* And at the heart of genuine learning is the capacity to genuinely change.

The Optimal State of Mind for Meaningful Learning

Our central task is to *counter downshifting.* The key to doing that is to recognize the alternative, which is the state of mind that we contend to be optimal for meaningful learning. There are at least two indispensable characteristics of that optimal state of mind:

1. A relaxed nervous system and a sense of safety and security that operates at mental, emotional, and physical levels.

2. Student self-motivation, which is critical to the expansion of knowledge at more than surface levels.

Relaxation: Safe Risk Taking

We have already demonstrated that threat is monitored by our perceptual system at subtle levels. When we perceive danger, we downshift by narrowing our focus, as we demonstrate in Chapter 6. Both our need for survival and our interest in novelty, enhancement, change, and variety lead us to constantly monitor the environment for inconsistency and incongruity, as well as opportunities.

To engage in more complex forms of learning, students often have to endure long periods of uncertainty, which can be threatening. There are times when the unknown is positively exciting and people are willing to take risks—if they feel a specific type of safety (Doll 1989). For teachers, it is a matter of taking students beyond their comfort zone without undue threat. This is precisely the characteristic of playfulness, which we discuss later.

To maximize learning, we need to establish an environment that allows for safe risk taking. In essence, we need to eliminate pervasive or continuous threat. That sense of safety that welcomes appropriate risks is one part of what we mean by relaxation.

In addition, students must have the capacity to actually deal with complex ideas and experiences. This includes a capacity to pay attention for long periods, to think systematically as well as creatively, and to collaborate actively. For all this to be possible, students must be physiologically well equipped. We emphasize the physical because the hippocampus and other portions of the brain and nervous system are extremely sensitive to stress. Students must have a nervous system that is sufficiently rested and that is neither in need of ongoing, intense sensory stimulation nor overagitated by other stimulants. This type of nervous system is the product of good nutrition, exercise, healthy relationships, rest, and other aspects of what is now being called "wellness."

MOTIVATION/CHALLENGE

Our purpose here is to identify some features of the innate drive that students have to act and to understand. Educators need to capitalize on these drives. In fact, this is precisely what exceptional teachers of gifted and talented students do. They provide opportunities for students to pursue their own interests. They support student creativity. They provide a rich and stimulating environment and in that context introduce students to more and more of what the world has to offer. That is the general philosophy that should apply to all students, everywhere.

Students' Specific Interests—Thematic Attractors. As much as possible, students must have a compelling interest in exploring or mastering a subject, topic, or skill—or be interested in the activities and procedures prescribed and demonstrated by teachers. The student must have a focal point and a desire for reorganization closely linked to an opportunity for self-enhancement.

Borrowed from the new science of complexity (Gleik 1987), the term *attractors* has been used to describe focal points around which we organize thoughts and ideas (Doll 1986). We suggest that the organizers of our life experiences could be called "thematic attractors." They operate in several ways. They access the deep meanings referred to in Chapter 8, and this gives them both direction and power. They provide a personalized focal point and framework around which patterns can form, so that attractors actually "seed" the felt meaning, much as an oyster builds a pearl around a fragment of grit.

Thematic attractors can best be explained, perhaps, by way of illustration.

• Consider the scientist in hot pursuit of some breakthrough discovery. Watson and Crick, the discoverers of the double helical structure of DNA, come to mind. So does Jane Goodall, who has spent the past 30 years seeking to understand chimpanzees. Much of what these scientists have done focuses on a dominant and often urgent theme.

• Look at comic strip characters, which often include thematic attractors. In "Calvin and Hobbes," Calvin regularly translates his daily experience into encounters with dinosaurs and alien beings. In one segment of another strip, "For Better or for Worse" (Johnston 1990), the father has a chance to leave work early and finds himself in a toy and hobby shop. He says to the proprietor that he would like a hobby—electric trains, perhaps. The proprietor somewhat ascerbically replies: "Electric trains, sir, are not a hobby. Electric trains are a way of life."

The deep meanings that dominate will be different for each person, as will their degree of intensity, manner of operation, selection of activities, and so on. However, even though people may have many interests, they are driven by their central theme, and they perceive and organize the world in terms of that theme. It is a way of life.

One feature of thematic attractors is the extent to which they influence and are influenced by expectations. The power of expectation is well illustrated in education by Rosenthal's work on the Pygmalion effect (Rosenthal and Jacobson 1968). He and others have shown that we are profoundly affected by our own beliefs about what we can and should be able to do, and that these beliefs, in turn, are influenced by the expectations of teachers and significant others.

Most students and educators have thematic attractors. It is evident in many of the students who compete each year in regional and national science contests. It is evident in the passion that people often have for sport and is often the dominant reason for the time that many adults spend in coaching. And it is evident in the political and social activities of many students.

We do not suggest that educators spend all their time seeking particular thematic attractors for each student. It often takes time to elicit what appeals to different people, but lessons that provide for individual choices and variations can accomplish this goal more easily.

Students' Predisposition to Learn. Fortunately, the "aha" of creative insight is also innately exciting and motivating. Moreover, we have demonstrated that people innately desire to make sense of experience and are stimulated by novelty. Hence educators can generate much of the excitement and energy they desire by introducing creativity into the lives of their students and by supporting their desire to know. The practical consequence is that a student's desire to know more about a subject is more important than a measure of performance at any point in time. That is why the setting of goals and the use of evaluation should not act to limit what a student can do or desires to do.

High Challenge and Low Threat. There is an optimal state of mind for expanding natural knowledge. It combines the moderate to high challenge that is built into intrinsic motivation with low threat and a pervasive sense of well-being. We call that a state of "relaxed alertness." Ongoing relaxed alertness is the key to people's ability to access what they already know, think creatively, tolerate ambiguity, and delay gratification, all of which are essential for genuine expansion of knowledge.

ELEMENTS OF INSTRUCTION INCORPORATING RELAXED ALERTNESS

Imagine leading athletes during a race or competition. They have a clear goal and put all their energy into achieving. They feel the thrill and excitement of participating, as well as highs and lows from moment to moment. And at the same time, to really accomplish what has to be done, they have to be relaxed because peak performance is impossible without sufficient relaxation. The same combination is necessary *and possible* for students.

Relaxed alertness is *not* the same as being calm and unchanging. Although ongoing, it is a dynamic state that is compatible with a great deal of change. Indeed, in the normal course of events, people have many different degrees of interest and many differences in mood, curiosity, predispositions, and intensity of excitement. There is the curiosity that we have when we want to find out why something works. There is a sense of excited expectancy that we have while anticipating the outcome or possible development of an issue or situation.

There is the overwhelming feeling of awe that often accompanies great art, music, and scientific discovery. There is even some fear of the unknown. Those "substates" are influenced by many variables, including the learner's history, values, and social world away from school. They are accompanied by often imperceptible physiological changes, such as changes in blood pressure, respiration, and hormone levels.

This range of change is vital. People need those shifts to maintain creative tension. Theater, including both comedy and drama, is built on the orchestration of changes in mood and perception. Music also depends, for much of its power, on the intermingling of degrees of tension and calmness. This instability is actually vital for healthy problem solving (McAuliffe 1990). Doll (1989) calls this state "dynamic tension." A good classroom works in the same way. Teachers do not have to be actors, nor do they have to provide their own version of *Sesame Street*. However, they must themselves be in a state of relaxed alertness most of the time and also be sufficiently at home with such media as art, music, and social interaction to orchestrate lessons appropriately.

THE IMPORTANCE OF TEACHER PRESTIGE

Anyone who has ever taught realizes just how much students notice. We have already discussed the fact that the brain is equipped with the capacity to continually perceive discrepancies in the environment. Students respond to subtle stimuli, including all the small signals that show what the teacher is really thinking and feeling. Because trust is such an important element in making learning "shifts," the role of the teacher becomes a critical one.

Many characteristics of the teacher go a long way toward ensuring maximum openness to learning and complex mapping. Most important, perhaps, is what Lozanov (1978a, b) calls teacher "prestige." Prestige does not refer to popularity, position, power, or fame. It refers to the *authority* that teachers have in the eyes of students by virtue of the sort of people they are and the knowledge they are able to share. There are two essential elements to prestige. One is what Lozanov calls "double planeness." The other element deals with how well teachers master and share subject matter.

Double Planeness. This aspect of prestige is closely related to what Rogers (1983) calls "congruence" or "empathy" and refers to the degree of congruence between the internal beliefs and values of an individual (in this case, the teacher) and their external behaviors, including body language. There is a level at which students respond to teachers who hold the students in contempt, no matter how bright their smiles and how open they claim to be. Moreover, double planeness largely operates below the level of consciousness. The subtle signs and surface indicators reflect what we actually are and not what we try to be. While we can fool ourselves into consciously denying these messages, such doubts and the discernment of hidden messages and weaknesses ultimately result in a lack of trust in the teacher and the teacher's message. Of course, this is a two-way street—a student's own biases may be "projected" onto the teacher. The consequence of a lack of trust shows some degree of downshifting and self-protection.

Expertise. The second aspect of teacher prestige involves the teacher's knowledge of subject matter. Expertise in the field of instruction is critical. This does not mean that the teacher must know all the answers. It means that the teacher has a "natural," lively grasp of the facts and also engages in discovery. In other words, the teacher models the fact that real experts also continue to learn. The teacher, therefore, demonstrates to students that in addition to mastering specific theories and procedures, all learning is open ended and real learning continues throughout life. As Bohm says, "all thoughts are incomplete" (Factor 1987). Teaching is more than knowing specific answers, but teachers must be deeply grounded in the subject matter. Having teachers instruct in areas in which they are poorly prepared is usually foolish. Students know the difference. The message to them is that teaching from the text or "as you go" is acceptable. Such practices foster and model mediocrity.

TYPES OF CONDITIONS AND "SUBSTATES" REFLECTING RELAXED ALERTNESS

Most of what generates relaxed alertness in the student is subtle. Besides the state of mind and prestige of the teacher, the atmosphere in the school and the community are critical influences on the learner's state of mind. As already pointed out, students respond to their global experience. Above all else, therefore, they must be in an *atmosphere* that can be described as one of relaxed alertness.

By way of guidance, Lozanov (1978a, b) suggests that educators strive to alternate and balance two specific substates in their students: "infantilization," or the childlike state, and "pseudo-passiveness," which we translate as passive listening. In the interplay between these two substates, we generate the overall atmosphere that is sought.

The Childlike State. "Childlike" does not mean childish. In essence, it is the sort of creative playfulness that children display. This state incudes a willingness to experiment, an openness to unexpected consequences, and a sense of positive anticipation or expectancy.

Playfulness can be generated in many ways, ranging from the teacher's clowning and miming to the use of puppets, songs, composed rhymes, and riddles. The artful teacher maintains prestige at the same time. Playfulness in that context can do a great deal to help students lose fear; break through to new knowledge; and go beyond what they, and often the teacher, believe to be their capacity to learn. The key is to build the play around the actual content. Thus a song may be written about the relationship between enzymes, and a dance may be used to explore the bonding of molecules. Many educators have discussed this notion (e.g., Canfield and Wells 1976, Dhority 1984).

It is important to avoid using playfulness simply to build mood. It must be part and parcel of the experience of content. The intelligent use of puppets, for example, or challenging games, demonstrations, and social interactions can all add to a sense of lightheartedness and creative participation, even while the content involves complex chemical formulas or a concept in physics. Geoffrey uses a stuffed animal—an orangutan named Regge—in his computer classes for adults. Regge starts out having a seat like all the other students, or as a co-instructor, and soon becomes a part of the class. This contributes significantly to a reduction in threat and a sense of warmth and lightheartedness. Invariably, one or two students are actually comforted by having Regge to touch and play with. Others are willing to explain things to Regge as a way of rehearsing what they want to display or say.

Passive Listening. This condition is akin to the state of mind of the audience at a good classical concert. They are relaxed and attentive, but open to the experience. This facilitates receptivity to incoming information. In fact, many educators use presentations with some type of musical accompaniment. This is a key ingredient in the work of many members of the Society of Accelerative Learning and Teaching, as reported in their journal (see Bibliography for address). Music can be used in many ways. Sometimes classical or relaxation music can be used as background for study. Leo Wood (personal communication April 1988) reports that his students even request specific pieces of classical music during their lab work in chemistry. Music can also be used to support or parallel a theme or lesson in history or geography. Documentaries use this feature. There is no reason why teachers should not. Music can also be used in the reading of stories. Optimalearning™ (Barzakov 1988)* offers perhaps the best set of related skills that we have encountered, including reading to music; selecting appropriate stories; and developing timing, intonation, and rhythm. Teachers can explore the power of music in many ways, be-

---

*Optimalearning™ by Barzakov Educational Institute, San Rafael, CA 94901.

ginning, we suggest, with occasional forays into the music that they and their students (with reservations) currently enjoy most. Excellent videos are also available—such as *Your Musical Heritage*, developed by Amanda Amend (Amend, Lynch, and Conrad 1989). This is a set of four instructional videos on how to use music in the classroom.

Visualization also makes use of and induces passive listening. There is a growing body of research on the power of visualization as an instructional tool (Galyean 1983). It works in many ways. "Best performance" imaging is now widely used by amateur and professional athletes and by many people in business. Visualization is also frequently used for the purpose of helping people to relax, to attain a state of positive expectancy, and to induce creative imagination. It is a very complex process, however; and it can be misused because success depends so much on teacher prestige and other factors. We therefore encourage teachers to receive some training before introducing visualization in the classroom. Incidentally, this is an area in which training is significantly ahead of research.

Both the childlike state and passive listening are familiar to all of us. Children learning to speak their native language spend much of their time playing with words, either with friends or parents or by themselves. Although we may not notice it, most experts also engage in some sort of play, ranging from making jokes to elaborate experimentation. Indeed, many programs invoke the power of play to both motivate and educate adults (Barzakov 1988, Dhority 1984). Similarly, when we hear a moving story or are engrossed in a play or film, we are "alertly" passive to some degree. The result, of course, is that both the plot and quite an impressive number of details become instantly etched in our memory.

ORCHESTRATED IMMERSION

A teacher can do many specific things to create a sense of relaxed alertness as a part of instruction. Many of them, such as the use of art and literature, work indirectly. They are basically ways of immersing students in "soft" environments. Additional ways of creating relaxed alertness should permeate all immersion. This illustrates our message that all elements of brain-based learning interpenetrate each other (see Chapter 9, "Orchestrated Immersion"). These are not just fun activities that make students feel good. Relaxed alertness is at its most powerful when introducing highly sophisticated information. The point is always to *challenge and "stretch" the learner so naturally and innocently that the process of mapping appears to be automatic.*

Using Themes Intelligently. In a state of relaxed alertness, students are challenged within a context of safety. Their sense of purpose is readily invoked by an appropriate theme that serves to orient and focus their experience. When students do what is important to them, they interpret their "work" differently. Whether someone wants to play ball for the school, master computing, or gain admission to a good college, if that challenge is deeply felt and is real, then much of what follows will automatically be linked to the pursuit of that goal. It becomes a thematic attractor. What follows makes sense and adds security and assurance—even when the day-to-day struggle is sometimes difficult or confusing.

Selecting Projects That Matter. For older students, we also recommend involvement with life-related, intellectually challenging problems, such as checking on the level of pollutants in local rivers. Problems relating to the "real" world add prestige and challenge. Apple Computers, for instance, working with the National Geographic Society and the Technology Education Research Center in Cambridge, Massachusetts, has established a network of school-based weather information stations. The students report their local conditions to a central computer, and a general area report is filed and fed back. The result is that students learn geography and demographics in the process because they want to know where relevant places are.

Equalizing Social Interactions. Teachers need to be especially aware of interpersonal aspects related to learning, such as status. Research suggests that shy and low-status learners do not become as engaged in the learning process as do high-status students or students who verbalize easily (Cohen 1984). High-status students, therefore, tend to benefit more from immersion. Relaxed alertness requires what we call "orderliness," discussed later in this chapter. Involving mutual respect and support among students, orderliness creates a sense of safety for risk taking so that students who would otherwise withdraw are encouraged to participate.

RELAXATION TECHNIQUES

Other techniques are more specifically directed toward inducing a general state of relaxed alertness independent of instruction. It makes sense that all of us learn how to reverse the "fight or flight" response. Recent research (Justice 1987, p. 79; Nadel personal communication 1987), for example, indicates that prolonged stress actually kills cells in the hippocampus and other areas of the brain. This is true for our entire society, not just schoolchildren. Needless to say, people in a downshifted family, workplace, community, or country are incapable of making the most intelligent and creative decisions. It is beyond the scope of this book to describe all the means of relaxation available, though some are elaborated on in our workbook.* We discuss two here, meditation and focusing.

Relaxation/Meditation. There is ample evidence at this point to suggest that relaxation practiced daily not only reverses the debilitating affects of stress (Murphy and Donovan 1988) but also helps to strengthen the immune system. Research at Ohio State University (Justice 1987, p. 158) found that medical students had a reduced helper-T-cell count on the day of examination. Helper T cells are critical in defending against bacterial infections and cancer. When half the group were taught relaxation techniques, their T-cell count increased.

Relaxation techniques that lower metabolic functions while heightening or maintaining conscious awareness are extremely powerful and practical. Since much relaxation is based on looking inward, it is not conducive for direct instructional purposes. It is helpful, however, for overall health and physical functioning. If practiced regularly, at least once or twice a day, it has the affect of a deep nap. Individuals can be trained to relax through audiotapes, relaxation training, or biofeedback. There is a wealth of assistance available, ranging from Transcendental Meditation (Bloomfield, Cain, and Jaffe 1975; Bloomfield and Kory 1976) and Benson's relaxation response (Benson 1976) to the relaxation tapes of Emmet Miller (1980). Because such relaxation reverses the debilitating affects of "distress," we also think that some type of relaxation needs to be incorporated into our social structure generally. However, there is much that must be understood when using relaxation techniques in the classroom. We therefore suggest that teachers receive training in researched methodologies and achieve some level of personal mastery before introducing the techniques into the classroom.

Focusing Exercises. Focusing and centering exercises are excellent for bringing conscious awareness to bear on what is being done. They are basically ways of "practicing" attention. Some exercises involve a detailed description of an object, scene, or process. Others are like the relaxed opening of the mind described by Gendlin (1981), which we discuss further in our treatment of contemplation in Chapter 11. Many of these techniques are particularly beneficial for children and learners who are hyperactive or easily distracted. Children may practice focusing on one thing at a time—very much like the *Karate Kid*, who was told to "wipe left, wipe right" while waxing the car. Focusing is often a natural part of performance in sports. It should be clear that sometimes students will *not* enjoy these procedures in the short term, even though they benefit from them substantially. A teacher, therefore, has the task of orchestrating what is done so that students are sufficiently challenged. This can only happen when such

---

*Available from 4C Connections, 331 S. Nordena St., Redlands, CA 92373.

exercises are a part of a larger plan that induces self-motivation and are shown to be deeply respected by the teacher.

GRADING AND EVALUATION

How do we reconcile relaxed alertness with evaluations? Evaluation is part of life. But simplistic types of evaluation, including tests and grading, frequently create stress; therefore, we urgently need to look for more diverse and supportive forms of evaluation.

Stress and the Immune System. Besides the debilitating effect of stress on the brain, stress from grading has also been shown to affect students' immune system. Joan Borysenko (1987) recalls her research conducted with McClelland and Benson at Harvard University, where they discovered "that the stress of examination periods reduced the level of a particular antibody in saliva, an antibody that is part of the first line of defense against colds." The drop in antibodies was highly correlated with the need for power.

Educative Feedback. Students need what Barzakov (1988) calls "educative feedback" in a practical, challenging, and nonthreatening form for much of their educational life. This type of evaluation has a great deal in common with good communication. "I found myself thinking . . . when you did that," or "What would happen if . . ." are examples of phrases that teachers can use as educative feedback. These phrases suggest not only general respect and acceptance but also further expansion of content issues. One of the authors, Renate (Nummela 1980), found that Teacher Effectiveness Training (see Gordon, T. 1974), practiced by teachers for a six-month period, positively affected a change in students' self-concept and attitude toward school. A sense of *mutual respect and problem solving* must be the primary objective.

Educative feedback also has a great deal in common with *reflective practice* (Schön 1983). Educative feedback provides necessary acceptance and support while presenting the student with new possibilities. Work is primarily collaborative and supportive so that even individual presentations are done in an atmosphere that helps that person to succeed.

ORDERLINESS AND CREATIVITY

One aspect of the learning atmosphere seems to be indispensable in establishing relaxed alertness. It is *orderliness*, which, in our view, is different from *order*. Orderliness is reflected in a pervasive sense of acceptable behavior as practiced by everyone in a school. This sense is marked by an understanding of interconnectedness and hence genuine respect for the feelings of and concern for others. It minimizes an emphasis on power or control. In terms of Doll's (1989) metaphor, there is "more dancing and less marching." Orderliness creates a safe context within which students can be creative, excited, and spontaneous.

The problem is that the brain downshifts in excessively unruly and unpredictable conditions or, for that matter, when there are few borders and too many choices. It also downshifts under coercion and threat. Creative teaching cannot flourish in total chaos. However, there will always be change, fluidity, disagreement, and a need for very different people to work together on a wide range of tasks with limited resources, and so on. How, then, do we arrive at the appropriate degree of fluid orderliness? We believe that given appropriate immersion strategies, teacher prestige, and relaxed alertness, the same self-organization that occurs within the individual also occurs in groups.

Most teachers are well trained in classroom control. The idea that students organized around a project will self-organize without interference from the teacher is difficult for most of us to believe. Over the years, Renate has sent more than 500 educational psychology students on school visits to look at discipline in classrooms. She has them assess the degree of innovative instruction by the teacher; total involvement in learning by students; and teacher prestige, as defined by Lozanov (1978a, b). The summary of these three factors is then linked to the number of discipline problems observed. The relationship between high scores on the three measures and the corresponding lack of discipline problems always amazes these college students.

We continue Bill Doll's narrative about his mathematics class to demonstrate what group self-organization looks like:

> We decided to give them flexibility in their intellectual and social organization—they solved the problems in their way and in their time. The patterns that emerged were both disorderly and coherent. Randomness was present in the way they approached their work—they skipped from problem to problem, they left problems unfinished, they interjected social comments into their conversation; they also did all the problems on the page, they went back to the unfinished ones, they put boundaries on their social conversation. Whether an observer saw randomness or progressive order depended on whether that observer was in the class for a few minutes or for the whole class period.

> While I was worried about the lack of linear order, about the direct challenge the students were giving to the "time-on-task" maxim, I became aware that over the period of the 45 to 60 minutes a new type of order was emerging—progressive, constructive, personal, interactive. Interest during the class was extraordinarily high, answers emerged from a variety of directions, those who were quiet often raised key questions, and Ron and I virtually never had to admonish students "to finish." While the process seemed disorderly from a segmented view, it had a

142

unity found only by looking at the whole class during the *entire* period (1989, p. 66).

In fact, more was happening than Doll discusses in the article. He and his co-teacher were working in consistent ways and with a powerful and practical theory in which they believed. This invariably led to increased prestige. They were, therefore, maintaining an atmosphere of orderliness within which teaching and learning flourished.

THE SCHOOL AS AN ORDERLY COMMUNITY

It is vital to maintain a sufficiently orderly atmosphere if we wish to really foster the conditions under which challenge and security can exist simultaneously. This becomes the concern and responsibility of the entire school community, from custodian and cook to student, teacher, and principal.

The most exciting example of a global approach to relaxed alertness that we encountered in our visit to innovative schools was at the Maharishi International University School in Fairfield, Iowa. The school consists of approximately 600 students. It is an unusual community because parents, teachers, and students all practice Transcendental Meditation and share a common philosophy. Children do not meditate, but they practice moments of silence during which they can remain active but focus on a special word. What struck us as most remarkable, however, was a series of "principles" taken from their "Science of Creative Intelligence." These are principles that all children learn from preschool on, and they focus on orderliness. Examples include "The inner determines the outer," "You water the root to get the fruit," "Order is everywhere [in nature]," "Everything in nature grows," and "The whole is bigger than the sum of its parts." As children play with puppetry, they are reminded that the puppeteer (the "inner") determines what happens outside with those who are watching (the outer). As children grow, they mark their progress on a ruler running on a wall and their names are written in at the appropriate point. This activity is tied to the principle that "Everything in nature grows." Sixth graders explained a quilt they had made by relating their work to the principles, including "The whole is greater than the sum of the parts."

The principles guide the understanding of content, and they link content and student behavior to one version of the laws of nature. We are not advocating that all schools be formulated after this one or that all educators select these particular principles. There are many sets of principles that can be used to orchestrate both behavior and content.

Even some of the brain principles spelled out in Chapter 7 can work in that way.

At one level, we were frustrated because so many features of the Maharishi school could not be translated into a public setting. Everyone in the school shared a specific focused philosophy and meditative technique. At a deeper level, however, the school illustrates the power of the general principles explored in this book. Students at this school, incidentally, are also immensely successful in winning state and national scholastic awards. As with so many other outstanding schools, we add this example to document processes and teaching that inspire young brains to learn and be at peace with themselves and their environment, while engaging in exciting, dynamic activity and learning.

As moderately self-contained communities, individual schools can determine their own models and protocols. The school can liken itself to a family, a well-run corporation, or a specially designed community. All the issues of priorities, courtesy, individual responsibility, cooperation, honesty, time consciousness, and forms of dress need to be attended to. What matters is that most of the members of the community take ownership of the decisions and genuinely implement them. They must grasp the effect of their own behavior on others and see the broader benefits and consequences of supportive, positive interactions. Thus the principal and vice principal, as well as teachers, must follow these guidelines in their interactions with peers and with students. Mutual respect is the common denominator.

Orderliness is vital for brain-based learning. Children and adults both respond to subtle signals and hidden messages and will therefore not respect the chosen guidelines unless all the people in authority genuinely practice what they preach. When mutual respect and responsibility drive the commitment to orderly behavior in the school, threat is lower because expectations become clarified and understood at deep levels of meaning.

* * *

Much of what influences learners is beyond the control of educators. A well-fed student with a supportive family, for instance, is in a much better position than a learner who is hungry or in a state of perpetual anxiety. Students respond to all the elements of their experience. In addition, because children learn from all experiences, the school alone cannot possibly account for all their learning. That is why the quality of the family, the community, and political and social institutions plays a critical part in how and what people learn. This global effect also demonstrates the reality of the concept of interconnectedness. It is therefore critical for schools to involve parents

144

and the community and for parents to take a lively interest in the education of their children.

The fact remains, however, that there is an optimal state of mind for learning and that schools can do much to make it happen. It is not our purpose to give an exhaustive list of activities, but rather to indicate the direction educators must follow in establishing relaxed and challenging environments. Teachers remain the key for establishing relaxed alertness in learning and in the classroom. Teacher perceptions add up to powerful invitations or limitations for learning. Teachers can limit what students learn because of their own personal prejudices, fears, and beliefs about what both they and their students can achieve. They can also take students far beyond the limiting expectations that would otherwise prevail. Among the teacher characteristics that matter are double planeness, joy of learning, knowledge and love of subject matter, artistry, and ability to organize the learning environment. Teacher education should therefore include a personal component, in which teachers reflect on their deeper meanings and, in an atmosphere of educative feedback, discover and move beyond their own limitations.

11

ACTIVE PROCESSING

According to Socrates, knowledge was to be sought
within the mind and brought to birth by questioning. He
contrasts perceiving, or the observation of things outside
oneself, with reflection, the discovery of what is within,
an activity he held to be common to both mathematics
and ethics. Socrates advocated reflection as opposed to
observation, an activity dependent upon a principle that
is important to any theory of reflective method: what we
are trying to do is not to discover something of which
until now we have been ignorant, but to know better
something which in some sense we know already; to
know it better in the sense of coming to know it in a
different and better way.

Paul Bitting and Renee Clift, in *Images of*
Reflection in Teacher Education, edited by
Waxman et al., 1988, p. 11

John Dewey pointed out many years ago that knowledge and experience are different (1965). We acquire knowledge—we learn—by processing experience. Students are immersed in global experiences that affect them deeply, irrespective of whether they want to be affected. Their job is to make sense of what is happening.

As we have shown, some processing takes place automatically as a consequence of the brain's ongoing search for meaningful patterns in experience. Educators can do a great deal to facilitate and guide the search, and that has been the thrust of the two preceding chapters.

Orchestrated immersion provides learners with rich, complex experiences that include options and a sense of wholeness. It presents what is to be learned in ways that allow for the perception of new patterns and relationships and make what is being learned intrinsically more meaningful.

Relaxed alertness ensures that students are challenged within a context of safety. A sense of purpose serves to orient and focus experiences. When students do what is important to them, they interpret their "work" differently. Intrinsic commitment includes a degree of excitement that energizes processing and patterning. Relaxed alertness also includes a personal sense of well-being and safety that allows students to explore new thoughts and connections with an expanded capacity to tolerate ambiguity, uncertainty, and delay of gratification.

ELEMENTS OF ACTIVE PROCESSING: CAPITALIZING ON EXPERIENCE

Orchestrated immersion and relaxed alertness are not enough. To maximize connections, gain deeper insights, and perceive the additional possibilities that are hidden in experience, we have to deliberately and consciously work for them. This work is roughly like processing the ore from mining to extract the maximum value. Students usually lack both the skill and the necessary awareness to search for deeper implications. That is why teachers may expend a great deal of effort in orchestrating an experience, only to discover that students have absorbed very little. Educators, therefore, need to deliberately work with students to help them more fully benefit from their experiences.

We call this aspect of brain-based learning active processing. *It is the consolidation and internalization of information, by the learner, in a way that is both personally meaningful and conceptually coherent.* It is the path to understanding, rather than simply to memory. We have all reflected at some time on the reasons for a situation turning out as it did. In our personal relationships, we often ask, "Why did that happen?" Professional athletes spend a great deal of time assessing and evaluating their performances. Those who regularly organize conferences tend to examine what worked and what didn't so that they will have even greater successes in the future. All of these are aspects of active processing. They involve an analysis of actual experience.

Active processing is extremely important in education. To some extent, it is often the only way for students to make sense of experience. Active processing also gives students opportunities to take charge of the direction and nature of the way they change. The pervasive objective is to focus on the process of our learning and extract and articulate what has been explored and what it means. In effect, the learner asks in as many ways as possible: "What did I do?" "Why did I do it?" and "What did I learn?" One student may take a class in computing, for instance, and find it exhilarating. Another may take the same class and feel frustrated and confused. Each is affected globally because almost all instruction influences the entire self in some way. The two students can ask the same question: "What is it about this experience that led to my feeling this way?" When they are assisted by a skilled teacher, they can each have crucial insights—felt meanings—that lead to personally appropriate understandings.

The key is to see that there are opportunities for students to learn not only about the subject in question, but also about themselves as people. Both are important. In effect, the questions "What does it mean?" and "Why do I or should I care?" generate felt meanings and invite an exploration of deep meanings. Such questions, therefore, contribute to and enhance intrinsic motivation. In active processing, students consistently examine precisely what is important to them, and often they find surprising new issues that are of importance. For that reason, it is imperative that we do not foreclose on the possibilities available to students. Though they need to master content areas, they must be free to do so in a way that expresses their own creative insights.

Active processing necessarily engages emotions, concepts, and values when meaningfulness is genuinely an issue. It sometimes seems to be therapeutic in nature, and it involves skills that counselors have. That is why we contend, in Chapter 8, that some aspects of counseling have a rightful place in the classroom. As Lozanov (1978a) recognized, for example, educators need to be equipped to deal with conflict, interpersonal communication, uncertainty, and other aspects of the changing personalities of their students.

Active processing is not just a stage in a lesson. It does not occur at one specific time, nor is it something that can be done in only one way. It is a matter of constantly "working" and "kneading" the ongoing experience that students have. It also requires that students stand back and examine what has transpired and what it means. This is an important process because the combination of perceived threat and the search for meaning often leads students to jump to conclusions and form initial impressions that interfere with real understanding. Learners need time to allow for new connections to be made. They need "space" for reflection. An example is the initial impression we may form that a computer is an alien rather than a useful assistant. We need to *relate* what we learn to what we know, but we can not afford to *reduce* it to what we currently think and feel. We have already introduced neuropsychologist Pribram's (1987) term "active uncertainty" to describe this time of openness and aliveness. It is critical to reorganization and making new connections in learning.

We see elements of active processing in the students we label as gifted, yet the capacity to reflect is something we are all born with—it simply needs to be developed. We have suggested that brain-based learning is built on a mixture of specifiable outcomes and private, unpredictable meanings. Some procedures may give rise to desired outcomes. At other times, those same procedures will lead a student into highly individual and personal explorations that are essential for those flashes of insight that indicate meaningful learning. For this reason, instead of the phrase "brain-based learning," we might more precisely label our approach "reflexive learning." The objective is for a student to make sense of personal experience.

What we have chosen to do is identify a series of processes that are effective both as vehicles for learning and as ways of assisting teachers in determining what is being learned. Without seeking to be exhaustive, we include the processes of reflection, contemplation, and creative elaboration; and we discuss performance and personal evaluations.

REFLECTION

Reflection is a critical aspect of all sophisticated and higher-order thinking and learning. As our opening quote suggests, the concept of reflection is not new. Reflection is as indispensable to great artists as it is to philosophers, statesmen, writers, and scientists. Unfortunately, it is infrequently used in schools. In our informal survey of schools we have visited, even the outstanding ones tended to leave reflection largely to chance or the counselor's office. Our main concern, therefore, is with extending reflection to all learning:

> Perhaps the single most glaring omission from the writing is adequate and explicit attention to the ultimate end of reflective practice: maximum learning and development by students in our schools. Most, although not all, discussions are focused on teacher development and professionalism as though those were ends in themselves. But schools exist to educate and help students, not teachers. While these are obviously not mutually exclusive, those in favor of reflective practice need to be much more specific about how students' skills in and love of learning, as well as their development as persons and citizens, will be enhanced by changes throughout the teaching and teacher education systems (Vaughan 1988, p. 48).

As we become more aware of the experiential nature of all learning, it will become more and more important for all students to reflect on their experiences for the purpose of adequately grasping the implications. At the moment, the closest that many schools come to reflection is with "wait time." This refers to a deliberate delay between a teacher's question and a student's answer; but wait time has as much to do with reflection as standing in line has to do with shopping.

We suspect that the power of reflection is actually cumulative. Not only do we want students to expand their natural knowledge, we also want them to desire that expansion. Reflection is powerful in part because it creates what Dewey called a "learning loop" (Fellows and Zimpher 1988).

When reflection is used in the classroom, students are also being subtly encouraged and predisposed to incorporate inquiry and evaluation as an habitual practice in all life experiences. . . . Essentially the act of reflection establishes within the teacher *and* the students simultaneously an open-mindedness and discernment, rational judgment, and creativity—all characteristics of the "educated" person (Fellows and Zimpher 1988, p. 19).

Reflection in learning is not a simple process. We have divided reflection into three main types.

Reflection on Feedback from Others. This type of reflection closely parallels two of Schön's notions. First, one of the best ways to teach learners is to have experts coach them on the job. This enables the coach and student to engage in "reflection in action," which, he believes, is one of the hallmarks of professional expertise. It is a sort of "on-the-spot experimenting," essential for dealing with the variety and uncertainty inherent in real situations, whether advocacy, painting, computing—or peer teaching.

Second, Schön advocates "reflection on action," a post hoc examination and analysis of what transpired. This type of reflection leads to the kind of further action that can be taken only after extensive deliberation (Schön 1983, 1990) and educative feedback after the event.

In both instances, learners can check their thinking and performance against that of others in the class or that of experts. Such learning is highly dependent on *guided modeling* and *approximation*. Students use whatever information is available to compare and contrast themselves to others. This comparison is not a direct copying; it employs a feedback process that allows for original work within definitive and agreed-on expectations and assumptions. It is used extensively by coaches in fields ranging from sports to music. Schön suggests that all professionals could benefit from training of this sort. Among the tools available to assist educators in the provision of appropriate and timely feedback are video cameras and computers.

Reflection Without Assistance. At times, we need to both reflect and self-correct, often while engaged in some activity, but without the assistance of others. This requires the ability to abstract, which does not usually develop until adolescence. It means that as a learner I have to develop the ability to observe myself as if I were a stranger on a video screen and learn how to make appropriate changes. Changing behavior this way is harder and usually comes only after *self-observation* becomes natural and changing makes sense. We suspect that this skill also relies on the further development of appropriate regions of the brain, perhaps in the frontal lobes, as MacLean (1978) suggests.

Teachers can introduce students to these self-observation skills through concrete games, such as role playing or imagining being someone else. Learning these skills can also be critical preparation for all types of reflection in adolescence and adulthood. In particular, reflection of this sort is an invaluable tool for teachers or teacher trainees to use in their interactions with students.

Personal Awareness of Deep Meanings. One essential thrust of reflection concerns the ways in which we are responding and changing as people. Students bring hidden expectations, preferences, beliefs, and life metaphors to any situation (e.g., Lakoff and Johnson 1980). These deep meanings influence interactions with others and with the environment. For example, a student whose deeply felt metaphor for school is "war" will behave differently at almost every moment from one whose metaphor is "growth" or "game." People in a war zone are quick to think of other people (such as students and teachers) in terms of allies and enemies. People who think in terms of playing games are better equipped to change sides and change their minds.

Metacognition—thinking about the way that we think, feel, and act—helps us to learn in much more depth because we begin to recognize and capitalize on personal strengths while improving or allowing for weaknesses. We are also better able to appreciate what is really important to us, and so access our own intrinsic motivation. Hence, active processing becomes a vehicle for increasing relaxed alertness.

CONTEMPLATION

Most of the procedures described under "Reflection" tend to be analytical. Paradoxically, however, one of the best ways to refine thought is to engage in some nonanalytic processes. Perhaps the best known of these procedures is the sort of contemplation that some sages have engaged in. Gendlin (1981), a psychologist from the University of Chicago, whom we mention in Chapter 10, has developed a fairly systematic, useful process that reinforces our own explorations. We have used this model with concepts, procedures, and situations that seem to be really resistant to understanding.

Focusing. Sometimes the act of trying to understand actually prevents understanding. That is why one of the basic steps in creative problem solving is to allow a question to *incubate*. We can facilitate this incubation by "letting go" of our current beliefs. Focusing assists. In some ways, it is like looking at a peaceful pond on a quiet day—or like being at a classical concert and observing and enjoying the music without analyzing it or expecting it to be played in a specific way. In a similar way, we can "place" an idea, concept, or procedure in the mind and then simply observe it without any form of analysis or deliberation. The objective, which requires both relaxation and patience, is to simply contemplate a subject *without* seeking to understand. On occasion this open focusing is the magic ingredient that allows the mind to relax and register the pattern that it has been seeking.

Felt Meanings. Geoffrey has used this procedure with the study of computers. Some people spend a lot of time studying computers without any breakthrough or sense of felt meaning. At one time, Geoffrey was in this position. Computers seemed to be represented by a dark, impenetrable block in his mind. He found himself inadvertently contemplating computers, however, while resting in the sun in the courtyard at the University of Queensland. Computing was the focus of his contemplation, but the meaning of computing was not specified in advance. Geoffrey experienced a feeling that some hidden barrier to understanding computers seemed to dissolve. It was not that computing was suddenly understood, but that it was now clearly possible to understand. Focusing, therefore, contributed to his acquisition of a felt meaning for computing.

CREATIVE ELABORATION

Reorganizing Experience. Creative elaboration emphasizes the reorganization of experience. One of the keys to effectively digesting and learning from experience is to deliberately set out to represent such learning in different ways and from different points of view. Elaboration is most successful when it engages all body/mind systems. In part, this is a way of generating associations with more of what we already know. Elaboration is also a way of recognizing and harmonizing with our own barriers and moving beyond our mind "sets." Robin Williams beautifully demonstrated this as a teacher in the movie *Dead Poet's Society*. He had his students jump on top of their desks to illustrate the possibility of seeing the world from different points of view.

Reperceiving Information. Reperceiving can be enhanced in many ways, among the most powerful of which are the varied uses of art. For example, Betty Edwards (1979) shows that we gain fresh insights by both literally and metaphorically turning the object of interest upside down. Another approach is to use what reflective practice calls "seeing as." The objective is to analyze a field of interest metaphorically. In other words, we see the content or subject as if it were something else. This use of analogies and metaphors is not only a way of introducing new material, but also of gaining a fresh perspective on a subject. Many people who are already moderately proficient in some field find it useful to explore it from a significantly different viewpoint. We previously mentioned Sam Crowell's course in which he uses the metaphor of the teacher as artist (Crowell 1989). As Crowell's students discovered, when the principles and methods inherent in the metaphor are brought to bear on the subject or field of primary interest, the latter is cast in a new and frequently interesting and powerful light.

Using Personal Analogies. A related type of elaboration can be described as "compare and contrast." Students need to take advantage of the brain's desire and ability to make multiple connections between what is new and what is known. The key is for each student to find some of their own analogies and metaphors so that what is learned can better fit into their personal world. In developing computer literacy, for instance, one solution is to find an appropriate way to introduce computers into our lives. Two executives we know placed their first computer in the kitchen because, to them, that was an easy and familiar context in which to learn about new gadgets (which is what a computer is). One reason that some children easily take to computers is that they treat computers as games and toys, and they already know a great deal about both.

COMBINATION PROCESSES

All the procedures described under "Reflection" and "Contemplation" can operate in different ways. There are also many procedures, such as journal writing, that do not fit comfortably under any specific umbrella term.

Student Journals. Writing in journals is a powerful way to process experience. A diary, of course, is a journal. And the novel began its life as a diarylike chronicle of opinions and events. What is popularly believed to be one of the first major novels in English, Richardson's *Pamela*, was constructed in letter and diary form.

A journal can be used in many ways. Barbara Flores (Flores and Garcia 1984, Flores et al. 1986) shows how powerful journals are as media for helping young children learn how to read and write. Ira Progoff (1980) has gone in a different direction with his development of the journal as a tool for what he calls "process meditation." This is an inner dialogue that allows writers to experience themselves from many different perspectives. The basic tool for teachers is to have students chronicle events and opinions on a regular basis. This is not intended to be a critical analysis or a research report, but an expansion of personal ideas, impressions, and feelings. The advantage is that students "bring to the surface" or "bring out" thoughts that might never otherwise emerge. In journals, they are literally exploring the landscape of their own locale memory system. The danger is that these impressions are very personal and intimate; it takes a sensitive and mature teacher, acting in a safe environment, to make journals work constructively.

Thinking Skills. A significant amount of time and effort is now being spent on the teaching of critical thinking. For example, see Brandt's (1986) "Frameworks for Teaching Thinking." We support the intent of those measures. It is clear that at the heart of reflection is the ability to question, analyze, compare, contrast, and organize thoughts. Students who have a grasp of critical thinking will be much better equipped to acquire natural knowledge in many subjects, as well as felt meanings. The full benefit of those skills will be realized when they can be used in any area of endeavor. In fact, instruction in critical thinking can be embedded in every subject in the curriculum.

ACTIVE PROCESSING IN ACTION

Here are some examples of the types of activities that can be used to encourage active processing.

Have students become resident experts is some field so that they are the ones who need to inform and assist other students. Their support may take the form of answering questions, helping to design projects, and providing advice. This takes advantage of peer teaching and provides invaluable feedback to teachers.

Simulate panels and discussion groups of various sorts, such as TV talk shows, presidential debates, United Nations forums, and congressional hearings. Simulate other real events. We know of a Spanish language class, for example, in which one half of the students act as the residents of a town, taking on the roles of shopkeepers and other inhabitants; and the rest of the class act as tourists.

Other classes engage in full congressional proceedings for the purpose of dealing with some social problem, such as pollution. One excellent example is the nationwide "law and community" project, in which students take the roles of advocates and jurors and argue socially relevant cases before panels of practicing lawyers and judges. At the college level, we have seen students develop sophisticated plans for community development: law students play a role in legal aid, engineering students participate in the development of solar power vehicles, and so on.

Elementary and secondary school students can also participate in community events, though in less sophisticated ways. In addition, students and teachers need to explore in more depth the power of the arts. For example, there are several outstanding programs in which students are given the opportunity to develop their singing, dancing, and other artistic talents and where their participation is directly linked to the content of their school curriculum in history or science.

There is a key to doing all this effectively. Some students may wish to develop professional expertise, whereas others may seek to win competitions. *It is extremely important, however, that many of the activities we discuss have no direct bearing on grades.* The students need to experience the joy of participating and to have the opportunity to be creative. They will receive more than enough feedback to give them a sense of what the community values. They must also have the freedom to experiment.

TESTING AND EVALUATION

It should be apparent that much of what is done to aid processing is open-ended. Students are invited to explore content in their own ways and express themselves uniquely. Yet it is also essential that students acquire socially prescribed information and skills. In practice, neither is possible with a system of testing and evaluation that is mechanical, limited, and fixed. The reason is that our methods of evaluation govern the way we teach and the freedom to learn. The result is precisely what we have—a majority of teachers teaching to simplistic tests, teaching for memorization, and thereby limiting what else students can learn and the connections they can make.

INDICATORS OF PERFORMANCE AND UNDERSTANDING

As already stated, a solution that we find extremely practical is to evaluate our students by combining measures of complex performance with indicators of understanding. Teachers must dramatically extend the range of observations that they can make of students. Standardized tests are not excluded. They simply become a relatively small part of the global evaluation process. Immersion and active processing tend to come together here. We take advantage of the entire gamut of activities in which the students engage for the purpose of genuinely grasping and coming to appreciate what they know.

This approach to evaluation can be systematized to some extent as follows, although this area is one educators urgently need to develop.

Performance in Multiple Contexts. Natural knowledge is knowledge that can be applied in real-world situations. Hence, we need to provide our students with realistic contexts within which to call on ideas and skills. Rather than ask questions about computers, for instance, we might ask them to build a database to record class attendance. Their reading skill is shown in their ability to follow instructions that come with new equipment or in their ability to find information on current events as reported in the press. And dealing with numbers is involved in everything from weaving and art to managing the finances for a class outing or field trip.

Ability to Question. It is a maxim in many professions that a key to success is not knowing the answer but knowing how to find it. Similarly, a manager knows that new employees are beginning to have a sense of felt meaning for the job when they ask penetrating questions. We therefore suggest that the same ability be invoked by educators as an indicator that a student is acquiring felt meaning. Critical indicators of acquiring felt meaning for a new subject include (1) being able to ask the right questions, (2) knowing how to find the answers, and (3) knowing what to do with the answers.

Appropriate Performance in Unexpected Situations. Students need to be able to do more than perform in scheduled, planned situations. Such performance is indicative of competence, but not necessarily of understanding and natural knowledge. Students need to be able to respond appropriately to unanticipated events. An expert, for example, is a person who can react appropriately but often unpredictably in unanticipated situations. A superb example is the capacity to engage in a conversation that unexpectedly calls one's knowledge into play. This happens all the time in the workplace and in social gatherings, whether the conversation is about computers, changes in Eastern Europe, art, or finance. Similar indicators of competence in spontaneous or unexpected interactions can serve to tell us that a child has genuinely begun to synthesize what has been learned. This does not exclude times when a problem will be presented for which there is no known answer. The expert is the person who can be reliably called on to work on and solve the problem.

EVALUATION GUIDELINES

We suggest that there are at least four relevant indicators that guide evaluation:

- The ability to use the language of the discipline or subject in complex situations and in social interaction.
- The ability to perform appropriately in unanticipated situations.
- The ability to solve real problems using the skills and concepts.
- The ability to show, explain, or teach the idea or skill to another person who has a real need to know.

The 15 questions in Figure 11.1 introduce general indicators of what should be taking place during brain-based learning. These questions underlie effective performance and the expansion of natural knowledge. They provide us with indicators concerning whether students are acquiring relaxed alertness, are being adequately immersed in orchestrated experience, and are being sufficiently active in processing their experience. Regardless of what particular educational model educators use, the key is the adequate engagement of the brain.

Figure 11.1 Checklist of Useful Questions

• Are students involved and challenged?
• Is there clear evidence of student creativity and enjoyment? Are students dealing appropriately with dissonance?
• Are students being exposed to content in many ways that link content to life?
• Are students' life themes and metaphors being engaged?
• Are there "hooks" that tie the content together in a big picture that itself can make sense to students?
• Is there some sort of continuity, such as through projects and ongoing stories, so that content is tied together and retains interest over time?
• Is there any sign of continuing motivation or student interest that expresses itself above and beyond the dictates of the class?
• Is the physical context being used optimally?
• What do the setting, decorations, architecture, layout, music, and other features of the context actually "say" to students?
• What sort of group atmosphere is emerging?
• Are there any signs of positive collaboration, and do they continue after the lesson and after school?
• Do students have opportunities to reorganize content in creative and personally relevant ways?
• Are there opportunities to reflect in an open-ended way on what does and does not make sense?
• Are students given the opportunity to apply the material in different contexts?
• Do students consciously and deliberately examine their performances in those different contexts and begin to appreciate their own strengths and weaknesses?

CAUTIONS ON EVALUATIONS

Brain-based teaching demands a critical look at current methods of evaluation. First, it is impossible to communicate the scope and depth of a student's abilities by means of a letter or numerical grade. In business, an employee often has a performance appraisal. It includes assessments by nominated people, as well as observed performance on complex tasks. When done well, this is a complex, global, and useful evaluation. This type of evaluation is also a helpful model for teaching.

Second, students' self-concept is also shaped by the type of feedback they get and the manner in which it is communicated. Whereas a student journal is an invaluable source of information regarding how a student really thinks, grading it or writing detached and insensitive comments can be quite destructive. All forms of assessment affect our feelings and perceived self. The more we risk personally, the more destructive simplistic evaluation will be.

Finally, there is a difference between looking for indicators and counting numbers of specific responses. One child may ask just one question and reveal profound understanding, whereas another may ask many questions and yet be relatively ignorant. There is a difference, therefore, between quality and quantity. That poses a challenge for teachers, because it is difficult to monitor what is happening in the classroom and also remember all the possible indicators and criteria. In our experience, the solution is for educators to acquire a grasp of these indicators as a part of *their own* natural knowledge. *Educators, in effect, must be experts at recognizing expertise in students.* This becomes easier when educators grasp the essence of levels of meaning and begin to identify real shifts in thinking.

ACTIVE PROCESSING IN TEACHER EDUCATION

Active processing—particularly reflection—is becoming important in teacher training. Pugach and Johnson report:

> Working with practicing teachers, we have focused on creating new meanings for immediate classroom problems—meanings that are meant to help teachers move from concentrating on immediate symptoms and frustrations to constructive responses based upon more disciplined self-inquiry into the situation (1988, p. 30).

The thrust of the process is self-inquiry through reflection. This certainly complements our conception of brain-based learning.

One excellent model is that of Donald Schön's "reflective practitioner" (1983), discussed earlier in this chapter. Schön's model, which involves teacher as coach and includes a significant amount of ongoing reflection, makes a great deal of sense from a brain-based perspective. It brings some sanity to education by taking us beyond our pervasive attempts to teach teachers by means of a limited, technical/rational approach.

* * *

As most of us reflect and understand, we acquire a greater insight into what we like to do and what we do best. The same applies to students. Their brains do not learn at the time, in the place, or in the ways that suit us. They change and develop and come to understand over time; and every subject and every experience will interact to enhance or impede that development. Active processing is a way to both facilitate and monitor changes over time. It requires a significant degree of patience and an appreciation of the fact that we are dealing with people, not machines. Above all, there is an interplay between mastery of prescribed content and the development of creative insight and autonomy as a human being. As teachers, we can facilitate, but not totally control, this process.

12

BRAIN-BASED LEARNING IN ACTION

*If the purpose of teaching is to promote learning, then we
need to ask what we mean by that term. Here I become
passionate. I want to talk about learning. But not the
lifeless, sterile, futile, quickly forgotten stuff that is
crammed into the mind of the poor helpless individual
tied into his seat by ironclad bonds of conformity! I am
talking about LEARNING—the insatiable curiosity that
drives the adolescent boy to absorb everything he can see
or hear or read about gasoline engines in order to
improve the efficiency and speed of his "cruiser." I am
talking about the student who says, "I am discovering,
drawing in from the outside, and making that which is
drawn in a real part of me." I am talking about any
learning in which the experience of the learner progresses
along this line: "No, no, that's not what I want" ;
"Wait! This is closer to what I am interested in, what I
need" ; "Ah, here it is! Now I'm grasping and
comprehending what I need and what I want to know!"*

Carl Rogers, *Freedom to Learn for the '80s,*
1983, p. 18

We have had the pleasure of meeting and observing many superb educators and of being introduced to a wide range of practical and sophisticated models of teaching. It is not our objective to describe any of those models in depth. Rather, we wish to illustrate brain-based teaching in operation, with a view to pointing out the importance of, and the dance between, the elements that we have identified. Most of the examples will deal with relaxed alertness and orchestrated immersion. Active processing occurs everywhere but is not used widely. Although the principles can be implemented in different ways, depending on the context, we believe that they apply universally. We have chosen to reflect their breadth of application by selecting examples from several different areas and levels of education.

THEMATIC TEACHING IN ELEMENTARY SCHOOL

Some schools have had success with both short- and long-term use of themes as organizers for specific lessons and an entire curriculum. Their first step is to find a way to integrate all the subject matter to be covered in the year's program in a way that is both coherent and meaningful. One solution is to begin with a general concept such as "the family," which we describe in Chapter 9.

Susan Kovalik (1989) frequently uses a picture and encourages teachers to search for different subject areas that are reflected in the picture. Examples range from biology and earth sciences to physics and social studies. The curriculum for the year can then be designed, with the added advantage that every subject can be related back to the thematic picture so that students grasp the interconnectedness of what they are learning.

A related approach is used in developing individual lesson plans. Martha Kaufeldt (1984) illustrates this in the book and videotape entitled *I Can Divide and Conquer*. The concept is "division," and the goal is to make division a theme for every activity that occurs during the day. Thus, parents may come for lunch and bring a pizza that must be divided into parts so that everybody has an equal share. People must have their fair share of time. The space in a room must be divided for different purposes. And so on. And throughout the day the teacher constantly talks about division and helps the students to recognize what and where it "is."

In such a classroom, both relaxed alertness and orchestrated immersion are featured prominently. Students are given maximum opportunity to explore areas of personal interest. They also engage in activities that are fun and nonthreatening but still demanding. They have opportunities to work privately and in groups. Parents and others from the community visit the class and participate in real ways (e.g., the pizza lunch), so that the content of instruction overlaps continually with real life. The entire physical context is used to support the lesson. And everything is constantly related back to the central theme for the year. Hence concepts and ideas are tied together in ways that innately make them more meaningful. There is also some active processing because teachers use the actual experience to "draw out" from students what division and other concepts really mean to them.

ECONOMICS IN A MIDDLE SCHOOL—
A LESSON USING ALL THREE ELEMENTS

In her video *Why Do These Children Love School?* Dorothy Fadiman (1988) shows a vignette of a class in the Peninsula School. Students are gathered around a large table in the classroom. The instructor goes to a cupboard and gets a paper bag, out of which he extracts a doughnut. "We are going to have an auction today," he says. "I am going to auction this doughnut." The students laugh, and their interest is aroused. The instructor has effectively capitalized on some aspects of their intrinsic motivation.

The teacher proceeds to tempt them with this delightful, freshly baked doughnut, having students savor the flavor and begin to bid. The action is heavy. Other goods are sold, and for one item someone bids $1, much more than its real market value. There is a gasp. Then laughter. The instructor asks why people bid, and there is a spirited discussion.

The instructor moves to the blackboard and begins to talk in a very different way. "We have been looking," he comments, "at supply and demand. I had a doughnut and you wanted it." Very quickly, he sketches some of the fundamental concepts of a market economy and of the power of advertising. He acknowledges that he deliberately tried to tempt them to buy. And he asks the students what they learned.

This is an excellent illustration of all three principles in operation because it also shows their interaction. The teacher generates and maintains relaxed alertness with his ongoing good humor and the challenge of the different procedures that he uses. This is also a superb example of orchestrated immersion. He blends everyday experience (of doughnuts and sales) with prescribed content (market economics) in a way that is a game, a "real" event, and a lesson. The "auction" generates real social relationships at many levels, ranging from the experience of bidding against each other to the observation of classmates behaving in unexpected ways. The teacher introduces props that focus attention. And he keeps the auction tight so that it is long enough to be real, but not so long that it becomes boring.

Active processing is then used quite intentionally. The instructor asks the students to reflect on their personal experience to draw out the new concepts. Thus students have to consciously think about what happened to them, such as being tempted, and consciously relate it to new ideas. This happens when the teacher introduces the notion of market economics. Note that this processing is also a continuation of the immersion. The experience is still ongoing, but it is now being mined for understanding and so takes on a different form.

In the video, one student is asked to comment on learning in the school generally. She says that they are obliged to think and reflect on what they have learned and that this helps them learn more. The question asked of that student for the purpose of reflecting on the school for the video is also active processing. She is given a real question with a real purpose and is obliged to bring into consciousness the way that the school works. Thus she is given an opportunity to think about learning itself.

CHEMISTRY IN SECONDARY SCHOOL

We have already mentioned Leo Wood. He teaches chemistry at Tempe High School in Tempe, Arizona, and has used Optimalearning™, a process developed by Ivan Barzakov (1988), to design his course. The content is the prescribed curriculum for grades 11 and 12. The school's student population is 37 percent minority, a percentage that also is reflected in Wood's chemistry classes. He has students for the same number of hours each week as do other chemistry teachers. And they have lab work, as well as regular classes. What, then, is different?

To begin with, Wood uses the overriding general theme we mentioned earlier, "Life Is a Miracle." Chemistry is then explored as "the central science that responds to the needs of society" (Wood 1986, p. 1). He shows that the miracle of life "is supported by chemical processes and substances which interact at all levels to allow for conditions necessary for the existence and maintenance of LIFE." Permeating the entire subject, then, are two types of principles that link the process of chemistry with living. First, at a general level, are his Ten Commandments of Success. Thus #7, "Thou Must Sweep Cobwebs From Thy Mind Before They Imprison Thee." In addition, he has posters of great works of art that celebrate life, and he plays appropriate selections of classical music as background to labwork. Second, at a specific, content-based level, are the essential chemical processes. This is an example of the thematical orchestration referred to in Chapter 9.

Wood also uses many techniques blended together in a learning model. These include reading with music; storytelling and metaphors; short lecturettes; the use of imagery to evoke a sense of expectancy and relaxation; songs, games, and skits; demonstrations; "grapples" or ways of connecting and relating subject matter to real-life situations and happenings; and both individual and group work. A beautiful illustration is a song he wrote that links the five essential chemical reactions of fusion, photosynthesis, combustion, respiration, and reactions of various types. He now has a tape and words to songs available for other teachers who want to use them or experiment in their own classes (Wood 1990).

The state of challenge and relaxed enjoyment in Wood's classes is specifically triggered by the use of techniques such as guided imagery. It is also a consequence of the blend of creative and challenging procedures that Wood uses and of the atmosphere he creates through music, materials, and genuine concern for students. Students are also immersed in multiple experiences that draw in a great deal of what is important to them in life. Thus the controversy over the alleged discovery of cold fusion in 1989 resulted in student-initiated discussions. They brought in articles and hotly debated the issues. The physical environment was used to the fullest through art, music, news of the day, and posters. A good interpersonal atmosphere was created that lasted well beyond school. Everyday phenomena, such as sunlight, were introduced in ways that were both interesting and relevant. And students had many opportunities to explore issues of personal interest. This combination of spontaneity and design is exactly what we mean by orchestration. Wood knows his subject intimately and cares about his students. He definitely has the prestige to totally engage his students.

Wood's results speak for themselves. On the average, he covers the required chemistry curriculum six weeks ahead of schedule. Yet his students achieve higher grades than do those in comparable classes, as tested on standardized measures; and he is particularly successful with minority students.

A College-Level Engineering Course—Integrating Subjects

Engineers have been criticized for not adequately considering the human and social implications of their actions; as a result, engineering educators are increasingly expected to produce baccalaureate engineers who are well-versed in humanities and social sciences. However, intense pressure to maintain, if not expand, technical requirements within engineering curricula all but eliminates any chance to offer more "stand-alone" humanities courses (Olds and Miller 1989, p. 1).

The Colorado School of Mines (CSM) has attempted to solve this problem by developing a program called "HumEn," in which aspects of the humanities were integrated directly into a prescribed undergraduate introductory course in chemical engineering. The materials included selections from Descartes, Bacon, Shakespeare (*The Tempest*), Mary Shelley (*Frankenstein*), and others. Among the issues explored were two questions: Do engineers and humanists approach and solve problems differently? Why is it important to recognize these differences, and how can we use them to our advantage?

Olds and Miller (1989, 1990) describe the course, which was team taught by an engineering and a humanities faculty member. This team emphasized class discussions rather than lectures; open-ended design problems in lieu of rote homework; small-group work; reading, writing (including a journal), and speaking; and discussions of connections, where appropriate, between technical and nontechnical aspects of the course. One of the design projects, for example, involved both a technical and a social analysis of the issues posed by acid rain. The usual amount of technical information was covered, but the course was extended by the addition of one extra class hour each week.

The pilot course was evaluated in several different ways and was contrasted to a "regular" group, which functioned as the control group. The preliminary evaluations are extraordinarily promising. Perhaps to be expected was clear evidence of a greater appreciation of nontechnical issues by the students in the pilot course. Moreover, the students enjoyed their course more than did students in the control group. In addition, "the HumEn students performed better than the control students on final examinations which were judged by department faculty to be of equivalent difficulty. Similar results were observed with other examinations and quizzes during the semester" (Olds and Miller 1989, p. 7). In addition, two independent consultants, funded by grants from the National Endowment for the Humanities, were quite positive:

> [The course] seems to be creating more favorable attitudes toward humanities and social sciences in general as well as greater awareness of non-technical criteria for making engineering design choices, while it seems to leave technical performance not only unimpeded but even improved (Olds and Miller 1989, p. 8).

The course is an excellent example of a mix of thematic teaching and the integrated curriculum. The engineering content has already been prescribed. A set of thematic questions were formulated, having to do with the approach to problems by humanists and scientists. Texts from the humanities were then selected with a view to casting light on the central themes of the course. In addition, some aspects of cooperative learning were included by virtue of the group projects and the focus on human issues and needs.

In addition, we see that all three elements of brain-based learning were in play and that they were not linear but permeated the entire program. First, the challenge inherent in *relaxed alertness* was present, both because the course was an element in the pursuit of a chosen career and because the selected issues touched the students personally. Relaxation was not specifically used, but the mix of activities was deliberately designed to make the course more "enjoyable." Hence, the preferred state of mind was induced to some extent by the course as a whole.

Second, that mix of activities and processes also constituted *orchestrated immersion* in appropriate experiences. Much of this was conscious. According to Olds and Miller (1989), team teaching, for instance, creates a "classroom structure [that] helps students to see the importance of humanities in the context of their technical education." The group work, the design projects, the literature, and the discussions helped to both foster relationships among all participants and enable them to perceive issues from several different perspectives.

Finally, *active processing* is evident in several ways. The design projects and the humanities readings clearly forced students to bring into consciousness and explore the issues in the materials. The discussions based on the thematic questions are excellent organizers. And the students kept personal journals which are superb vehicles for personal reflection.

TEACHING COMPUTING TO ADULTS

Brain-based learning applies to adults as well as children, and many of the techniques described previously can be adopted in adult education.

Geoffrey has taught courses on entry-level computing for adults, including teachers. The setting for these computer courses includes a projector and screen showing the instructor's computer screen. A portable tape deck is playing the *Pastorale Symphony*. A database of names and fields for attendance has been created and is on the screen when people enter. Chairs are arranged in a semi-circle facing the screen. Before the course officially begins, but after most people have arrived, we ask for a volunteer who has never used a computer. Usually there are one or two enthusiastic beginners. One is selected and is asked to check with people that their names were spelled correctly and to enter them as present. We call for another volunteer with some background in the selected program to show our novice how to move the cursor and enter information.

This is an excellent process. All students pay attention because they check their own name, want to be registered, and have some empathy with the volunteer. The first volunteer is immediately engaged in actual computing, and they are all immersed in a real experience with computers.

In this class, we use metaphors drawn from experience. For example, we bring in a TV, a typewriter, and a dual-drive tape deck and show that computers are very much like all those items connected to each other. When we discuss the creation of new files and the deletion of old ones, we compare them to opening and closing bank accounts. And when we show people how to use software, we take full advantage of the metaphor of menus. We literally ask people to think of a restaurant menu. There are different sections, such as for entrees and desserts; and within each of these there are still more selections. That is very much how menus work on a computer. Thus, even though all the items may not be familiar, the general notion of how software is organized becomes clear—and students relax.

One of the most striking phenomena in the world of computing is the difference between the way that experts learn new products and the procedures they develop for novices. Experts typically play games, push a product to its limits, invent new ways to use it, make puns on terms, and basically explore the product in creative ways. Most of us relish that sort of activity when we feel secure. Hence, it is precisely the sort of activity that students ought to experience as well. In our computer courses for teachers, for example, after a substantial number of new terms have been introduced—say, after half a day of instruction on some type of software—students are invited to "speak" the software. They pretend that they are purchasing software in a store or are at a computer hackers' party. In our experience, they subsequently relate to the terms more easily and remember them better.

HOME STUDY

"3rd Home-Taught Youth Off to Harvard"

This headline appeared in the *Los Angeles Times* on December 31, 1987. It tells the story of Reed Colfax, one of four brothers who were taught exclusively on a family ranch in Boonville in Mendocino County, California. Reed, like his two older brothers (the youngest of the four was only 12 at the time), had never taken a formal test before having to take the Scholastic Aptitude Test for college entrance. The boys learned algebra and geometry as they and their parents built a house; and they learned science, including genetics and embryology, while raising livestock. They also used textbooks, buying several on any one subject and then as a family deciding which they liked most. "When we started out here, we did hard physical work outside, or we did schoolwork, so schoolwork was always a break for us," said Reed, a long-distance runner, jazz enthusiast, and guitarist. Another son, Drew, said, "I think the four of us know more about the anatomy of an animal than anyone at Harvard. . . . I just had a white rat dissection lab that was so boring. It was 'Here's the stomach and here's the heart.' "

The boys are not geniuses, according to their father. Rather, they are highly motivated and enjoy learning. And he believes that the methods themselves are important because two sons, Reed and Garth, were adopted. Mr. and Mrs. Colfax, however, were also well equipped. Miki, the boys' mother, is a former high school English and creative writing teacher; and David, their father, has a doctorate in sociology from the University of Chicago.

> "When Grant [the first son] was accepted, the story was 'Bumpkin Goes to Harvard,'" said David Colfax, who serves on the Mendocino County School Board. "Now the hook on the whole story is what are we doing right? . . . It raises a lot of questions about education in America" ("3rd Home-Taught Youth Off to Harvard," 1987, p. 21).

Our point is not that home study is better than schooling, but that the Colfaxes show the power of orchestrated immersion of the learners in complex experiences, embellished by reading and theory, and built around personally meaningful challenges. The students were also guided by highly educated, intelligent, and knowledgeable teachers (their parents). All the elements of brain-based learning described previously are evident. That is what works. That is the picture toward which schools must move if they are to teach to the possibilities inherent in the human brain.

One of the best examples of a school that implements what the Colfaxes did is the Peninsula School (referred to previously). In this school, all subjects relate to each other and are embedded in authentic experience. For example, weaving is used to make mathematics real and to generate a sense of wholeness and a desire for completion. Team games, such as hockey, become avenues for conflict resolution and reflection on the nature of communication and choice. Manual skills, such as carpentry, come alive in the minds of students and generate self-esteem. Thus, as shown in Fadiman's (1988) video about the Peninsula School, a graduating class actually built a sophisticated playground structure as a gift to the school. And former students and their parents met with the parents of incoming students to reassure them and demonstrate that the Peninsula process works. These and other levels of interaction and creativity occur within a tradition that has been evolving for decades.

SCHOOL-COMMUNITY PARTNERSHIP

Orchestrated immersion, high challenge, felt meanings, active processing, and thematic teaching—these and many other aspects of brain-based learning are evident in an ongoing national competition among U.S. high school students in government classes. In this program, entire classes, whose instructors choose to participate, engage in mock congressional hearings on the U.S. Constitution and Bill of Rights, as a celebration of the Bicentennial of the U.S. Constitution.

This is how the competition works: Students are treated as experts on particular topics, and they are asked to testify before a panel of judges, who themselves play the role of congressional committee members. The judges are interested and qualified members of the community. Each competing class has six groups, or teams; and every member of the class must participate. Hence the members work together to develop their understanding and presentations. They are also assisted by volunteers from the community.

Each team must make a presentation and respond to questions on topics such as political philosophy, the establishment of government, and fundamental rights and responsibilities of citizens. These topics are included in the program's core textbook, *We the People*, published by the Center for Civic Education* (1987). The center also provides the students with questions on each topic, and the "congressional committee" selects one question to ask the students at the "hearing." For example, on the subject of political philosophy, one question for the 1988–89 academic year was as follows:

How do the Declaration of Independence and the Constitution reflect the ideas of the natural rights philosophy?

• Has the understanding of what constitutes basic human rights changed since the days of the Founders? Explain your answer.

• What do you think should be the role of the government in securing basic rights for all individuals?

Provision is made for timekeeping, judging criteria, feedback to students, and conflicts and protests. There is an intraschool competition, and the winning class goes on to compete with other schools from the same congressional district. Ultimately, winners from each state compete in Washington, D.C.

In 1990, students at Reed High School, in Washoe County, Nevada, placed fourth nationally. Their teacher (or, should we say, facilitator) was Denton Gehr. One of the volunteers who helped coach the students was Larry Struve, director of the Nevada Department of Commerce and vice-chair of the Nevada Commission on the Bicentennial of the U.S. Constitution. He stated:

Because of the way in which the students were involved in researching their topics, they "hungered" for as much information and knowledge on constitutional history as was possible in the time allotted before the competition. In effect, *the learning process was taken out of the hands of the government teacher and placed into the hands of the students themselves,*

---

*Center for Civic Education, 5146 Douglas Fir Rd., Calabasas, CA 91302.

who went to the library for independent research, challenged each other, participated in special fund-raising events, and interviewed community resource people to get different insights on the topic [emphasis added] (Struve, personal communication 1990).

Struve saw firsthand the "phenomenal excitement generated by the students." He added that many of the students also publicly commented at a Washoe County Partners in Education Program, attended by several hundred community leaders supporting this competition and related programs, that they felt they had learned more from this one experience than from four years in conventional classes.

Another project coach was Thomas Jefferson scholar Clay Jenkinson, who came to Reed under the auspices of the Nevada Humanities Committee (Melton 1990).

The extra effort the students put into the project is an indicator of both motivation and growth in understanding—essential to brain-based learning. They worked together in collaborative groups. Students were immersed in vivid, real experiences in which content came to life, supported by the willing and enthusiastic participation of community members and by a teacher who allowed them to teach themselves.

In addition, students discussed and analyzed what they were told and what they read, and thus formed personal opinions that nevertheless reflected genuine expertise in a given field. The community took pride in the accomplishments of the students (Melton 1990). Of critical importance in this example of brain-based learning is the marriage between school curriculum and life experience.

METACOGNITIVE TEACHING

One of the more sophisticated approaches that illustrate active processing is what Sam Crowell calls "metacognitive" teaching (personal communication 1989). He either models or includes students in a process and then stops to ask, "What did we do? What did you experience?" The objective is to create the exact circumstances of a concept that is being taught.

For example, one way to make downshifting more than a retreat to surface knowledge is to give students an appropriate experience to reflect on. In her teacher education classes, Renate places the students in cooperative groups and then gives them highly competitive quizzes. The students instantly downshift and revert to entrenched strategies, ranging from an emphasis on short-term and unthought-out responses to petulance. In short, these college students behave like children often do in school. Renate then stops the class and together they review the responses and reflect on what happened and on the

169

downshifting process as an experience. In this way—provided there is a general atmosphere of relaxed alertness and trust—students move immediately to deeper levels of understanding because the experience includes dealing with the impact of the process on themselves, including emotional involvement.

In another teacher education course, Renate's colleague, Phyllis Maxey Fernlund, uses the metacognitive approach in a social studies methods course (personal communication 1989). As an exercise, she asks the teachers to discuss how their values interact with the process of designing a lesson and to explore the values implicit in their choices. The teachers in her class often deny that they have values or claim that their teaching is value free. By reflecting on the underlying assumptions in the phrase "value free," these teachers come to terms with their values. If "value free" means that they plan to give students in their classrooms abundant choices, then they are compelled to recognize that giving students choices is part of their value system. This exercise is also a part of the democratic process. Students learn this process not as an abstract concept but in relation to their own thinking and behavior. Both Crowell and Maxey Fernlund teach content, but they also help their students grasp the concepts by becoming aware of the impact their experience has had on them. These instructors also model superb brain-based learning.

* * *

There are specific models available for teaching to the human brain. They are useful and important, but they must be used appropriately. The key is for educators to appreciate what must actually take place for students to learn effectively. Any model or procedure must be used with those more fundamental procedures in mind. Once that happens, educators begin to discover and create procedures that suit them, assist their students, and make both learning and teaching enjoyable and satisfying.

CONCLUSION:
TRANSFORMATION AND TRANSITION

"The ground itself is moving" [Emory 1969]: our
underlying frames, gestalts, paradigms, big pictures are
everywhere in doubt. The task is to understand how we
acquire frames, how we communicate them, and how we
change them in ourselves and others.

Peter Vail, *Management as a Performing Art*,
1989, p. 106

WHERE ARE WE NOW?

The focus on specific outcomes is deeply entrenched in our educational system. Legislatures request minimum competencies, expressed in outcomes that are easily subjected to quantitative evaluation. Prescribed outcomes are, indeed, very important. Unfortunately, they are heavily geared toward taxon learning and the memorization of surface knowledge even though they speak of teacher "artistry" or "creative and responsible decision making." The answer is not a matter of doing what we do better and faster, the answer lies in thinking differently. What does "time on task" really mean from the point of view of a brain looking for meaning? What is "wait time" when it is used artificially without sensitivity to context? How can excellent models of teaching like the inquiry method and Synectics™, now being taught in teacher education programs, be effectively brought into the average classroom? Are such models effective if we don't relate our teaching to the adult world our students will enter or to personally relevant subject matter? Are they used for separate and discrete lessons the teacher designs for students while ignoring the impact of more subtle teaching behaviors?

Testing, grading, and a focus on uniform outcomes are not limited to the United States. The British government's reform program for secondary education calls for the "creation of a new statutory framework for a national curriculum with clear objectives and national

171

assessment at the ages 7, 11, 14, and 16. This will end the huge variation in standards between schools and different areas and arrest the
current trend at the age of 14 whereby girls drop sciences and boys
drop languages" (Baker 1989, p. 3). Such frameworks say little about
how this teaching will be accomplished. Will girls suffer through bad
teaching to get the required course content, but end up despising math
and science?

If students are to become genuinely more proficient, more
capable of dealing with complexity and change, more highly motivated, and more capable of working both autonomously and with
others, then we have no choice but to teach for meaningfulness.

TEACHER TRAINING

By the time most teachers experience innovative and creative ways
of teaching, they also have experienced a minimum of 14–16 years
of lecture and memorization. It is extremely difficult to turn the resulting ingrained habits around in the three to four courses required
by most state legislatures for teacher credentialing. In addition, many
of those education courses are taught by professors or graduate students
educated in the traditional mode, not by the type of teachers we have
been discussing or through reflective practice. To this day, courses on
educational psychology are assessed through multiple-choice tests
scored by the computer or the Scantron method to make scoring and
grading less time consuming.

Many education professors are adept at teaching in more
creative ways. However, most basic courses are filled with more than
60 students who are geared for content and the all-important grade
needed for acceptance into a practicum or student teaching. Professors
are under pressure to do the writing, research, supervision, and con-
sulting they need for promotion and tenure; and students are under
pressure to fulfill the specified requirements and get the grade. Everyone is caught in the pursuit of outcomes for short-term goals. It is no
wonder that creative solutions are hard to come by. This is, of course,
an excellent example of a system that generates downshifting. Unfortunately, a downshifted society tends not to make good decisions.
Perceived short-term needs and established methods of acting override
what individuals may wish to do or the changes they would like to
implement. Many, perhaps most, education professors would prefer to
teach differently and move away from standard evaluations. But even
their own performance is evaluated by narrow standard forms and
procedures extremely resistant to change. Universities are also deeply
entrenched in the lecture mode of teaching.

In addition, schools on the whole, particularly urban schools, are overwhelmed by social problems that often make much innovative instruction look foolish, particularly when viewed at superficial levels. The demands on teachers today are enormous. They frequently become surrogate parents, police and truant officers, and welfare workers. They are the factory foremen who have to produce the workers that business needs, while operating with a false sense of what is required in a context that ignores essential information. They are asked to exhibit compassion and consideration while implementing a system that discounts many of the essential needs and characteristics of students. And most educators are tested and evaluated according to standards that force them to choose between good teaching and personal survival. In Peter Vail's terms, it really is like having to maneuver a canoe in the rapids of white water, without even being sure where the white water is (Vail 1989).

CAN WE SUCCEED?

We have acknowledged that many of the methods discussed here have been around for a long time. What possible reason is there for assuming that things will finally change?

The pessimist has a strong case. We have seen innumerable efforts at creative, worthwhile methods of instruction go the way of other movements and fragmented approaches. Education has an extraordinary capacity for rebuffing the new and turning back to the tried and true. This is a clear indicator of a downshifted profession. For example, we currently talk of how to facilitate "teacher induction." This term is used to mean that we need to "induce" new teachers to continue teaching, not that we need to change schools to keep creative, enthusiastic teachers. "Induction" itself is a military term for a specific process. When the military metaphor is applied to teaching, then we know that bringing new methodologies and fresh thinking to schools will be difficult because the context is not supportive.

There is also a move toward developing a way to assess teachers on a national basis, similar to the medical profession, in order to elevate the prestige of teachers. But how can a commission to evaluate educators be effective when the research is only beginning to define what education can and should be? The danger is that national standardization will result in one more bureaucratic structure implementing standards based on outmoded conceptions of teaching. The result could easily be the further entrenchment of counterproductive belief systems and a bureaucratic entity that continues to reinvent and perpetuate those systems.

Fortunately, we did not write this book without hope. Optimists might suggest that we are at a point in history where education lags so far behind that we have no choice but to change drastically. They could argue that education is being supported by government and private industry in the push for change. And we are developing a more comprehensive picture of learning, which includes information on the brain and physiology, so that we are actually better equipped to attain our goals.

We also know that change is possible because there are so many superb educators and schools that have succeeded. They are distributed throughout the United States and other countries, in developed and depressed areas, in cities, and in the country. Moreover, wherever we have traveled, we have met large numbers of educators and students with a desire for genuine and profound change. Many of them are successfully networking with each other. And there is evidence of calls for significant parental involvement and community support, as illustrated by the Comer approach, already mentioned (Comer 1987).

Finally, we do not view education as a closed system. Enthusiasm, creativity, and success generate their own momentum. To a large extent, therefore, success is a state of mind. While we do not underestimate the problems, we are very excited about the possibilities.

WHERE TO BEGIN?

T*he single most important step we can take to ensure success is to appreciate that all the factors that influence our students also affect us and our development.* We all innately seek to make sense of our own life experiences. We are driven by our own amalgams of drives, needs, purposes, and constructs. We react to our peripheral environment, both consciously and unconsciously. Our emotions, senses, physical well-being, social relationships, and individual styles all interact with our work and affect it. We are motivated in some ways and demotivated in others by a system of external rewards and punishments. We downshift under threat and respond positively to challenge. And we are capable of enormous creativity, but still operate within the limits of our own internalized social-suggestive norms.

The task, then, is for educators to deeply understand the way in which the brain learns. The more profound the understanding, the easier it is to actually see what is happening in a classroom and to creatively introduce the necessary changes. It is impossible to become an effective brain-based teacher by simply memorizing educational theory and techniques. The grasp of design and artistry, the recognition of levels of meaning, the use of indicators of understanding, the three elements of brain-based learning, and the brain principles need to become the natural knowledge of educators. Then they can be invoked as readily as experts invoke the concepts and procedures of their domains.

THE COMMUNITY OF EDUCATORS

It is impossible for educators, acting alone, to remedy all the ills in education. Nor should that be the objective. A way to begin is by defining our task in terms of making brain-based learning work. That means that we need to be able to elicit and maintain a state of relaxed alertness in students. We have to design appropriate experiences within a well-orchestrated environment. We need to ensure that students both can and do process that experience in multiple ways so that they successfully acquire deeper insights and a more profound understanding of their subjects and themselves. It must be possible for us to confirm that real learning is taking place. And we must be able to sustain this process over time.

There is a double bind that is explored throughout this book. Educators need to be creative—and they need to change. However, change, particularly in view of the demands of society, is a risk that leads to quite dramatic downshifting. And it is difficult for a downshifted person to access creativity. One solution is a group effort.

Restructuring is more likely to succeed when undertaken at the school level. Thus, the ideal context would be one in which an entire school or an entire department embarks on the course with the intention of developing slowly and consistently over time. Charmaine Della Neve (1985), at Drew Elementary School, began brain-compatible learning with a small group of teachers. Eventually, all the teachers joined her; and the school is successful today even though the enthusiasm of teachers varies significantly. Hightstown High School in New Jersey (Shalley 1987) is separated into "houses," each of which has a particular subject focus. The humanities "house" chose to integrate its curriculum, while the rest of the school did not. In both of these cases, restructuring depended on someone with leadership abilities and the conviction that this type of learning could work.

In the absence of leadership from others, educators should voluntarily meet with colleagues from other subject areas. Science, art, language, mathematics, social studies, and all the other subject areas overlap sufficiently. Collaborating with colleagues and learning from them is also a way of bringing enthusiasm and recognition to faculty. This may have to begin with the best and brightest, because faculties are definitely mixed in terms of expertise and willingness to engage in creative and cooperative ventures.

CHANGING THINKING

We suggest that teachers and educators do not change much in their schools or classrooms until their own thinking has begun to shift. It could lead to discouragement if tomorrow they decided to implement specific techniques or methods we have introduced in the book. Instead, we suggest that teachers first acknowledge the interactive processes of immersion, relaxed alertness, and active processing in their personal lives. How is this done?

First, *find new ways to reflect on and process your own experience.* Begin by searching for different ways to see. It helps, sometimes, to see things upside down first to gain a new perspective. Both authors of this book have taken this advice to heart. For example, to our knowledge, Geoffrey is the only person ever to obtain permission from the custodians of the Tate Gallery in London to look at works of art upside down. He was looking at a work called "Linear Construction No. 2." It seemed almost to disappear into itself, so he lay down to see it differently. "I'm dreadfully sorry, Sir," said a voice. "You can't do that. It distracts the public."

Deciding not to take that lying down (so to speak), Geoffrey approached the voice's superior. The latter asked which work of art was to be so examined, gave permission, and then asked politely, "Excuse me, sir, but are you an Australian?" He seemed satisfied with an answer in the affirmative.

Second, *explore what interests you.* If you wish to include music in the classroom, we suggest that you immerse yourself in it first. Sit on the beach on a windy day and listen to Beethoven's *Fifth* as the waves roll in. Listen to George Winston's *December* while watching the rain come down in a forest. Play Vivaldi's *Four Seasons* while watching a brook run in springtime, or create your own experience with music. When you feel the music and your rising enthusiasm, or when the use of music begins to make sense and you can think of a time and place where it might fit, that is the time to introduce it to the classroom. Play it first as a background, perhaps, and let new ideas and connections unfold.

The same is true of art. Visit an art gallery with someone who loves and knows art and can explain the hidden nuances and meanings expressed by the artist. Enroll in an art class and play with paints and hues and colors. If time does not allow for that, make a lunch date with someone totally enthusiastic about art. Buy some meaningful posters for your classroom. Begin by putting up posters that you enjoy, and work toward orchestrating art to complement your thinking and, finally, a lesson you are planning.

RELAXED ALERTNESS

In our experience, many people find it difficult to reconcile being relaxed and alert with being a teacher. Fortunately, we are not talking of perfection. What we are talking about is change. And what counts most is a turning around. Most of the engagement in learning and health that we want for our students, teachers must provide for themselves.

The two dominant characteristics of relaxed alertness are a degree of general relaxation and intrinsic motivation. Because that is what we seek to create in students, that is what we need in ourselves. Teachers may find it helpful to participate in programs such as "The Turning Point,"* which provides seminars on teaching and learning from within, or other similar programs.

RELAXATION

Take time out to genuinely relax. Reflect on how it feels to be happy and relaxed and begin to do the things that help you and your students experience this while actively engaged in learning. We suggest approaching this in two phases. The first involves relaxation techniques, and the key to that, after finding the right one, is persistence. The second involves life management, and the key to that is support.

We do not believe that relaxation techniques should be restricted to any one particular method, but to maximize the functioning of our own brains and manage the myriad of stresses, we find these techniques absolutely essential. Such techniques instill a general state of relaxed alertness and reverse the fight-or-flight syndrome with its debilitating hormones and their potential effect on brain functioning.

As we point out in Chapter 10, the evidence suggests that meditation twice a day for 20 minutes will, over time, trigger changes in our blood pressure, metabolism, capacity to sleep, and bodily stress. Fortunately, there are many well-researched procedures currently available. As already suggested, Transcendental Meditation (TM) is still available. Benson (1976), a Harvard physician who carried out some of the first research on TM, has developed a modified approach that he calls the *relaxation response*. The time requirements are the same, but the mental exercise is slightly different. Other relaxation procedures abound, ranging from the progressive relaxation of Jacobson (1938) to the visualization exercises available on cassettes everywhere. Jacobson's approach is to alternately stretch and then relax each muscle system so that at the end of about 20 minutes the entire body is relaxed. Visualizations vary enormously; each person must find what

---

*The Turning Point, P.O. Box 8166, San Bernadino, CA 92412. Telephone: (714) 867-2107.

works best. Stress management, which is much more complex, includes an exploration of our own deep meanings and changes in perception.

INTRINSIC MOTIVATION

Intrinsic motivation means that we do something for the joy of it and not for what we can get or to fulfill other people's goals and expected outcomes. It is a point acknowledged by some in the business world. Thus, "the most successful firms attract and retain employees by providing an environment that is intellectually engaging" (Applegate, Cash, and Mills 1988). Indeed, there is a strong link between distress and meaninglessness. Where an opportunity is provided to make work meaningful, distress is significantly reduced.

It is essential, therefore, to find a way to love what we do or do what we love. Once again, regain enthusiasm for the subject you are teaching. Begin to talk to others about their "loves" and look for ways that your subject can be expanded and connected to others. Reclaim your own creativity because it is absolutely vital to making genuine changes in the classroom. *In brain-based learning, the emphasis is on the teacher's creativity, and not on the ability to implement what others have created.*

TEACHER PRESTIGE

Much of what we seek to implement depends more on educator prestige than on the methods used (see Chapter 10). A teacher's prestige, in the eyes of students, is critical if they are to access what Lozanov (1978a, b) calls their "hidden reserves" of initiative and creativity. Prestige is responsible, in large measure, for the extent to which a teacher can be trusted. This trust opens the learner to input from the teacher.

Prestige can be developed in many ways. One, as Carl Rogers (1983) noted, is for teachers to have positive regard for students. This follows necessarily if they are to trust us. As we strive for double planeness, we may find that we actually do not like teaching or being with students.

The difficult aspect of prestige is that it cannot be imposed. We can make students fear us. We can elicit all sorts of other responses, as well, so that students want to please us. But what we need is students who are willing to risk. And they will risk in our classes when they sense at a deep level that risk taking is okay and the teacher deeply supports their exploration.

Double planeness is acquired as a result of self-knowledge. Hence, as teachers, we need to put effort into monitoring the reasons why we do what we do. In effect, it is a matter of probing our own deep meanings. This is not done overnight. Nor is it solely a matter of going to a counselor or therapist. We have pointed out that our emotions and beliefs interpenetrate our own understandings. Hence, we need to acquire the tools for probing ourselves, privately and with others, as a part of what motivates us. In other words, we need to consistently engage in reflection on our own experiences. Active processing, therefore, needs to be regularly introduced into our own lives.

HINTS ON ORCHESTRATING THE ENVIRONMENT

Decide on a metaphor for your classroom. Choose one that will provide the most productive environment for human learners. This means a lively—and alive—environment, based on a comfortable, organized model. A well-run home or small community is better than a factory and production line.

For example, a good home or a healthy family has certain important characteristics. It consists of a coherent group. Everyone has responsibilities. People talk to each other but generally respect and tolerate each other. Problems are worked out in the group and with the help of others. The family members affect each other—when one person wins, everyone feels successful. Plants and living things other than humans are welcome and are taken care of by designated individuals. In a classroom with such a metaphor, fun, hard work, and responsibility are not strangers.

For older students, the corporate family might provide a better model. The work of students becomes meaningful. They work with outside agents such as business or community groups, and they bring what they have learned back to class. They discuss their projects with fellow students.

TEACHING DESIGN

Teachers can begin by designing a thematic unit. As we discuss in Chapter 9, thematic units engage emotions, social relationships, and complex cognitive processing through intellectual challenge. Look at the curriculum guide and organize what is to be taught by finding an object, picture, or work of art that represents the subject matter on a broad level. If the subject is history and you are studying the Industrial Revolution, for example, begin by finding a provocative painting about this time in history. Imagine what it was like to live then and intrigue students with the reality of these times. Perhaps you begin by reading a brief story, or telling one. How would their (the students') lives be different if they were living at that time? How did democracy help people in the Industrial Revolution? Find a story about a union boss—

have students rewrite it as a brief play. Find a poignant part of a poem or story and read it to music. Engage students' imagination and understanding and then allow them to reconstruct this time period through group and individual projects, demonstrations, drama, and collections of art and music, which say more than a textbook can ever say. What you will find is that students will be thinking and talking about the Industrial Revolution not only in class but at lunch and at home. You will also find that your students will be teaching you.

SIGNIFICANT REORGANIZATION AND CHANGE

Teachers often respond enthusiastically to genuinely creative teaching. In fact, we believe that many teachers would intuitively prefer to teach in the ways we have described. Panic sets in , however, in part because of the fear that such teaching does not appear to take into consideration what they are supposed to cover in the text and the curriculum guide. The problem is that an overemphasis on output, performance, and the short term prevents us from really using our brains and maximizing learning. A deep shift in the appreciation of outcomes is needed. We simply must part with the idea that specific pieces of information "taught" to learners for rewards is an effective use of our brains or theirs. That type of teaching does not work well and does not engage the brain sufficiently. For the shift to occur, we need to seek the patterns that connect. The answer lies in teaching for meaning.

Change, of course, takes time. All learning is developmental, including the learning of educators. Many of the changes that are needed will also appear in unexpected ways and from unpredictable sources. Some of the most unlikely people will become the most valuable colleagues and collaborators. The transition from fragmentation to a higher degree of order is not easy. It is clear, however, that when the right conditions are established, the transition can occur. Setting out to participate in the change is exciting, challenging, and immensely rewarding.

From this hour I ordain myself loos'd of limits and imaginary lines,
Going where I list, my own master total and absolute,
Listening to others, considering well what they say,
Pausing, searching, receiving, contemplating,
Gently, but with undeniable will, divesting myself of the holds
    that would hold me

Walt Whitman, "Song of the Open Road,"
Leaves of Grass, [1892] 1958

BIBLIOGRAPHY

Adams, M.J., and A. Collins. (1977). *A Schema-Theoretic View of Reading*. Technical Report No. 32. Cambridge: Bolt Beranek and Newman.

Altweger, B., C. Edelsky, and B. Flores. (1987). "Whole Language: What's New?" *The Reading Teacher* 41, 2: 144–154.

Amabile, T. (1983). *The Social Psychology of Creativity*. New York: Springer-Verlag.

Amabile, T. (1985). "Motivation and Creativity: Effects of Motivational Orientation on Creative Writers." *Journal of Personality and Social Psychology* 48, 2: 393–397.

Amabile, T. (1986). "Social Influences on Creativity: The Effects of Contracted-for Reward." *Journal of Personality and Social Psychology* 50, 1: 14–23.

Amend, A., D. Lynch, and P. Conrad, creators. (1989). *Your Musical Heritage*. (videotape). Cedar Rapids, Iowa: Kirkwood Productions, Kirkwood Community College.

Ames, K. (Fall/Winter 1990). "Why Jane Can't Draw (or Sing, or Dance . . .)" *Newsweek* (Special Issue). *Education: A Consumer's Handbook*.

Anderson, J.R. (1980). *Cognitive Psychology and Its Implications*. San Francisco: W.H. Freeman and Company.

Anderson, R.C., R.E. Reynolds, D.L. Schallert, and E.T. Goetz. (1976). *Frameworks for Comprehending Discourse*. Technical Report No. 12. Urbana-Champaign: University of Illinois, Laboratory for Cognitive Studies in Education.

Anderson, R.C., R.J. Spiro, and M.C. Anderson. (1977). *Schemata as Scaffolding for the Representation of Information in Connected Discourse*. Technical Report No. 24. Urbana-Champaign: University of Illinois, Center for the Study of Reading.

Applegate, L.M., J.I. Cash, and D.Q. Mills. (November/December 1988). "Information Technology and Tomorrow's Magic." *Harvard Business Review* 66, 6: 128.

Asher, J. (1982). *Learning Another Language Through Actions: The Complete Teacher Guide Book*. Los Gatos, Calif.: Sky Oaks Productions.

Asimov, I. (1983). *The Foundation Trilogy*. New York: Ballantine Books.

Bach, R. (1977). *Illusions*. London: Heinemann.

Baker, K. (1989). "The British Government's Reform Program for Secondary Education." In *Education: Pathways to Reform*, pp. 2–6. Proceedings of the IPA Education Policy Unit Conference (Chair: Dame Leonie Kramer). Australian Capital Territory (ACT), Australia: Institute of Public Affairs Limited, Education Policy Unit.

Barzakov, I. (July 14, 1988). Unpublished workshop notes. *Optimalearning*™ *Workshop*.

Bateson, G. (1980). *Mind and Nature: A Necessary Unity*. New York: Bantam Books.

Benderly, B.L. (September 1989). "Everyday Intuition." *Psychology Today* 23, 9: 35–40.

Bennett, E.L., M.C. Diamond, D. Krech, and M.R. Rozenzweig. (1964). "Chemical and Anatomical Plasticity of the Brain." *Science* 146: 610–619.

Benson, H. (1976). *The Relaxation Response*. New York: Avon.

Biehler, R.F., and J. Snowman. (1990). *Psychology Applied to Teaching*. 6th ed. Boston: Houghton-Mifflin.

Bitting, P.F., and R.T. Clift. (1988). "Reflection upon Reflection: The Classical and Modern Views." In *Images of Reflection in Teacher Education*, edited by H. Waxman, H.J. Freiberg, J. Vaughan, and M. Weil. Reston, Va.: Association of Teacher Educators.

Bloom, B., M. Englehart, E. Furst, W. Hill, and D. Krathwohl. (1956). *Taxonomy of Educational Objectives: The Classification of Educational Goals. Handbook 1: Cognitive Domain.* New York: Longmans Green.

Bloomfield, H.H., M.P. Cain, and D.T. Jaffe. (1975). *TM: Discovering Inner Energy and Overcoming Stress.* New York: Delacourt Press.

Bloomfield, H.H., and R.B. Kory. (1976). *Happiness: The TM Program, Psychiatry and Enlightenment.* New York: Dawn Press, Simon and Schuster.

Bohm, D. (1987). *Unfolding Meaning: A Weekend of Dialogue with David Bohm.* London: Ark Paperbacks.

Boorstin, D.J. (1988). *The Image: A Guide to Pseudo-Events in America.* New York: Macmillan.

Borysenko, J. (1987). *Minding the Body, Mending the Mind.* Reading, Mass.: Addison-Wesley.

Boyer, E.L. (1983). *High School: A Report on Secondary Education in America.* New York: Harper and Row.

Brandt, R.S., exec. ed. (May 1986). "Frameworks for Teaching Thinking." *Educational Leadership* 43, 8: (Whole Issue).

Brandt, R.S. (1986). "On Improving Achievement of Minority Children: A Conversation with James Comer." *Educational Leadership* 43, 5: 13–17.

Bransford, D., and M. Johnson. (1972). "Contextual Prerequisites for Understanding: Some Investigations of Comprehensive Recall." *Journal of Verbal Learning and Verbal Behavior* 11: 717–721.

Brown, G.I. (1971). *Human Teaching for Human Learning: An Introduction to Confluent Education.* New York: Viking.

Bruner, J., J. Goodnow, and G.A. Austin. (1967). *A Study of Thinking.* New York: Wiley.

Caine, G., and R.N. Caine. (1989). "Learning about Accelerated Learning." *Training and Development Journal* 43, 5: 64.

Caine, G., and R.N. Caine. (1990). "What We Know about Learning." *Data Training* 9, 3: 26–32.

Caine, R.N., and G. Caine. (1990). "Understanding a Brain-Based Approach to Learning and Teaching." *Educational Leadership* 48, 2: 66–70.

Campbell, J. (1982). *Grammatical Man: Information, Entropy, Language, and Life.* New York: Simon and Schuster.

Campbell, J. (1989). *The Improbable Machine.* New York: Simon and Schuster.

Canfield, J., and H. Wells. (1976). *One Hundred and One Ways to Enhance Self-Concept in the Classroom.* Englewood Cliffs, N.J.: Prentice-Hall.

Carbo, M., R. Dunn, and K. Dunn. (1986). *Teaching Students to Read Through Their Individual Learning Styles.* Englewood Cliffs, N.J.: Prentice-Hall.

Carnegie Forum on Education and the Economy. (1986). *A Nation Prepared: Teachers for the Twenty-First Century.* Report of the Task Force on Teaching as a Profession. 3rd printing. New York: Carnegie Corporation of New York.

Carnegie Foundation. (1988). *An Imperiled Generation—Saving Urban Schools.* Special Report. Princeton, N.J.: Carnegie Foundation for the Advancement of Teaching.

California English/Language Arts Framework. (1988). Sacramento: California State Department of Education.

California History/Social Science Framework. (1988). Sacramento: California State Department of Education.

California Science Framework. (1990). Sacramento: California State Department of Education.

Carrington, P. (1977). *Freedom in Meditation*. Garden City, N.Y.: Anchor Press, Doubleday.

Center for Civic Education. (1987). *We the People*. Calabasas, Calif: Center for Civic Education.

Cermack, L.S., and F.I.M. Craik, eds. (1979). *Levels of Processing in Human Memory*. New York: Wiley.

Chang, T.M. (1986). "Semantic Memory: Facts and Models." *Psychological Bulletin* 99, 2: 199–220.

Chi, M.T.H. (1976). "Short-Term Memory Limitations in Children: Capacity and Processing Deficits." *Memory and Cognition* 4: 559–572.

Chopra, D. (1990). *Perfect Health: The Complete Mind/Body Guide* New York: Harmony Books.

Clark, B. (1986). *Optimizing Learning*. Columbus, Ohio: Merrill.

Clynes, M. (1977). *Sentics: The Touch of Emotions*. New York: Anchor Press, Doubleday.

Cohen, E.G. (1984). "Talking and Working Together: Status, Interaction and Learning." In *The Social Context of Instruction* (pp. 171–187), edited by P.L. Peterson, L.R. Wilkinson, and M. Hallihan. New York: Academic Press.

Cohen, E.G., and R.A. Lotan. (1990). "Teacher as Supervisor of Complex Technology." *Theory into Practice* 29, 2: 78–84.

Cohen, E.G., R.A. Lotan, and L. Catanzarite. (1990). "Treating Status Problems in the Cooperative Classroom." In *Cooperative Learning: Research and Theory*, edited by S. Sharan. New York: Praeger.

Cohen, E.G., R.A. Lotan, and C. Leechor. (April 1989). "Can Classrooms Learn?" *Sociology of Education* 62: 75–94.

Combs, A.W., ed. (1962). *Perceiving, Behaving, Becoming: A New Focus for Education. 1962 Yearbook of the Association for Supervision and Curriculum Development*. Alexandria, Va.: ASCD.

Combs, A.W., R. Blume, A. Newman, and H. Wass. (1974). *The Professional Education of Teachers*. 2nd ed. Boston: Allyn and Bacon.

Combs, A.W., A.C. Richards, and F. Richards. (1976). *Perceptual Psychology: A Humanistic Approach to the Study of Persons*. New York: Harper and Row.

Combs, A.W., and D. Snygg. (1949). *Individual Behavior: A Perceptual Approach to Behavior*. New York: Harper and Row.

Comer, J. (November 1987). "Building Quality Relationships" In *Making Schools Work for Underachieving Minority Students: Next Steps for Research, Policy and Practice*. Proceedings of the conference on "Our National Dilemma." ERIC document ED 294949, Speeches/Meeting Papers.

Coughlin, E.K. (May 23, 1990). "Renewed Appreciation of Connections Between Body and Mind Stimulate Researchers to Harness Healing Powers of the Arts." *The Chronicle of Higher Education* 36: A6.

Cousins, N. (1989). *Head First: The Biology of Hope*. New York: E.P. Dutton.

Cowan, P.A. (1978). *Piaget with Feeling: Cognitive, Social and Emotional Dimensions*. New York: Holt, Rinehart and Winston.

Craik, F.J.M., and R.S. Lockhart. (1975). "Levels of Processing: A Framework for Memory Research." *Journal of Experimental Psychology: General* 104: 268–294.

Crowell, S. (1989). "A New Way of Thinking: The Challenge of the Future." *Educational Leadership* 47, 1: 60.

Davis, G.A., and M.A. Thomas. (1989). *Effective Schools and Effective Teachers*. Boston: Allyn and Bacon.

Deci, E.L. (1980). *The Psychology of Self-Determination*. Lexington, Mass.: D.D. Heath.

Deci, E.L., and R.M. Ryan. (1987). "The Support of Autonomy and the Control of Behavior." *Journal of Personality and Social Psychology* 53, 6: 1024–1037.

Della Neve, C. (October 1985). "Brain-Compatible Learning Succeeds." *Educational Leadership* 43, 2: 83–85.

Dewey, J. (1962). *Reconstruction in Philosophy*. New York: The Beacon Press.

Dewey, J. (1965). *Experience and Education*. New York: Collier.

Dewey, J. (1966). *Democracy and Education: An Introduction to the Philosophy of Education*. New York: The Free Press.

Dhority, L. (1982). Unpublished workshop notes.

Dhority, L. (1984). *Acquisition Through Creative Teaching (ACT)*. Sharon, Mass.: Center for Continuing Development.

Diamond, M. (March 23, 1985). *Brain Growth in Response to Experience*. Seminar, University of California, Riverside.

Diamond, M. (January 1987). "Brain Growth in Response to Experience." Paper presented at *Educating Tomorrow's Children* seminar. California Neuropsychology Services, San Francisco.

Diamond, M. (1988). *Enriching Heredity: The Impact of the Environment on the Anatomy of the Brain*. New York: The Free Press.

Diamond, M., A. Scheibel, G. Murphy, and T. Harvey. (1985). "On the Brain of a Scientist: Albert Einstein." *Experimental Neurology* 88: 198–204.

Dienstbier, R.A. (January 1989). "Arousal and Physiological Toughness: Implications for Mental and Physical Health." *Psychological Review* 96, 1: 84–100.

Dillon, R., and R. Sternberg, eds. (1986). *Cognition and Instruction*. Orlando, Fla.: Academic Press, Inc., Harcourt, Brace, Jovanovich.

Doll, W.E.J. (1986). "Curriculum Beyond Stability: Schön, Prigogine, Piaget." Unpublished manuscript.

Doll, W.E.J. (1989). "Complexity in the Classroom." *Educational Leadership* 47, 1: 65–70.

Dolson, D.P., project leader. (1984). *Studies on Immersion Education: A Collection for United States Educators*. A report prepared under the direction of the Office of Bilingual and Bicultural Education. Sacramento, Calif.: California State Department of Education.

Dunn, R. (1978). *Teaching Students Through Their Individual Learning Styles: A Practical Approach*. Reston, Va.: Reston Publishing Company.

Eccles, J.C. (1989). *Evolution of the Brain: Creation of the Self*. London: Routledge.

Edwards, B. (1979). *Drawing on the Right Side of the Brain*. Los Angeles: J.P. Tarcher.

Eisler, R. (1987). *The Chalice and the Blade*. San Francisco: Harper and Row.

Ekman, P. (1985). *Telling Lies*. New York: W.W. Norton.

Emery, F., ed. (1969). *Systems Thinking*. New York: Penguin Books.

Epstein, H. (1978). *Education and the Brain: The 77th Yearbook of the National Society for the Study of Education*. Chicago: The Yearbook Committee and Associated Contributors, University of Chicago Press.

Factor, D. (1987). "Introduction. D. Bohm." In *Understanding Meaning: A Weekend of Dialogue with David Bohm*. London: Ark Paperbacks.

Fadiman, D. (1988). *Why Do These Children Love School?* (videotape). Menlo Park, Calif.: Concentric Media.

Fellows, K., and N.L. Zimpher. (1988). "Reflectivity and the Instructional Process: A Definitional Comparison Between Theory and Practice." In *Images of Reflection in Teacher Education*, edited by H.C. Waxman, H.J. Freiberg, J.C. Vaughan, and M. Weil. Reston, Va.: Association of Teacher Educators.

Finn, C. (1989). "Reforming Secondary Education in the United States." In *Education: Pathways to Reform*, pp. 22–28, 32. Proceedings of the IPA Education Policy Unit Conference (Chair: Dame Leonie Kramer). Australian Capital Territory (ACT), Australia: Institute of Public Affairs Limited, Education Policy Unit.

Flores, B., and E. Garcia. (1984). "A Collaborative Learning and Teaching Experience Using Journal Writing." *Journal of the National Association for Bilingual Education* 8, 2: 67–83.

Flores, B., E. Garcia, S. Gonzalez, G. Hidalgo, K. Kaczmarek, and T. Romero. (1986). *Holistic Bilingual Instructional Strategies*. Phoenix, Ariz.: Exito.

Flores, B., and E. Hernandez. (December 1988). "A Bilingual Kindergartner's Sociopsychogenesis of Literacy and Biliteracy." *Dialogue* 5, 3: 2.

Forem, J. (1974). *Transcendental Meditation*. New York: E.P. Dutton.

Fulghum, R. (1988). *All I Really Need to Know I Learned in Kindergarten*. New York: Ivy Books.

Galyean, C. (March 1983). "Guided Imagery in the Curriculum." *Educational Leadership* 40: 53–58.

Gardner, H. (1982). *Art, Mind and Brain: A Cognitive Approach to Creativity*. New York: Basic Books.

Gardner, H. (1985). *Frames of Mind: The Theory of Multiple Intelligences*. New York: Basic Books.

Gazzaniga, M. (1985). *The Social Brain: Discovering the Networks of the Mind*. New York: Basic Books.

Gazzaniga, M. (1988). *Perspectives in Memory Research*. Cambridge: The Massachusetts Institute of Technology Press.

Gendlin, E.T. (1962). *Experiencing and the Creation of Meaning*. Glencoe, Calif.: The Free Press of Glencoe (a division of Macmillan).

Gendlin, E.T. (1981). *Focusing*. 2nd ed. New York: Bantam Books.

George, J.C. (1972). *Julie of the Wolves*. New York: Harper and Row.

Girdano, D., and G.S. Everly. (1986). *Controlling Stress and Tension: A Holistic Approach*. 2nd. ed. Englewood Cliffs, N.J.: Prentice-Hall.

Gleick, J. (1987). *Chaos: Making a New Science*. New York: Viking.

Goodman, K. (1986). *What's Whole in Whole Language?* Portsmouth, N.H.: Heinemann.

Goodman, K., and Y. Goodman. (1979). "Learning to Read is Natural." In *Theory and Practice of Early Reading*, edited by L. Resnick and P. Weaver. Hillsdale, N.J.: Lawrence Erlbaum.

Gordon, T. (1974). *T.E.T.: Teacher Effectiveness Training*. New York: David McKay.

Gordon, W. (1961). *Synectics: The Development of Creative Capacity*. New York: Harper and Row.

Gregory, R.L., ed. (1987). *The Oxford Companion to the Mind*. Oxford: Oxford University Press.

Gruneberg, M.M., and P.E. Morris. (1979). *Applied Problems in Memory*. London: Academic Press.

Halgren, E., C.L. Wilson, N.K. Squires, J. Engel, R.D. Walter, and P.H. Crandall. (1983). "Dynamics of the Hippocampal Contribution to Memory: Stimulation and Recording Studies in Humans." In *Molecular, Cellular and Behavioral Neurobiology of the Hippocampus*, edited by W. Seifert. New York: Academic Press.

Hainstock, E.G. (1971). *Teaching Montessori in the Home: The School Years*. New York: New American Library.

Hand, J.D. (1984). "Split Brain Theory and Recent Results in Brain Research: Implications for the Design of Instruction." In *Instructional Development: The State of the Art. Vol. 2*, edited by R.K. Bass and C.R. Dills. Dubuque, Iowa: Kendall/Hunt.

Harman, W. (1988). *Global Mind Change*. Indianapolis: Knowledge Systems.

Harste, J.C. (1989). *New Policy Guidelines for Reading: Connecting Research and Practice*. Urbana, Ill.: National Council of Teachers of English and the ERIC Clearinghouse on Reading and Communication Skills.

Hart, L. (1975). *How the Brain Works: A New Understanding of Human Learning, Emotion, and Thinking*. New York: Basic Books.

Hart, L. (1983). *Human Brain, Human Learning*. New York: Longman.

Hartshorn, H., and M. May. (1928). *Studies in Deceit*. New York: Macmillan.

Haynes, N.M., J.P. Comer, and M. Hamilton-Lee. (Spring 1989). "School Climate Enhancement Through Parental Involvement." *Journal of School Psychology* 27, 1: 87–90.

Hermann, D.J., and J.R. Hanwood. (1980). "More Evidence for the Existence of Separate Semantic and Episodic Stores in Long-Term Memory." *Journal of Experimental Psychology: Human Learning and Memory* 6, 5: 467–478.

Hindle, B. (December 1982). "Now and Then: Necessity Is *Not* the Mother of Invention." *American Heritage* 34, 1: 8–9.

Holden, C. (1979). "Paul MacLean and the Triune Brain." (Comments and Notes). *Science* 204, 4397: 1066–1068.

Hooper, J., and D. Teresi. (1986). *The Three-Pound Universe: The Brain, from Chemistry of Mind to New Frontiers of the Soul*. New York: Dell.

Hooper, K. (1988). *Interactive Multimedia Design*. Technical Report No. 13. Cupertino, Calif.: Apple Computer Inc.

Horne, J.A. (1989). "Sleep Loss and Divergent Thinking Ability." *Sleep* 11, 6: 528–536.

Houston, J. (1981). "Education." In *Millenium: Glimpses into the 21st Century*, edited by A. Villoldo and K. Dychtwald. Los Angeles: J.P. Tarcher.

Hughes, M. (Winter 1984). "Using the Means of Suggestion to Harmonize with Barriers." *The Journal of the Society for Accelerative Learning and Teaching* 9, 4: 257–269.

Hunt, M. (1982). *The Universe Within: A New Science Explores the Human Mind*. New York: Simon and Schuster.

Hunter, M. (1990). "Preface: Thoughts on Staff Development." In *Changing School Culture Through Staff Development: 1990 Yearbook of the Association for Supervision and Curriculum Development*, edited by B. Joyce. Alexandria, Va.: ASCD.

International Association for the Evaluation of Educational Achievement (IEA). (1988). *Science Achievement in Seventeen Countries: A Preliminary Report*. New York: Pergamon Press.

Isaacson, R.L. (1982). *The Limbic System*. 2nd ed. New York: Plenum Press.

Jacobs, H.H., ed. (1989). *Interdisciplinary Curriculum: Design and Implementation*. Alexandria, Va.: ASCD.

Jacobs, W.J., and L. Nadel. (1985). "Stress-Induced Recovery of Fears and Phobias." *Psychological Review* 92, 4: 512–531.

Jacobson, E. (1938). *Progressive Relaxation*. Chicago: University of Chicago Press.

Jaques, E. (1986). "The Development of Intellectual Capability: A Discussion of Stratified Systems Theory." *The Journal of Applied Behavioral Science* 22, 4: 361–383.

Jelen, H.G., and K.K. Urban. (1988). "Assessing Creative Potential World-Wide: The First Cross-Cultural Application of the Test for Creative Thinking-Drawing Production (TCT–DP)." *The Creative Child and Adult Quarterly* 14, 3: 151–167.

Jenkins, J.R., and S.L. Deno. (1971). "Influence of Knowledge and Type of Objectives on Subject Matter Learning." *Journal of Educational Psychology* 62: 67–70.

Jensen, E.P. (1988). *Super Teaching: Master Strategies for Building Student Success.* Dubuque, Iowa: Kendall/Hunt Publishing Company.

Johnson, D.W., G. Murayama, R.T. Johnson, D. Nelson, and L. Skon. (1981). "Effect of Cooperative, Competitive and Individualistic Goal Structures on Achievement: A Meta-analysis." *Psychological Bulletin* 89: 47–62.

Johnston, L. (1990). "For Better or for Worse." (syndicated comic strip). *Los Angeles Times.*

Joyce, B., ed. (1990). *Changing School Culture Through Staff Development: 1990 Yearbook of the Association for Supervision and Curriculum Development.* Alexandria, Va.: ASCD.

Justice, B. (1987). *Who Gets Sick: Thinking and Health.* Houston, Tex.: Peak Press.

Kaufeldt, M. (1984). *I Can Divide and Conquer.* Oak Creek, Ariz.: Susan Kovalik and Associates.

Kelly, G. (1955). *The Psychology of Personal Constructs.* New York: Norton.

Klausmeier, H.J., and P.S. Allen. (1978). *Cognitive Development in Children and Youth: A Longitudinal Study.* New York: Academic Press.

Kline, P. (1988). *The Everyday Genius: Restoring Children's Natural Joy of Learning—and Yours Too.* Arlington, Va.: Great Ocean Publishers.

Koestler, A. (1972). *The Roots of Coincidence.* London: Hutchinson.

Kohn, A. (1986). "How to Succeed Without Really Vying." *Psychology Today* 20, 9: 10.

Kohn, A. (1987a). "Art for Art's Sake." *Psychology Today* 21, 9: 52–57.

Kohn, A. (1987b). "It's Hard to Get Left Out of a Pair." *Psychology Today* 21, 10: 52–57.

Kohn, A. (December 4, 1989). "Reward and Creativity." *Los Angeles Times,* Metro, B2.

Kolb, B., and I.Q. Whishaw. (1985). *Fundamentals of Human Neuropsychology.* 2nd ed. New York: W.H. Freeman.

Kovalik, S. (1986). *Teachers Make the Difference—With Integrated Thematic Instruction.* Oak Creek, Ariz.: Susan Kovalik and Associates.

Lakoff, G. (1987). *Women, Fire, and Dangerous Things.* Chicago: University of Chicago Press.

Lakoff, G., and M. Johnson. (1980). *Metaphors We Live By.* Chicago: University of Chicago Press.

Leonard, G. (1981). *The Transformation.* Los Angeles: J.P. Tarcher.

Leonard, G. (1987). *Education and Ecstasy: And the Great School Reform Hoax.* rev. ed. Berkeley, Calif.: North Atlantic.

Levy, B. (1972). "Do Teachers Sell Girls Short?" *Today's Education* 61: 27–29.

Levy, J. (May 1985). "Right Brain, Left Brain: Fact and Fiction." *Psychology Today* 19: 38.

Lolas, F., and H. Mayer, eds. (1987). *Perspectives on Stress and Stress-Related Topics.* Heidelberg, Germany: Springer-Verlag.

Lozanov, G. (1978a). *Suggestology and Outlines of Suggestopedy.* New York: Gordon and Breach.

Lozanov, G. (1978b). *Suggestology and Suggestopedia—Theory and Practice*. Working document for the Expert Working Group, United Nations Educational, Scientific and Cultural Organization (UNESCO). (ED–78/WS/119).

Lund, R.D. (1978). *Development and Plasticity of the Brain: An Introduction*. New York: Oxford University Press.

Luria, A.R. (1973). *The Working Brain: An Introduction to Neuropsychology*. New York: Basic Books.

Luria, A.R. (1980). *Higher Cortical Functions in Man*. 2nd ed. New York: Basic Books.

Lynch, D., and P.L. Kordis. (1989). *Strategy of the Dolphin*. New York: Morrow.

Lynch, G. (1986). *Synapses, Circuits, and the Beginnings of Memory*. Cambridge: The Massachusetts Institute of Technology Press.

Lynch, J.J. (1985). *The Language of the Heart: The Body's Response to Human Dialogue*. New York: Basic Books.

MacLean, P.D. (1969). "New Trends in Man's Evolution." In *A Triune Concept of the Brain and Behavior*. Papers presented at Queen's University, Ontario, 1969. Ann Arbor, Mich.: Books On Demand, University Microfilms International.

MacLean, P.D. (1978). "A Mind of Three Minds: Educating the Triune Brain." In *The 77th Yearbook of the National Society for the Study of Education*, pp. 308–342. Chicago: University of Chicago Press.

Marsh, H.W., and R. Shavelson. (1985). "Self-Concept: Its Multifaceted, Hierarchical Structure." *Educational Psychologist* 20, 3: 107–123.

Martel, L.D. (1989). *A Working Solution for the Nation's Schools: The Validation Report on Integrative Learning at the Guggenheim School*. Syracuse, N.Y.: Center for the Study of Learning and Retention, Syracuse University.

Maslow, A.H. (1968). *Toward a Psychology of Being*. New York: D. Van Nostrand.

McAuliffe, K. (February 1990). "Get Smart: Controlling Chaos." *Omni* 12, 5: 43.

McCabe, M.E., and J. Rhoades. (1988). *The Nurturing Classroom: Developing Self-Esteem, Thinking Skills and Responsibility Through Simple Cooperation*. Willits, Calif.: ITA Publications.

McCarthy, B. (1981). *The 4MAT System—Teaching to Learning Styles with Right/ Left Mode Techniques*. 2nd ed. Barrington, Ill.: Excel.

McCloskey, M., and J. Santee. (1981). "Notes, Comments, and New Findings. Are Semantic Memory and Episodic Memory Distinct Systems?" *Journal of Experimental Psychology: Human Learning and Memory* 7, 1: 66–71.

McGuinness, D., and K. Pribram. (1980). "The Neuropsychology of Attention: Emotional and Motivational Controls." In *The Brain and Psychology*, edited by M.D. Wittrock. New York: Academic Press.

Melton, R.L. (May 10, 1990). "Reed Students Prove They Know Their Bill of Rights." *Reno Gazette-Journal*, 1E.

Merritt, S. (1989). *Successful, Non-Stressful Learning: Applying the Lozanov Method to All Subject Areas*. San Diego: Stephanie Merritt.

Miller, E.F., and S. Halpern. (1980). *Letting Go of Stress* (audiotape). Stanford, Calif.: Halpern Sounds.

Miller, G.A. (1956). "The Magical Number Seven Plus or Minus Two: Sum Limits to Our Capacity for Processing Information." *Psychological Review* 6, 3:81–97.

Minsky, M. (1975). "A Framework for Representing Knowledge." In *The Psychology of Computer Vision*, edited by P.H. Winston. New York: McGraw-Hill.

Montessori, M. (1965). *The Montessori Method*. Cambridge, Mass.: Robert Bentley.

Moraes, E.R. (1986). "Sociolinguistic Determinants of Academic Achievement in Brazilian Public Schools." Paper presented at annual meeting of the American Educational Research Association, San Francisco.

Moss, D.M., and E. Keen. (1981). "The Nature of Consciousness: The Existential-Phenomenological Approach." In *The Metaphors of Consciousness* (Ch. 4, pp. 107–120), edited by R.S. Valle and R.V. von Eckartsberg. New York: Plenum Press.

Murphy, M., and S. Donovan. (1988). *The Physical and Psychological Effects of Meditation.* San Rafael, Calif.: Esalen Institute.

Muuss, R.E. (1988). *Theories of Adolescence.* 5th ed. New York: Random House.

Nadel, L. (1989). "Down's Syndrome in Neurological Perspective." Unpublished manuscript.

Nadel, L., and J. Wilmer. (1980). "Context and Conditioning: A Place for Space." *Physiological Psychology* 8: 218–228.

Nadel, L., J. Wilmer, and E.M. Kurz. (1984). "Cognitive Maps and Environmental Context." In *Context and Learning*, edited by P. Balsam and A. Tomi. Hillsdale, N.J.: Lawrence Erlbaum.

Naranjo, C., and R.E. Ornstein. (1973). *On the Psychology of Meditation.* New York: Viking.

Nelson, C.A., and F. Horowitz. (1983). "The Perception of Facial Expressions and Stimulus Motion by Two and Five Month Old Infants Using Holographic Stimuli." *Child Development* 54, 4: 868–877.

Nummela, R., and D. Avila. (1980). "Self-Concept and Teacher Effectiveness Training." *The College Student Journal* 14, 3: 314–316.

Nummela, R., and T. Rosengren. (1986). "What's Happening in Students' Brains May Redefine Teaching." *Educational Leadership* 43, 8: 49–53.

Nummela, R., and T. Rosengren. (1988). "The Brain's Routes and Maps: Vital Connections in Learning." *NAASP Bulletin* 72: 83–86.

O'Keefe, J., and L. Nadel. (1978). *The Hippocampus as a Cognitive Map.* Oxford: Clarendon Press.

Olds, B.M., and R.L. Miller. (1989). "Meaningful Humanities Studies for Engineering Students: A New Approach." Unpublished manuscript. A Report on the Colorado School of Mines HumEn Program.

Olds, B.M., and R.L. Miller. (June 1990). "Meaningful Humanities Studies for Engineering Students: A New Approach." (summary). In *1990 ASEE Annual Conference Proceedings* (pp. 1040–1043), Toronto.

Oliver, D., and K. Gershman. (1989). *Education, Modernity, and Fractured Meaning.* Albany: State University of New York Press.

Olton, D.S., J.T. Becher, and G.E. Handelmann. (1979). "Hippocampus, Space and Memory." *Behavior and Brain Science* 2: 313–365.

Ornstein, R., and P. Ehrlich. (1989). *New World, New Mind: Moving Toward Conscious Evolution.* New York: Doubleday.

Ornstein, R., and D. Sobel. (1987). *The Healing Brain: Breakthrough Discoveries about How the Brain Keeps Us Healthy.* New York: Simon and Schuster.

Ornstein, R., and R.F. Thompson. (1984). *The Amazing Brain.* Boston: Houghton-Mifflin.

Ortony, A. (1980). "Metaphor." In *Theoretical Issues in Reading Comprehension*, edited by R.J. Spiro, B.C. Bruce, and W.F. Brewer. Hillsdale, N.J.: Lawrence Erlbaum.

Overly, N., ed. (1979). *Lifelong Learning: A Human Agenda. 1979 Yearbook of the Association for Supervision and Curriculum Development.* Alexandria, Va.: ASCD.

Papalia, D.E., and S. Wendkos Olds. (1981). *Human Development.* 2nd ed. New York: McGraw-Hill.

Pelletier, K.R. (1977). *Mind as Healer, Mind as Slayer: A Holistic Approach to Preventing Stress Disorders*. New York: Dell.

Pichert, J.W., and R.C. Anderson. (1976). *Taking Different Perspectives on a Story*. Technical Report No. 14. Urbana-Champaign: Center for the Study of Reading, University of Illinois.

Popham, W.J. (February 1968). "Probing the Validity of Arguments Against Behavioral Goals." Paper presented at the annual convention of the American Educational Research Association, Chicago.

Postman, N., and C. Weingartner. (1969). *Teaching as a Subversive Activity*. New York: Dell.

Pribram, K., ed. (1969). *On the Biology of Learning*. New York: Harcourt, Brace and World.

Pribram, K. (1971). *Languages of the Brain*. Monterey, Calif.: Brooks/Cole.

Pribram, K. (January 1987). "A Systematic Analysis of Brain Function, Learning and Remembering." A paper presented at *Educating Tomorrow's Children* seminar, Neuropsycholoby Services, San Francisco.

Prietula, M.J., and H.A. Simon. (January-February 1989). "The Experts in Your Midst." *Harvard Business Review* 1: 120.

Prigogine, I., and I. Stengers. (1984). *Order Out of Chaos: Man's Dialogue with Nature*. Toronto: Bantam Books.

Progoff, I. (1980). *The Practice of Process Meditation*. New York: Dialogue House Library.

Pugach, M.C., and L.J. Johnson. (1988). "Promoting Teacher Reflection Through Structured Dialog." In *Images of Reflection in Teacher Education*, edited by H.C. Waxman, H.J. Freiberg, J.C. Vaughan, and M. Weil. Reston, Va.: Association of Teacher Educators.

Purkey, W.W. (1970). *Self-Concept and School Achievement*. Englewood Cliffs, N.J.: Prentice-Hall.

Quina, J. (1989). *Effective Secondary Teaching: Going Beyond the Bell Curve*. Cambridge: Harper and Row.

Restak, R. (1984). *The Brain*. Toronto: Bantam Books.

Rico, G.L. (1983). *Writing the Natural Way: Using Right-Brain Techniques to Release Your Expressive Powers*. Los Angeles: J.P. Tarcher.

Rogers, C. (1962). "Toward a Theory of Creativity." In *A Source Book for Creative Thinking* (pp. 64–72), edited by S. Parnes and H. Harding. New York: Scribner's Sons.

Rogers, C. (1983). *Freedom to Learn for the '80s*. Columbus, Ohio: Merrill.

Rosenfield, I. (1988). *The Invention of Memory*. New York: Basic Books.

Rosenthal, R., and L. Jacobson. (1968). *Pygmalion in the Classroom*. New York: Rinehart and Winston.

Rumelhart, D.E. (1980). "Schemata: The Building Blocks of Cognition." In *Theoretical Issues in Reading Comprehension*, edited by R.J. Spiro, B.C. Bruce, and W.F. Brewer. Hillsdale, N.J.: Lawrence Erlbaum.

Sagan, C. (1977). *The Dragons of Eden*. New York: Ballantine Books.

Schank, R.C., and R.P. Abelson. (1975). "Scripts, Plans and Knowledge." In *Advance Papers of the Fourth International Joint Conference on Artificial Intelligence*. Tbilisi, Georgia, U.S.S.R.

Schön, D.A. (1983). *The Reflective Practitioner*. New York: Basic Books.

Schön, D.A. (1990). *Educating the Reflective Practitioner*. San Francisco: Jossey-Bass.

Schrage, M. (December 7, 1989). "America's Sense of Design Finally Starting to Take Shape." *Los Angeles Times*, D1.

Sculley, J. (participant). (October 20, 1989). *Fortune 500 Summit*. CSPAN.

Selye, H. (1978). *The Stress of Life*. rev. ed. New York: McGraw-Hill.

Shalley, C. (1987). "Humanities Program: Hightstown High School. Curriculum for the Integrated Humanities Program at Hightstown High School, Hightstown, N.J." Unpublished manuscript.

Shoben, E.J., K.T. Westcourt, and E.E. Smith. (1978). "Sentence Verification, Sentence Recognition, and the Semantic Episodic Distinction." *Journal of Experimental Psychology: Human Learning and Memory* 4, 4: 304–317.

Singer, J. (1977). "Ongoing Thought: The Normative Baseline for Alternative States of Consciousness." In *Alternate States of Consciousness*, edited by N.E. Zinberg. New York: The Free Press.

Smith, F. (1973). *Psycholinguistics and Reading*. New York: Holt, Rinehart and Winston.

Smith, F. (1986). *Insult to Intelligence: The Bureaucratic Invasions of Our Classrooms*. Portsmouth, N.H.: Heinemann Educational Books.

Society of Accelerative Learning and Teaching. (n.d.). *Journal of the Society for Accelerative Learning and Teaching*, edited by Pedro Portes. Department of Psychology, Iowa State University, Ames, IA 50011.

Sperry, R. (1968). "Hemisphere Disconnection and Unity in Conscious Awareness." *American Psychologist* 23: 723–33.

Sperry, R. (1986). "The New Mentalist Paradigm and Ultimate Concern." *Perspectives in Biology and Medicine* 29, 3: 413–422.

Spielberger, C.D., ed. (1972). *Anxiety: Current Trends in Theory and Research*. Vols. 1 and 2. New York: Academic Press.

Spiro, R.J. (1980). "Constructive Processes in Prose Comprehension and Recall." In *Theoretical Issues in Reading Comprehension*, edited by R.J. Spiro, B.C. Bruce, and W.F. Brewer. Hillsdale, N.J.: Lawrence Erlbaum.

Spiro, R.J., B.C. Bruce, and W.F. Brewer, eds. (1980). *Theoretical Issues in Reading Comprehension*. Hillsdale, N.J.: Lawrence Erlbaum.

Springer, S., and G. Deutsch. (1985). *Left Brain, Right Brain*. 2nd ed. New York: W.H. Freeman.

Squire, L. (1986). "Mechanism of Memory." *Science* 232: 1612–1619.

Squire, L.R., C. Cohen, and L. Nadel. (1984). "The Medial Temporal Region and Memory Consolidations: A New Hypothesis." In *Memory Consolidation* (pp. 185–209), edited by H. Weingartner and E.S. Parker. Hillsdale, N.J.: Lawrence Erlbaum.

Stucki, M., H.R. Kaufmann, and F. Kaufmann. (1987). "Infants' Recognition of a Face Revealed Through Motion: Contribution of Internal Facial Movement and Head Movement." *Journal of Experimental Child Psychology* 44, 1: 80–91.

Swanson, L.W. (1982). "Hippocampal, Long-Term Potentiation: Mechanisms and Implications for Memory." *Neurosciences Research Program Bulletin* 20: 613–764.

"3rd Home-Taught Youth Off to Harvard." (December 31, 1987). *Los Angeles Times*, 21.

Tilley, A., J. Horne, and S. Allison. (1985). "Effects of Loss of Sleep on Retrieval from Semantic Memory at Two Different Times of Day." *Australian Journal of Psychology* 37, 3: 281–287.

Toepfer, C.F. (1980). "Brain Growth Periodization Data: Some Suggestions for Re-thinking Middle Grades Education." *High School Journal* 63, 6: 222.

Tulving, E. (1986). "What Kind of a Hypothesis Is the Distinction Between Episodic and Semantic Memory?" *Journal of Experimental Psychology: Learning, Memory, and Cognition* 12, 2: 307–311.

U.S. News and World Report (October 27, 1986).

Vail, P.B. (1989). *Management as a Performing Art*. San Francisco: Jossey-Bass.

Valle, R.S., and R.V. von Eckartsberg, eds. (1981). *The Metaphors of Consciousness*. New York: Plenum Press.

Vaughan, J. (1988). "The Potential of Reflective Practice: Rainbow or Reality." In *Images of Reflection in Teacher Education*, edited by H.C. Waxman, H.J. Freiberg, J.C. Vaughan, and M. Weil. Reston, Va.: Association of Teacher Educators.

von Eckartsberg, R. (1981). "Maps of the Mind, the Cartography of Consciousness." In *The Metaphors of Consciousness*, edited by R.S. Valle and R.V. von Eckartsberg. New York: Plenum Press.

Vygotsky, L.S. (1978). *Mind in Society*. Cambridge: Harvard University Press.

Wallace, R.K. (1986). *The Maharishi Technology of the United Field: The Neurophysiology of Enlightenment*. Fairfield, Iowa: Maharishi International University (MIU) Neuroscience Press.

Waxman, H.C., H.J. Freiberg, J. Vaughan, and M. Weil, eds. (1988). *Images of Reflection in Teacher Education*. Reston, Va.: Association of Teacher Educators.

Wentworth, P. (1950). *Through the Wall*. New York: Harper and Row.

White, G.M. (1967). *The Elicitation and Durability of Altruistic Behavior in Children*. Research Bulletin No. 67-27. Princeton, N.J.: Educational Testing Service.

Whitehead, A.N. (1979). *Process and Reality*. New York: The Free Press.

Whitman, W. [1892]. (1958). *Leaves of Grass*. New York: The New American Library.

Whitten, W. (June 1990). "The Joys of Mastery: A *New Age Journal* Interview with George Leonard." *New Age Journal* 36: n.p.

Winner, E. (1982). *Invented Worlds*. Cambridge: Harvard University Press.

Winner, E. (1988). *The Point of Words: Children's Understanding of Metaphor and Irony*. Cambridge: Harvard University Press.

Wittrock, M.C., ed. (1980). *The Brain and Psychology*. New York: Academic Press.

Wood, L. (1988). *Buff Chemistry Guide*. Tempe, Ariz.: Tempe High School.

Wood, L., and G. Odell. (1989). *Chemistry Songs*. Tempe, Ariz.: Tempe High School.

Wurman, R.S. (1989). *Information Anxiety*. New York: Doubleday.

Yingling, C. (January 1987). "Neuroscience, Cognitive Science, and Education: Partners in Progress or Strange Bedfellows?" A paper presented at *Educating Tomorrow's Children* seminar, California Neuropsychology Services, San Francisco.

Zahourek, R. (1988). *Relaxation and Imagery: Tools for Therapeutic Communication and Intervention*. Philadelphia: W.B. Saunders.

CURRENT ASCD NETWORKS FOR BRAIN-BASED EDUCATORS

ASCD sponsors numerous networks that help members exchange ideas, share common interests, identify and solve problems, grow profession- ally, and establish collegial relationships. Several may be of particular interest to readers of this book:

CLEARINGHOUSE FOR LEARNING/TEACHING STYLES
AND BRAIN BEHAVIOR

Contact: Kathleen Butler, consultant and director of The Learner's Di- mension, 7 Lakeview Drive, Columbia, CT 06237. Telephone: (203) 228-3786.

TEACHING THINKING

Contacts: Robin Fogarty, editor, Skylight Publishing, Inc., 200 E. Wood Street, Suite 250, Palatine, IL 60067. Telephone: (708) 991-6300. Esther Fusco, 24 Hopewell Drive, Stony Brook, NY 11790. Telephone: (516) 661-5820.

TEACHING FOR MULTIPLE INTELLIGENCES

Contact: David G. Lazear, consultant, Illinois Renewal Institute, 200 E. Wood Street, Suite 200, Palatine, IL 60067. Telephone: (708) 991-6300.

For more information about these and other ASCD networks, call ASCD's Field Services Department at (703) 549-9110, ext. 506 or 502. Or write to ASCD at 1250 N. Pitt Street, Alexandria, VA 22314.